Second Edition

Culturally and Linguistically Responsive Teaching and Learning

Classroom Practices for Student Success

Author
Sharroky Hollie, Ph.D.

Foreword
Becky Allen, M.A.Ed.

SHELL EDUCATION

Publishing Credits

Corinne Burton, M.A.Ed., *Publisher*; Conni Medina, M.A.Ed., *Managing Editor*; Aubrie Nielsen, M.S.Ed., *Content Director*; Tara Hurley, *Assistant Editor*; Don Tran, *Graphic Designer*

Image credits

p. 192 Sara Krauss; All other photos courtesy of Baba Riley

Shell Education

5301 Oceanus Drive
Huntington Beach, CA 92649-1030
http://www.shelleducation.com
ISBN 978-1-4258-1731-2
© 2018 Shell Educational Publishing, Inc.

Table of Contents

Foreword

I have long believed that the best gift anyone can give someone else is the gift of an education, truly the great equalizer for opening future possibilities for all students. I spent over 25 years teaching Earth science to young teens, eventually channeling my passion for education into leading professional learning for other teachers and launching a constant quest to find and share the best-available research in our profession. When I accepted the role of professional development coordinator for Hopkins, it was not with the goal of leading equity-related work; I just wanted to bring solid research-based practices to our classrooms and develop a stronger sense of community among staff across the district. Dr. Hollie's work with culturally responsive strategies was exactly the vehicle we needed.

In his introduction to this second edition of his groundbreaking original text, Dr. Hollie notes that he wanted to incorporate his own learning that resulted from his interaction with teachers and leaders across the country. I can only hope that I played a small role in that journey. Dr. Hollie first arrived in Hopkins Public Schools at the invitation of our high school teacher-leaders and principal who felt the urgency of implementing culturally responsive practices into the high school culture. Recognizing that this was valuable work for *all* of our schools, our district leadership decided to implement CLR training districtwide. In the subsequent years that Dr. Hollie was actively coaching and leading in Hopkins Schools, he and I had many conversations, and they were often very intense. He challenged me, and because of him, I can say with certainty that I am more aware of my biases, more intentional in leading change, and more committed than ever to finding a way for all individuals to be "VABBed" in our school community.

Dr. Hollie's culturally responsive practices brought the essential element that was missing in our previous equity work—the "how-to" for creating an equitable classroom. He provided us with practical strategies that shifted our teaching practice and increased student engagement and, more importantly, inspired us to develop CLR mindsets. As Dr. Hollie says in chapter one, to fully embrace CLR, "…educators have to shift their beliefs, attitudes, and knowledge to a stance that sees what the student brings culturally and linguistically as an asset…." It is the blend of the skillset and mindset that validates and affirms a student's home culture and language while bridging and building him or her to the academic setting.

The academic setting is where we have the capacity to prepare a student to be college- and career-ready. Good educators know that a student's education goes beyond academic standards; we are obligated, even compelled, to provide the life-essential skills of discourse, problem-solving, and adaptability. Through Dr. Hollie's work, we have been given effective tools to build capacity with academic vocabulary, literacy, language, and situational appropriateness. The language of cultural responsiveness has been introduced to our teachers across the grade levels, from early childhood through high school. The common strategies and language are also threaded through classrooms across all grades and disciplines. Every day, I am inspired by the impact of CLR practices when used intentionally by adults who love teaching children.

Successful implementation of this work is, of course, not done through the efforts of one person, and I lean on the instructional coaches within the district to assist in promoting and sustaining CLR practices. These are the people with the relationships and influence; they are the ones who intentionally implement these practices daily and keep them alive in Hopkins, and the work continuously proves inspirational. One teacher recently shared, "Using CLR strategies has transformed my students' learning. It has increased student engagement and accountability." That is the impact of cultural responsiveness.

In this second edition, Dr. Hollie puts an emphasis on mindset and the realization that becoming a CLR educator is a journey. Dr. Hollie celebrates the passionate teachers who coined such phrases like "VABBulous" and "Who have you VABBed today?" He challenges us to intentionally interrupt our traditional practices and balance them with responsive and culturally responsive practices, to create experiences that resonate with all students, and to name our underserved and give them a voice. This is not merely "pedagogy"—I have learned that culturally responsive teaching goes far beyond the strategies and activities in the classroom, relying heavily on our minds and on our hearts. As Dr. Hollie notes in his final chapter of this edition, we need to "love outrageously."

Dr. Sharroky Hollie has shared his gift with all of us through his work on culturally and linguistically responsive teaching and learning. This text is the perfect resource to begin the journey of becoming a CLR practitioner. He is leveling the playing field for students while raising all educators to their highest level of performance. He reminds us that educators, like students, respond best when we build the relationship first. Be intentional. Go slow to go fast. And, most importantly, love the students—outrageously!

—Becky Allen, M.A.Ed.
Professional Development Coordinator,
Hopkins Public Schools

Adjunct Professor,
University of Minnesota

Introduction

I try to practice what I preach as often as possible. My vision is for you to be culturally responsive in all that you do, so I do my best to model being validating and affirming in all that I do. A core principle of responsiveness is to have an ongoing willingness and open-mindedness to change. This second edition of *Culturally and Linguistically Responsive Teaching and Learning* is the best example I can provide for modeling change because so much has changed about my knowledge, beliefs, and experiences in cultural and linguistic responsiveness (CLR) since the first edition released five years ago. I am grateful to have this opportunity to share my fresh perspectives and new learnings about CLR. These changes have not been linear by any measure. They have been incremental, sometimes haphazard and other times intentional. It has been an evolutionary experience for me and has led me to what I now understand as the *journey to responsiveness*. In essence, we are all on a journey to being better for our students in culturally and linguistically responsive ways. Just like in the first edition, I will share with you the *how* of that "mo' betta" responsiveness through a cultural and linguistic lens. What you can expect in this second edition is more clarity in terminology and concepts, new examples and anecdotes from my travels across the country, updated research in anthropology and in our four focus areas of instruction, and finally, an alignment with my recent work in *Strategies for Culturally and Linguistically Responsive Teaching and Learning* (Hollie 2015).

The most impactful change for me has been the theme of the journey to responsiveness, which is addressed in the first chapter. As a culturally responsive educator or any global citizen, you have to always ask yourself, *Where am I in my journey to responsiveness?* This is almost a daily reflection, where you inquire inwardly, *Am I being culturally and linguistically responsive to those most in need of it?* Throughout the book, your journey to responsiveness is examined through assessments of your mindset and skillsets.

My goal is to focus you on recognizing the necessary shifts in your mindset to be culturally and linguistically responsive and for you to recognize the ways in which you need to develop your skills in how you talk to your students, how you build rapport and relate to them, and how you teach them.

In this second edition, I have elevated the concept of validation and affirmation, building and bridging, or what I now affectionately refer to as *VABBing* and being *VABBulous*. In truth, I cannot take credit for these terms. This is how teachers who are practicing the work of CLR at the deepest levels recognize cultural and linguistic responsiveness. VABBing is the soul of cultural and linguistic responsiveness, and so I spend more time on the concept with more clarity and depth than before. Linked to VABBing is situational appropriateness, another aspect of the approach that I now see more clearly and poignantly. While VABBing is the soul of CLR, situational appropriateness is the grit, the goal. We want all students and persons in general to understand the most appropriate cultural and linguistic behaviors for any situation without losing who they are culturally and linguistically. But in order to teach situational appropriateness, you must be skilled at validating and affirming, and willing to validate and affirm (Muhammad and Hollie 2011). I extend ideas developed in the first edition to give a concrete framework for what it means to *Validate* and *Affirm* (VA) and what it means to *Build* and *Bridge* (BB).

CLR: cultural and linguistic responsiveness

VA: Validate and Affirm

BB: Build and Bridge

VABBing: validating, affirming, building, and bridging

Finally, since the first edition, I have deepened my knowledge in the four focus instructional areas for cultural and linguistic responsiveness: classroom management, academic vocabulary, academic literacy, and academic language. A big difference in this second edition is explicitly asking, *To what extent is your instructional practice culturally and linguistically responsive?* I believe that cultural and linguistic responsiveness is a lens that should be used to look at all that we are doing in schools—organizationally and instructionally. This lens makes the case that CLR is not something that you *do* but something that you *have* in all that you do. This lens opens up a CLR possibility to a litany of things that come with the institutionality of schooling—programs, grants, initiatives, philosophies, standards, policies, and on and on. When it comes to instruction, we use the CLR lens to examine how culturally and linguistically responsive we are in our classroom management practices, our academic vocabulary building, our academic literacy growth, and our academic language focus. As always, I have culled the latest research to see what the experts are teaching us about advances in the four instructional areas and how that new information mirrors our principles of cultural and linguistic responsiveness. In my continued studies, however, something that has not changed—and never will—is that the core of my CLR focus is instruction. Research has consistently shown that what happens in terms of quality of classroom instruction has the most impact on improved student achievement (Dean, et al. 2013).

Fostering student engagement in learning activities is a primary goal for all teachers. Similarly, as I wrote the first edition of this book, I wanted to provide features that would engage the reader in thinking about personal perspectives about culturally and linguistically responsive pedagogy. To this second edition I bring deeper insights into the *journey to responsiveness*. These heightened understandings are embedded in questions and statements designed to invite teachers to examine their *mindsets* and *skillsets* as they reflect on the content and how they can incorporate the ideas into their professional learning experiences and collaboration with colleagues.

This book has three parts:

- **Part 1**: **Understanding Mindset** consists of chapters 1 and 2, which concentrate on the framework and pedagogy of CLR.

- **Part 2**: **Building Skillsets** includes chapters 3, 4, 5, 6, and 7, which focus on the infusion of CLR into everyday teaching.

- **Part 3**: **A Personal Coda** culminates the book with chapter 8, which shares more personal insight on what it means to be a responsive teacher.

The features found throughout the book include the following:

- Each chapter opens with an *Anticipation Guide*, which offers a number of statements related to the chapter topic. This guide invites you to specify whether you agree or disagree with each of the statements listed.

- At the end of each chapter is a *Reflection Guide*. This invites you to reconsider what you have read and your responses to the statements in the Anticipation Guide.

- *Pause to Ponder* is another feature designed to engage your attention on critical issues in your classroom, school, or district. These activities are presented to prompt exploration of your thoughts and the material and its relevance to your current situations.

- Sidebars are interspersed throughout the chapters. This content serves to augment ideas in the text.

- The appendices present a collection of practical, evidence-based instructional activities, which have been successfully implemented in schools across the nation. This section also includes a glossary of terms associated with CLR, an updated list of culturally authentic texts, and a Learning Environment Survey designed for collegial observations of the quantitative and qualitative aspects of the classroom.

The goal of this second edition is the same as the first edition: I want to illuminate how and where cultural and linguistic responsiveness fits into the overall work of equity and, to a certain extent, the bigger picture of "diversity." My focus is narrower, though, than most academics and other experts in this field. I am focused on culture from an anthropological framework, not a race ideology; on pedagogy, not content; and lastly, on this work being teacher driven (grassroots) and not institution-driven (regardless of the institution). The chapters are curated to address this narrow focus.

Chapter 1 establishes the concepts and terminology for CLR. How we use words in CLR is extremely important. I am a parser of words (some say I should have been an attorney), and I think that precision with our word use is critical. This first chapter sets the tone for CLR work, with more attention paid to your individual mindset, which is necessary for responsiveness overall. Chapter 2 explains the pedagogy of CLR, turning the page to what is required for developing skillsets or instructional practices. I deeply dive into what it means to validate and affirm instructionally and what it means to build and bridge academically. Chapters 3 through 7 follow the sequence of CLR infusion into everyday teaching. Chapter 3 covers classroom management with a new emphasis on distinguishing cultural behaviors from unacceptable behaviors. Chapter 4 discusses academic vocabulary, with a provocative look at how to validate and affirm youth vocabulary, including slang, profanity, and racially charged terms. Chapters 5 and 6 bookend each other, with the former focusing on literacy skills, particularly the importance of using culturally authentic texts, and the latter on academic writing and speaking, expanding the view of nonstandard (what I call *unaccepted*) languages compared to academic language in the context of situational appropriateness. Chapter 7, known as the Blumenbach chapter, again challenges you to look at your learning environment and its responsiveness to your students in terms of images on the walls, display cases, materials, resources, and texts.

In the end, I want you to feel empowered, inspired, and equipped to be better—*mo' betta*, that is. In this context, Chapter 8 is my expression of the depth of emotion that I carry for CLR and what you can do to observe and achieve success. What I love about what I do—write about and teach people to be culturally and linguistically responsive—is that CLR is truly about the journey, the process. I am so different in this work than I was 25 years ago, or even two years ago. I am better in my responsiveness. I am hoping that this book will support and guide you to your next step in your journey to responsiveness.

Understanding Mindset

Part

1

The Journey to Responsiveness

Chapter 1

Anticipation Guide

What do you think of when you encounter the term *culturally responsive teaching*? Do you agree or disagree with the following statements about the concept?

_____ Culturally responsive teaching is meant to help with race relations among educators and students.

_____ All students can achieve highly when given the opportunity to learn.

_____ Racial identity and cultural identity are synonymous.

_____ Nonstandard English is a simplified version of Standard English.

_____ Socioeconomic status is the most critical factor in student success.

Your Journey to Responsiveness

Where are you in your journey to responsiveness? I need you to answer this question by the end of the chapter because where you are in your journey will determine how receptive you are to the rest of the chapters in the book. Cultural responsiveness, no matter how you are viewing it now, begins with you and where you are in your heart and mind. Before we begin what will be, in effect, a reflective process, I want to make sure that you recognize that you are beginning or have been involved in an ongoing progression to better serve all your students in a way that validates and affirms who they are culturally and linguistically. The recognition of your process and knowing where you are in it will keep you centered and focused on the overall goal: better academic outcomes for all students and a deeper understanding of their cultural selves in the context of academia (school culture) and mainstream culture. There is a caution, however. You must be certain, confident, and capable on this journey because there will be hurdles, challenges, pitfalls, and bumps along the way—sometimes in the form of negativity, or what I call *resistance*, and sometimes in the form of struggles, which are expected and can be positive.

What is the journey to responsiveness? It involves two initial phases followed by a landing phase. Phase one is courageously conversing about race when necessary. Note the word *courageously*. This is not the conversation with your neighbor, with your family, or the conversation you had on November 9, 2016, the day after a historic presidential election. The conversation I am referring to is different than those because it requires four parts. Glenn Singleton describes these parts in his concept of *Courageous Conversations* (2015). The four parts are:

1. You had the opportunity to speak your truth. You were able to get things off your mind, off your chest.

2. You listened to someone else with an open mind.

3. The conversation was uncomfortable. You felt a healthy tension, anxiousness.

4. The conversation was real talk, adult language, no minced words; all cards were put on the table.

If you have had ongoing courageous conversations about race, when necessary, that included these four parts, then you are well on your way to responsiveness. Think. When was the last time that you had a courageous conversation about race?

Next, you recognized that there was more to this journey than conversation and consideration about race. While discussing race is inescapable in the context of the United States, there is a glass ceiling with the conversation. At some point, there is no place to go with it. Actions have to be taken, steps have to be made toward justice, fairness, and success for your students. In your journey, you recognized this and began to advocate for those who cannot advocate for themselves. You became a voice for the voiceless or the unheard. You spoke up in a meeting about unfairness. You risked your position by fighting for a policy, procedure, or practice that was to the benefit of those who have not traditionally benefitted from schooling in the United States. The second phase is *advocacy*. Have you been an advocate recently? For whom? In what ways? After advocating, you realized that there is more to this journey.

The *landing phase* of the journey causes you to look up at the sky and wonder about the possibilities. And if it is a clear evening, with stars illuminating the sky, then you will see "Planet Responsiveness," your landing spot for the journey. It is there— or here, where I am—that you will spend the rest of your time exploring "cultures." The cultures referred to are not based on race, nor ethnicity alone. The cultures on Planet Responsiveness speak to who we are, wholly related to our identities and how they are manifested in the context of institutions such as schools. If you are on Planet Responsiveness, then you are learning about your students culturally and linguistically every day. You are making efforts to engage them in ways that first validate and affirm, and then build and bridge. This is achieved in how you talk to your students, how you build rapport and relationships with them, and how you teach them.

This chapter and those that follow are going to teach you how to move through the three phases. The concepts and activities will work most effectively and efficiently once you land on Planet Responsiveness. I am waiting for you, whether you are here already or on your way. With the journey to responsiveness comes changes and shifts in your mindset, which are recognitions of your dispositions, perspectives, biases, prejudices, ignorance, misunderstandings, and misgivings about the cultures and languages of others. The rest of the chapter is organized around what it takes to change your attitude about culture and language.

Changes in Mindset

The journey to responsiveness happens in two ways: a change in mindset and a change in skillset. The focus of this first chapter is the change in mindset. As the initial step to changing the instructional dynamic in the classroom and the overall school climate, educators have to see their students' cultural and linguistic behaviors differently. A change in mindset is rooted in four areas, which form the organization of this chapter. These areas are:

1. Speaking a common language—CLR terminology

2. Defining CLR technically and conceptually—VABB

3. Listening to your deficit monitor

4. Identifying the beneficiaries of responsiveness

Phases in the Journey to Responsiveness

Phase 1—Converse: Participate in courageous conversations about race.

Phase 2—Advocate: Become an advocate for constructive change.

Phase 3—Explore: Appreciate the possibilities for change and strive to fulfill them.

What's in a Name? Everything!

Unfortunately, the term *culturally responsive teaching* has become a cliché, buried in the grave of educational terms that are cast about like ghosts in books, state mandates, district initiatives, and conference themes. When a term in education becomes clichéd, it becomes meaningless; it loses its power. Over the years, I have seen a steady increase in educators saying they are culturally responsive or that culturally responsive teaching is a part of their goals. Long ago, I received an email from an educator in the Midwest who said that her superintendent had now branded the district "culturally responsive." However, she was not sure what that meant and needed to know immediately—before the ubiquitous one-day mandated district professional development program. Throughout my home state of California, many districts want to be culturally responsive, or at least they think they do. In reality, what they are seeking is how to address racial issues under the cover of *culturally responsive teaching*. And why not? The term sounds appropriate and informative, seems to address the sensitive issues of race in a nonthreatening way, and serves a purpose in situations where the achievement gap persists and where negative attitudes about race, culture, and language remain stubbornly in place. But turning the meaning of culturally responsive teaching into a quick fix for race relations, diversity issues, and achievement-gap woes is a fleeting solution. The authenticity and relevance of the term is steeped in transforming instructional practices to make the difference for improving relationships between students and educators and increasing student achievement. This is my point: what you label actions to address sensitive issues must have meaning backed by tangible outcomes. There must be an investment in cultural and linguistic responsiveness like any other program, approach, or initiative.

Speaking a Common Language

Being culturally and linguistically responsive begins with understanding its meaning and having consensus about how to name it. My term, *culturally and linguistically responsive teaching and learning (CLR),* speaks to its comprehensiveness and complexity. There is an in-depth focus on culture and language. This focus is a benefit to both teachers and learners. The use of the word *responsive* is strategic and purposeful because it forces a thought process beyond such common monikers as relevance, proficiency, or competency. To be responsive, educators must be willing to validate and affirm students through instruction, which leads to the pedagogical skillset (the topic of Chapter 2). Let's begin by speaking a common language.

Multiple names and definitions have been given to culturally responsive teaching over the past 50 years. These variations include, among others, culturally responsive pedagogy, culturally compatible teaching, culturally relevant teaching, culturally connected teaching, culturally responsive learning, culturally matched teaching, cultural proficiency, cultural competency, and culturally appropriate teaching (Gay 2000). Within the past five years, Paris and Alim have introduced another term, *culturally sustaining pedagogy* (2014).

While CSP advances the theory of culturally relevant teaching, the multiple definitions have contributed to its clichéd use that has diluted its meaning. Furthermore, some superficial interpretations have led to obscure attempts at implementation in districts (focused on professional development), schools (focused on curriculum

Defining Culturally Responsive Pedogogy

Gloria Ladson-Billings defines *culturally responsive teaching (CRT)* as "a pedagogy that empowers students intellectually, socially, emotionally, and politically by using cultural and historical references to convey knowledge, to impart skills, and to change attitudes" (1994, 13).

Geneva Gay defines *culturally responsive pedagogy (CRP)* as "the use of cultural knowledge, prior experiences, frames of reference, and performance styles of ethnically diverse students to make learning encounters more relevant to, and effective for them" (2000, 31).

Sharroky Hollie defines *cultural and linguistic responsiveness (CLR)* as "the validation and affirmation of the home (indigenous) culture and home language for the purposes of building and bridging the student to success in the culture of academia and mainstream society" (2012, 23).

Django Paris and H. Samy Alim explain *culturally sustaining pedagogy (CSP)* as having "as its explicit goal supporting multilingualism and multiculturalism in practice and perspective for students and teachers. CSP seeks to perpetuate and foster—*to sustain*—linguistic, literate, and cultural pluralism as part of the democratic project of schooling and as a needed response to demographic and social change. CSP, then, links a focus on sustaining pluralism through education to challenges of social justice and change in ways that previous iterations of asset pedagogies did not" (2014, 14).

initiatives), and classrooms (focused on instructional strategies). My proposal is that you explicitly look at cultural relevancy as theory on a continuum and know where you fall philosophically. As a result, you will know better where you stand, which will increase your chances of being culturally responsive. Figure 1.1 provides a continuum to consider. Of course, this consideration requires you to deeply study the various viewpoints of what makes each one different in the progression. Think of the theory as a hamburger and the different names for it as different types of hamburgers. When it comes to hamburgers, think of the types you prefer and the accompaniments of each. In order to be culturally responsive, you need to know what type of burger you are eating. Just don't go for the bun and meat with lettuce and mayo. In others words, know your brand.

The continuum in Figure 1.1 illustrates the evolution of culturally relevant theory through the years 1994–2014.

Fig. 1.1 Continuum of Culturally Relevant Theory

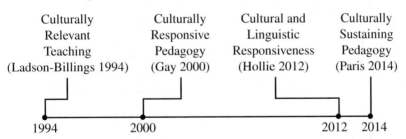

Almost any innovation that has had staying power in education and is still in use today has maintained its terminology and meaningfulness. The term for that innovation will not have changed, although its interpretation may have evolved in a consistent way. An example that comes to mind is *cooperative learning*, a concept put forth in the late 1960s (Johnson, Johnson, and Holubec 1994; Kagan and Kagan 2009). The term *cooperative learning* has remained intact for almost four decades and has furthermore evolved to include the concept of *collaborative learning*. When most educators encounter the term *cooperative learning*, there is consensus on its meaning. My point is that cooperative learning has had staying power because it has not been subjected to multiple terms and interpretations, as is the case with culturally responsive teaching.

I believe that clarity can sometimes be more important than agreement. Being clear on what is meant by culturally and linguistically responsive teaching is certainly one of those cases. In training over 100,000 educators, observing in over 2,000 classrooms, and speaking to hundreds of audiences across the country, I have found that most teachers and administrators appreciate the focus on clarity as opposed to forcing agreement or buy-in.

Pause to Ponder

What is your term for cultural relevancy? Why did you choose that term? In which situations have you used the term? In those situations, was there consistency in the use of terms and their meanings? Do you think it is necessary for individuals to use the same terms and definitions?

For the purposes of my work and this book in particular, I advocate a singular use of the concept and terminology. If an educator desires to be culturally and linguistically responsive or a school is looking to implement the approach, I recommend that all stakeholders agree upon one term and one meaning—preferably the one used in this book. As a result of the work in which I have been immersed since 2000, I have adopted the term *cultural and linguistic responsiveness (CLR)* for three reasons:

1. I have found that many so-called followers of culturally responsive teaching are actually most interested in *racially* responsive teaching. There is a tendency to be more focused on racial identity rather than the myriad cultural identities in our collective diversity. My focus on culture, language, gender, class, and religion is anthropologically based, not race based. Conflating culture and race is a common misinterpretation among some individuals who work with diverse groups of students. CLR makes clear the distinction and fosters understanding of the need to avoid such identity confusion.

2. I use CLR in order to emphasize the language aspect of culture. I believe that there is nothing more cultural about us as humans than the use of our home language. Linguistic identity is a crucial aspect of who we are. By itself, the term *culture* subsumes language; consequently, linguistic identity is obscured. By including "linguistic" in the term CLR, the intentionality of the language focus is demonstrated as equal to what we typically consider as culture. In short, we are what we speak, and to a large extent, our language is a representation of our heritage, including family, community, and history.

3. CLR is a pedagogy. Pedagogy is a five-star word frequently thrown around in academic circles with the result that some people consider the term to be jargon. I consider pedagogy to be a powerful term in its meaning and its functionality in CLR. I define *pedagogy* as the "how" and "why" of teaching, the strategic use of methods, and the rationale behind why instructional decisions are made. Pedagogy is usually the most often missed facet of culturally responsive teaching. Without the pedagogy, there is only theory on how to respond to students' cultural and linguistic needs, and theory alone does not adequately serve teachers and students.

To sum up, what a concept is called matters. In society, how we label something speaks to what it means to us symbolically. *Cultural and linguistic responsiveness* is the concept that is developed in this book.

Defining CLR Technically and Conceptually: VABB

Most proponents of culturally relevant teaching will point to *The Dreamkeepers*, Gloria Ladson-Billings's (1994) groundbreaking book, as the star in the culturally responsive universe. This work has defined what many have come to know about the approach, and her description of six culturally relevant teachers is a must-read for those interested in being culturally responsive. She provides a classic definition of *culturally responsive teaching*: "A pedagogy that empowers students intellectually, socially, emotionally, and politically by using cultural and historical referents to convey knowledge, to impart skills, and to change attitudes" (1994, 13). Teachers practicing culturally relevant teaching know how to support student learning by consciously creating social interactions that help them meet the criteria of academic success, cultural competence, and critical consciousness. In addition to the work of Ladson-Billings, advanced students of culturally responsive teaching will point to the contributions of Ramírez and Castañeda (1974). Many cite this reference as the earliest introduction of culturally responsive teaching, showing that the concept itself goes back many years. While Ramírez and Castañeda may have introduced culturally responsive teaching to the research, Ladson-Billings put it on the national map.

Geneva Gay's text, *Culturally Responsive Teaching: Theory, Research, and Practice* (2000), is by most accounts the second most influential work on culturally responsive teaching. She added pedagogy to the concept and became the leader in the second wave of books and articles that would build upon Ladson-Billings's work. She defines culturally responsive pedagogy as "the use of cultural knowledge, prior experiences, frames of reference, and performance styles of ethnically diverse students to make learning encounters more relevant to, and effective for, them" (Gay 2000, 31). This pedagogy teaches *to and through* the strengths of these students. It is culturally validating and affirming. In addition to the focus on pedagogy, Gay provides positive achievement data supporting the work from districts and schools across the nation. This addition of results data was important to establish the credibility of culturally responsive teaching, which had been an easy target for critics of the approach. Unfortunately, some criticism can still be found today. Goodwin (2011) cites that there is no research that supports culturally responsive teaching correlated to student achievement. But this statement is based on research from the 1970s and does not account for the evolution of the theory since that time, not to mention any recent research. Other researchers who have made important contributions to the literature of culturally responsive teaching include Delpit and Dowdy (2002), Hollins (2008), Irvine (1991), and Villegas and Lucas (2007). These researchers agree on a key element of culturally responsive teaching: it responds to students' needs by taking into account cultural and linguistic factors in their worlds.

This view of CLR from the research perspective is central to the content of this book as well as to the work I do with educators around the country. Therefore, *technically*, cultural and linguistic responsiveness means the *validation and affirmation* of indigenous (home) culture and language for the purpose of *building and bridging* the students to success in the culture of academia and in mainstream society. *Conceptually*, CLR is going to where the students are culturally and linguistically, for the aim of bringing them where they need to be academically. *Metaphorically*, CLR is the opposite of the sink-or-swim approach to teaching and learning in traditional schools. CLR means that teachers jump into the pool with the learners, guide them with appropriate instruction, scaffold as necessary, and provide for independence when they are ready. Validation, affirmation, building, and bridging is known as *VABB*. I want you VABBing your students. I want you to be VABBulous in all that you do with your students. Your teaching should be VABBilicious. I think that you get the point. VABB is CLR.

Validation

Validation is the intentional and purposeful legitimatization of the home culture and language of the student. Such validation has been traditionally delegitimatized by historical institutional and structural racism, stereotypes, and generalizations primarily carried forth through mainstream media. In the institution of schools, students are invalidated when they are told over and over that they are rude, insubordinate, defiant, disrespectful, disruptive, unmotivated, and lazy. These labels over time chip away at students' cultural and linguistic value in the context of school. To validate is to provide a counter narrative to students, letting them know in explicit terms that they are not those labels but that they are culturally and linguistically misunderstood.

Affirmation

Affirmation is the intentional and purposeful effort to reverse the negative stereotypes, images, and representations of marginalized cultures and languages promoted by corporate mainstream media, including music, film, and television. The messages are often subtle and play out through the instructional materials, textbooks, and how the Internet is used in schools. To affirm requires intentionally providing images, texts, and narratives that give students alternate perspectives and the tools to critically analyze media and materials as consumers.

Building

Building is understanding and recognizing the cultural and linguistic behaviors of students and using those behaviors to foster rapport and relationships with the students. In other words, you are building stock with your students, making an investment.

Bridging

Bridging is providing the academic and social skills that students will need to have success beyond your classroom. If building is the investment, then bridging is the return. Bridging is evident when your students demonstrate that they are able to successfully navigate school and mainstream culture.

This definition of CLR is meant to be broad, covering a range of cultural identities and languages. It centers on ethnic identity in the cultural context and on nonstandard languages in the linguistic context because they are the core of who we are in terms of childhoods and upbringing, our families. But in no way is the definition exclusive to any one group. Indeed, CLR is a universal concept. Cultural responsiveness is for everyone. Later in the chapter, I distinguish the different identities that comprise who we are as humans and the cultures that come with those identities. We explore why it is necessary to validate and affirm all that your students are, culturally and linguistically. Before going there, though, I need you to reflect. Given the positive intent of VABBing, why would it be so difficult to do? Given that hardly anyone would argue against the idea of VABBing, why don't our schools VABB on general principle? The next section is the second step in changing your mindset: knowing your biases.

Pause to Ponder

What could prevent you from VABBing a student or a colleague?

Listening to Your Deficit Monitor

What can block you from VABBing your students, colleagues, or even family and friends are your hidden biases. Banaji and Greenwald (2013) teach us that these hidden biases are bits of knowledge about social groups that, once lodged in our minds, can influence our behavior toward members of particular social groups, but we remain oblivious to their influence. As humans, we all have "first thoughts" that are based on prejudices, ignorance, misperceptions, or misinterpretations. These first thoughts keep you from VABBing because they ask, *Why would I validate and affirm a behavior that I view as negative or bad?* In order to VABB, you must be aware of your first thoughts; you have to always listen to your deficit monitor but with the promise that these first thoughts will not be your last thoughts.

Your *deficit monitor* is that internal signal that warns you when you are looking at students' behaviors solely as negative, as lacking, or as liabilities, without consideration that they might be culturally or linguistically based and, therefore, assets. Those who practice responsiveness as a way of being constantly ask reflectively, *What will prevent me from validating and affirming a student culturally and linguistically?* This reflection keeps us honest about our potential for bias, prejudice, misinformation, and ignorance. We have to be omni-aware of our implicit biased thinking so that we can combat it with the cultural lens of validation and affirmation. "Every man has reminiscences which he would not tell to everyone but only to his friends. He has other matters in his mind which he would not reveal even to his friends, but only to himself, and that in secret. But there are other things which a man is afraid to tell even to himself, and every decent man has a number of such things stored away in his mind" (Banaji and Greenwald 2013, 24). If we stay stuck in the deficit lens, then we are unlikely to validate and affirm. This can affect our instructional practices and the school climate and organizational issues related to equity and institutional racism. Being attuned to your deficit monitor is the key to cultural responsiveness in the classroom. It highlights the path to teaching in a way that validates and affirms.

Eliminating the Deficit Perspective

When it comes to consideration of the cultures and languages of underserved students, many educators' beliefs, attitudes, and mindsets are deficit oriented. In essence, this means that the students are blamed for their failures and are seen as the problem. The students are myopically viewed as lacking *something*. The view of an educator with a deficit mindset is reflected in such observations as these:

- If we had better students, then we would have better schools.

- Our scores were good until *they* started coming here.

- Everyone in our school seems to be doing well except for *those* kids.

- What is *wrong* with them?

Culturally and linguistically, underserved students are all too frequently seen as deficient, deviant, defiant, disruptive, and disrespectful. What they bring to the classroom culturally and linguistically is not seen as an asset but as a liability.

The reality is that our biases never completely go away. They simply recede or change, which is why it is important for you to know your biases, to be in control of your thought processes, and to be prepared to go responsive when necessary. I offer these three steps to check in with your biases:

1. Check Your Filter: I cannot stress enough the value of knowing where your information comes from, how your knowledge base developed, and how your experiences have shaped what you believe.

2. Question Your Belief System: Once you realize that you have received inaccurate information about the cultures and languages of others, you are compelled to then question everything that you believe and seek out accurate information. I often share Gandhi's wise words on this topic: "A man is but the product of his thoughts; what he thinks, he becomes." Psychology research tells us that most of what we believe is formed between infancy and pre-adolescence, and we spend the rest of our lives debunking or reconfirming what we believe. Know that if you are getting your information from mainstream media—and that includes all the various streaming and online outlets—then you have received tainted, biased, one-sided, and shaded perspectives about the cultures and languages of others.

3. Listen To Your Deficit Monitor: I believe that we all have an internal voice, sound, or feeling that tells us when we are thinking with prejudice, bias, ignorance, or misinformation. This is our internal warning to stop thinking this way. The question is, do we listen to it? For me, it is a voice that tells me that I am thinking with inaccuracy, half the story, or negative thoughts. I listen most of the time to my monitor and stop thinking in deficit terms. And when I do, I pivot and begin the process of validation and affirmation.

Biased thoughts happen as fast as you can blink your eyes (Gladwell 2005). They are otherwise known as snap judgments and occur in fast-thinking mode. Ross (2014) noted that if you are human, then you are biased. Specifically, he says, "Unconscious influences dominate our everyday life. What we react to, are influenced by, see or don't see, are all determined by reactions that happen deep within our psyche" (10). What we need to do is slow our thinking down by doing the three steps outlined above. But it takes a lot of practice, which is why I suggest you pay attention to your everyday biases when you are grocery shopping, going to the movies, or walking your dog. Since, as a human, you are having first thoughts anyway, why not use the opportunity to check your filter, question your belief system, and listen to your deficit monitor?

I want to put these three steps to the test by using myself as an example. I recognize my many biased thoughts every day. In the winter of 2017, I visited Chicago. As I made my way out of the airport to the rental car shuttle, the cold hit me hard. I knew it would be cold, but I did not expect the freeze to take effect as soon I hit the outside. When I got to the shuttle stop, I noticed a man in shorts and flip-flops. I was shocked! It was 15 degrees. I felt like ice, and this guy looked like he was heading to Santa Monica Beach in California, where I am from. My first thought was, *What the hell is he doing out here like that?* My next thought was, *This is what* they *do.* "They" for me was white people. And as soon as I had this thought, I began my internal process:

1. I checked my filter: Where did I get my information from about Caucasians and liking the cold? I had to search my mind and experiences. And I realized it was mainly from media and also the geography of where "they" live, as far as I knew. In either case, I was misinformed or not fully informed.

2. I questioned my belief system: What did I believe about Caucasians and the cold? More importantly, what did I believe about this man? The bottom line is I could not draw any conclusions. I had to acknowledge my stereotyping.

3. I listened to my deficit monitor: I stopped thinking with a stereotype and looked at this gentleman anew, comfortable with the fact that I had no idea why he was dressed in shorts and flip-flops in 15-degree weather. In truth, it did not matter.

In order for you to effectively VABB, you are going to have to go through the same process and eventually put it on automation. Again, I suggest you start at home, but eventually it will be about recognizing the biases and ignorance you have about your students. You cannot VABB without recognizing your first thoughts, but remember that they will not be your last thoughts. The key to being willing to recognize when you are thinking with prejudice is to know who you are culturally and linguistically, which is the next step in the changing of your mindset.

Pause to Ponder

Think of the last time you had a biased thought and how you responded. What cultural behaviors are you seeing in a negative way as it applies to your students?

Knowing Your Cultural Identity

The research is clear. The better you know who you are racially, ethnically, and nationally, the more likely you are to validate and affirm others (Villegas and Lucas 2004; Villicana, Rivera, and Dasgupta 2011). The concept is simple. When you love yourself and know who you are culturally and linguistically, you are likely to love others. The worrisome part of this concept is its opposite. If you do not love who you are culturally, then you are unlikely to be validating and affirming or to change your instruction to fit your student population. Similar to listening to your deficit monitor, knowing your identity is a prerequisite to changing your skillset or instruction in the classroom and the school climate. Discovering yourself culturally is a liberating experience because it gives you empathy. Empathy will open up your teaching and allow you to be more validating and affirming. In other words, when you are able to consider your cultural background with confidence, then you are able to walk in the shoes of your students. That walk begins with your understanding and accepting the fundamental difference between race and culture first and then seeing how the concept of the "rings of culture" connects to VABBing overall. Before distinguishing race from culture, I want to look at the bigger picture of CLR.

Purpose of Culturally and Linguistically Responsive Pedagogy

Given the historical context for who benefits most from culturally and linguistically responsive pedagogy, it is easier to understand why we need CLR. Inject the topics of race, culture, and language into almost any conversation, and you are very likely to find an intense and provocative discussion. Enter those same topics in a discussion among educators, and you encounter a surly tension with a tempered vibe. When the topics of race, culture, and language are coupled with the pressure of increasing standardized test scores, educators are faced with simple but complex choices for addressing the real issues of diversity and improving student achievement.

The simplicity of the choices is often provided through state, federal, and district curricular mandates with quick-fix-it programs that ultimately do not address the diversity issues with substantive and sustaining change. Such mandates invariably replicate the persistent stagnation and failure of the school as an institution to meet the needs of underserved students. The difficulty of making appropriate choices is either masked in the negative beliefs, attitudes, and expectations about certain students, or it is clouded by the desire and the intention to make changes but without the knowledge of how to do so instructionally. Culturally and linguistically responsive pedagogy deals with the complexity of both these negative mindsets and the well-intentioned desires to make changes that will matter.

It is worth restating: The first purpose of CLR is to refute deficit thinking by having educators undergo a change in heart and in mind about underserved students. I call this change a *mindset shift*, or as my colleague Kiechelle Russell dubbed it, a "mindshift." In order to be culturally and linguistically responsive, educators have to shift their beliefs, attitudes, and knowledge to a stance that sees what the student brings culturally and linguistically as an asset, a capability, and an element that can be built upon. In this mindshift, students are not the problem but rather the source of the solution.

A second purpose for CLR pedagogy is to clarify what is meant specifically by culture while simultaneously giving educators an awareness of some of the noted cultural and linguistic behaviors of underserved student populations. There is a lingering confusion between race and culture and the various identities that comprise who we are culturally. We are made up of at least seven separate identities, of which all but one have an unrelated cultural connection. The seven identities are race, gender, nationality, religion, ethnicity, class, and age.

These identities examined in isolation say something about who we are and why we enact certain behaviors, or make what I call *cultural determinations*. The exception is race. In other words, our behaviors are culturally determined by these identities only. But race determines nothing about our behavior. For example, there are some behaviors that we do simply because of how old we are or the decade we grew up in and nothing else. Some decisions and behaviors are based on our socioeconomic identity and nothing else. Before examining other examples, I want to clearly eliminate racial identity as the one factor that has nothing to do with cultural determination.

Our racial identity is very clear: it is the biological DNA representation that gives us our blood lineage and inherited physical traits, such as bone structure and eye color. Other than that, racial identity really tells us nothing about who we are as individuals. In *The Myth of Race: The Troubling Persistence of an Unscientific Idea*, Sussman states, "Anthropologists have shown for many years now that there is no biological reality to the human race. There are no major complex behaviors that directly correlate with what might be considered human 'racial' characteristics" (2014, 2). The salient point is that racial identity has nothing to do with our cultural identity. Racial identity does not necessitate or affect any of our other identities—age, religion, gender, ethnicity, or nationality. There is nothing that we do racially that is connected to who we are mentally or behaviorally. Although we are locked into our racial identity by birth and perhaps genomes, we remain free to be who we are ethnically or otherwise.

On the other hand, by acknowledging our various cultural identities in explicit terms, we are acknowledging a cultural complexity that truly speaks to the kaleidoscope that has been guised under the narrowness of racial identity and the thickness of racism for too long. From an ethnocultural perspective, being African American does not mean that one is Black, if Black is seen as an ethnic identity no different from Irish, Armenian, or Jewish. Being Caucasian American does not mean that one is ethnically White Anglo-Saxon Protestant or Catholic. Villegas and Lucas (2007) define culture as the way life is organized within an identifiable community or group. This includes the ways in which a community uses language, interacts with one another, takes turns to talk, relates to time and space, and approaches learning. The group patterns that exist reflect the standards or norms used by community members to make sense of the world. Clifford Geertz defined culture as "an historically transmitted pattern of meanings embodied in symbols, a system of inherited conceptions expressed in symbolic forms by means of which 'men' communicate, perpetuate, and develop their knowledge about and attitudes toward life" (Sussman 2014, 161). Simply, cultural identity is the way we see the world.

Culture or ethnic identity differs from race, nationality, and socioeconomic identity in that our ethnocultural identity is passed down from generation to generation. Sometimes, who we are ethnoculturally can be mistaken for our national cultural identity and/or our socioeconomic cultural identity. In fact, there are behaviors that we exhibit based simply on our nationality or our economic status. Consider these two questions:

- Why do you celebrate the Fourth of July if you are a United States citizen?

- Where do you wash your clothes?

Before answering the first question, though, ask yourself if you celebrate the Fourth of July because you are White Anglo-Saxon or Mexican (ethnically and not racially speaking) or because you are a citizen of the United States. For the second question, by knowing where you wash your clothes, I can (most of the time) accurately guess your economic status. If you regularly wash your clothes at a Laundromat, washhouse, or building complex, my guess would be that you are of a lower or working socioeconomic class. If you wash your clothes in your home, then my guess would be middle class. If someone washes your clothes for you, then you might be upper class. The point is that the Independence Day that you celebrate is determined not by your ethnocultural identity but by your national cultural identity. The way you wash your clothes is not determined by your Black or White ethnicity but by your economic identity.

Some people find it difficult to determine which vocabulary to use to describe their Rings of Culture. In addition to confusion around ethnicity and race (see sidebar on page 37 for clarification), there are evolving terms for identifying gender and orientation with which not everyone may be familiar. Educators should familiarize themselves with the terminology associated with these rings and understand their connotations.

The central focus of CLR is the ethnocultural identity of students, but not to the exclusion of the other identities that define culture. Additionally, educators have to be responsive to gender culture, orientation culture, national culture, socioeconomic culture, and age culture—or what I call the *Rings of Culture*. Figure 1.2 illustrates the Rings of Culture. Each of these rings is a potential source of responsiveness for the educator. Notice that race does not appear in the figure.

Fig. 1.2 Rings of Culture

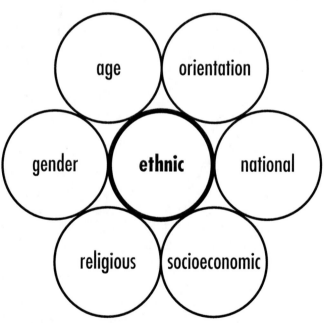

Pause to Ponder

Who are you? Identify the Rings of Culture for yourself. For each ring, provide a behavior or attribute that you do solely linked to that identity. Two hints: Ethnic identity is your home culture (heritage) and race is not a culture, so it is not a ring. Consider how you might learn about your students using the rings. I have completed the Rings of Culture diagram for myself as an example.

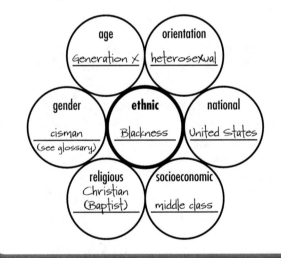

age	**orientation**
Generation X	heterosexual

gender	**ethnic**	**national**
cisman (see glossary)	Blackness	United States

religious	**socioeconomic**
Christian (Baptist)	middle class

What educators must not do is to mistake one of these cultures for another, and they certainly should not confuse any of these with race, which often happens in the classroom. Such mistakes affect the dynamics of instruction. Sometimes, educators will make judgments about African American students' behaviors as being Black ethnically when in actuality the behaviors are more in alignment with lower socioeconomic behaviors. For example, consider the familiar stereotype about some African American or Black students being unlikely to do their homework. Educators who make these assumptions about Black students generalize a socioeconomic behavior (doing homework) as an ethnocultural behavior. Indeed, the fact that some educators would conclude that Black students are less likely to do homework causes these educators to miss the opportunity to be responsive to the economic culture. Similarly, a persistent cultural myth about Mexican American students is that they value labor over education and often drop out of school because they are not interested in education. In fact, it is often structural economic pressure and depressed wages for Mexican American workers that often burden youth to forgo education to attend to immediate needs. Once again, this would be a consequence of generalizing a socioeconomic behavior as an ethnocultural behavior.

The Link Between the Rings of Culture and VABB

An understanding of the Rings of Culture is directly linked to the process of validating, affirming, building, and bridging, especially as it applies to ethnocultural identity. Recall that part of the purpose of CLR is to make legitimate and positive those cultural and linguistic features that have been made illegitimate and negative by institutions and mainstream media. It is the ethnocultural identity that needs to be most validated and affirmed. The issue for educators is to appropriately identify those ethnocultural behaviors. For this reason, I rely on anthropological research, going back to when the original distinctions were made between race and culture. As early as the 1800s all the way up until the 1930s, the use of race as culture had been institutionalized (for example, put in textbooks) and was considered, simply put, racist. Since my focus is not on race, I strongly encourage you to research the racist history of eugenics and other so-called scientists.

What is significant for culturally responsive educators is the work of Franz Boas, the father of American anthropology. Boas distinguished race from culture in a way that debunked what had gone heretofore. He introduced what is now known as the Iceberg Concept of Culture, uprooting the idea that race is behaviorally based. Figure 1.3 shows the Iceberg Concept of Culture. It is from the Iceberg that I pull general ethnocultural behaviors, which are our home cultural behavior because we learn them from when we are born from those who are raising us, and they learned them the same way. Therefore, these behaviors represent our heritage.

Notice that the iceberg is divided into three sections: surface, shallow, and deep. To be culturally responsive, your emphasis will be on the shallow and deep behaviors, not the superficial. In fact, if you only focus on superficial culture, you are doing a disservice to cultural responsiveness overall because you are ignoring who your students really are at the deepest levels. Take a moment and look at those behaviors; they are comprehensive and expansive. For me, this list of elements of culture shows the complexity of culture and illuminates how we as educators often simplify who our students are culturally and linguistically.

Fig. 1.3 The Iceberg Concept of Culture
Like an iceberg, nine-tenths of culture is below the surface.

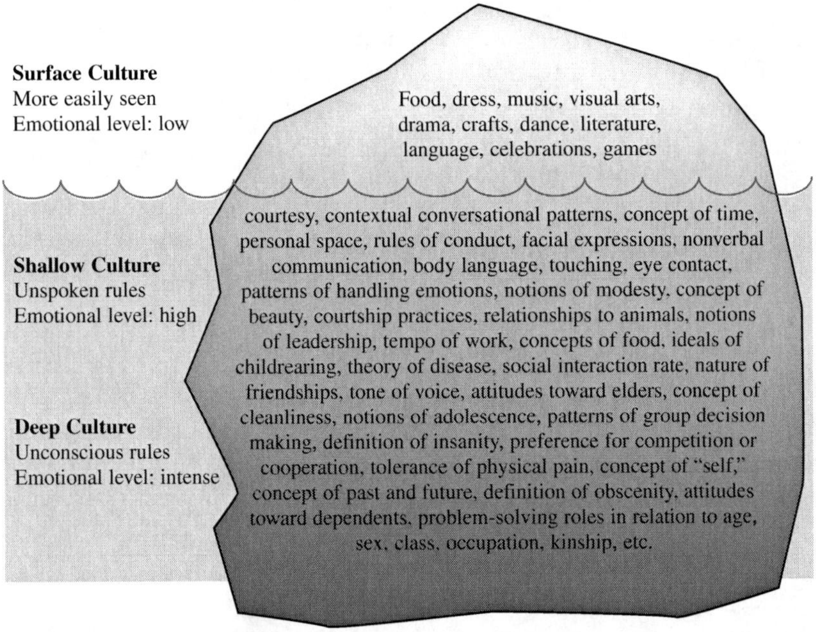

Surface Culture
More easily seen
Emotional level: low

Food, dress, music, visual arts, drama, crafts, dance, literature, language, celebrations, games

Shallow Culture
Unspoken rules
Emotional level: high

Deep Culture
Unconscious rules
Emotional level: intense

courtesy, contextual conversational patterns, concept of time, personal space, rules of conduct, facial expressions, nonverbal communication, body language, touching, eye contact, patterns of handling emotions, notions of modesty, concept of beauty, courtship practices, relationships to animals, notions of leadership, tempo of work, concepts of food, ideals of childrearing, theory of disease, social interaction rate, nature of friendships, tone of voice, attitudes toward elders, concept of cleanliness, notions of adolescence, patterns of group decision making, definition of insanity, preference for competition or cooperation, tolerance of physical pain, concept of "self," concept of past and future, definition of obscenity, attitudes toward dependents, problem-solving roles in relation to age, sex, class, occupation, kinship, etc.

(Fatlu and Rodgers 1984)

In the milieu of the classroom, we focus on the most common ethnocultural behaviors, based on the work of Boykin (1983). Many of these behaviors are in stark contrast to the behaviors validated by school and mainstream culture. These behaviors include preferences for variation and spontaneity, sociocentricity, high-movement contexts, approximation of time, collaboration, inductive reasoning, verbal overlap, and pragmatic, interpersonal, and affective language use. These cultural behaviors, which are typically viewed negatively in the culture of school, are the ones that need to be validated and affirmed. Students whose cultural norms mirror those of mainstream culture are already being VABBed. These expected behaviors of the school and mainstream culture include a focus on prompting, independence, low-movement contexts, competition, deductive reasoning, and verbal communication. Once educators have validated and affirmed students' home cultural norms and mores, they can then begin practicing CLR notably by building awareness of and bridging toward the cultural norms and mores of the school and mainstream culture. To be clear, the focus of your validating and affirming will be around the behaviors listed above because these are the behaviors that are the most common to the culture of your classroom. Throughout the rest of this text and in other CLR resources, you will see these specific behaviors referenced.

Focus on Linguistic Behaviors

Similar to culture, the linguistic behaviors of students have to be validated and affirmed in the context of their home language for the purposes of building and bridging to proficiency in Standard English and Academic Language. In order to be linguistically responsive, educators have to subscribe to the following three linguistic absolutes:

1. All language is good for the communicative purposes it serves. There is no such thing as proper English, bad English, street speech, or "gutter talk" in the context of interpersonal communication.

2. All linguistic forms are rule governed and systematic and are not randomly formed or put together haphazardly. They are regular in their phonological and syntactic patterns.

3. As infants and toddlers, beginning as early as pre-birth, we learn the language that is spoken in the home by the primary caregivers.

Understanding these three linguistic principles allows for an open-minded discussion around nonstandard languages.

The issue of the use of nonstandard linguistic forms extends beyond the United States. Corson (1997) reveals that formal educational policies for the treatment of nonstandard varieties of language are conspicuous by their absence in most educational systems. He points out that these varieties are nonetheless brought into the work of the school in one way or another. Educators have to recognize that children coming from these backgrounds often possess two or more linguistic varieties—one of which they use in their home and community and another that they use in school. Still, other forms may exist. The bottom line is that students speaking nonstandard language varieties are frequently penalized for using language that is different from the linguistic capital that has high status in the school.

Corson (1997) chronicles how the history of prejudice against the users of nonstandard varieties of a dominant language probably can be traced to the Ancient Greeks. Evidence shows that the use of different Greek dialects was used as a way of stereotyping other Greeks. A Roman playwright, Publilius Syrus, wrote that "speech is a mirror to the soul; as a man speaks, so is he" (Syrus). In France, the purpose of the *Académie française* was to maintain the purity of the

French standard variety. A national policy such as this has a direct impact on schooling for French children. Similarly, in Spain and Portugal, the standard varieties are elevated. Sometimes, negative consequences affect those speakers of nonstandard varieties.

In the United States, William Labov's studies (1972) of Black American and Puerto Rican vernaculars of English have proven to be groundbreaking. He found that people from different sociocultural backgrounds speak different kinds of English that, in important aspects, deviate systematically and regularly from one another. These findings helped to overturn the common stereotype that these and many other varieties of language are incorrect forms of English. Labov's legacy has been the evidence that nonstandard language varieties have their particular norms and rules of use. Therefore, these language forms deserve respect and valuation. However, the institution of education itself as a standard and routine practice devalues varieties that are very different from the dominant form.

The nonstandard languages that become the focus of applying linguistically responsive pedagogy are tied to the specific populations described here. These languages are Hawaiian Pidgin English (HPE), Chicano English (CE), American Indian dialects, and African American Vernacular English (AAVE). Each of these linguistic entities has its rule-governed system. Inclusive of all the language dimensions, examples of specific features of these languages are provided in Chapter 6.

Labov (1972) has argued that there is no real basis for attributing poor performance to the grammatical and phonological characteristics of any nonstandard variety of English. He found that it was not African American Vernacular English itself but teachers' low expectations based on linguistic misperceptions that were the culprit of academic failure. The students were deemed deficient because their language variety was wrongly judged in the context of school language. Generally speaking, educational policy for the use of nonstandard language forms is limited mainly because of simple ignorance about the range of varieties that can and do coexist in a single linguistic space (Corson 1997).

When educators recognize students' linguistic behaviors or the use of the rules of home languages as positives and not deficits, they can then begin to validate and affirm students' language. Consequently, teachers can begin the process of building and bridging that will enable students to succeed within the context of school culture and language.

Pause to Ponder

Including the unaccepted languages defined above, what are the various home languages in your class and school?

Identifying the Beneficiaries of Responsiveness

Without a doubt, the changing of an educator's mind-set and skill set benefits all students, regardless of their culture. Validation and affirmation is for everyone. There are some students, however, who will benefit more from this than others. Identifying who these students are focuses your advocacy and instruction. Since the beginning of state-mandated standardized testing, there are four groups—Mexican American, African American, Hawaiian American, and American Indian—that have been traditionally underserved, failing academically or behaviorally because the school is not culturally responsive (Hollie 2012; New American Foundation 2008). Through advocacy, CLR teaching and learning calls for specific discussions around certain students and particular issues that directly affect them. For instruction, educators implementing CLR identify the most underserved—any student who is not successful academically, socially, and/or behaviorally because of the school's unresponsiveness to the student's needs.

The Benefits of Culturally and Linguistically Responsive Pedagogy

The simple answer to the question of who benefits from culturally and linguistically responsive pedagogy is *all students*. A more specific answer delves into who these students are most likely to be in the sense of culture (not race) in the classroom. A survey of any past or recent standardized data gives the answer of who is and who is not achieving in our schools. In the context of academic failure and behavior issues, CLR most benefits *any* student who is identified as *underserved* as opposed to the more commonly labeled *underachieving* or *underperforming* student.

According to my definition that follows, the school as an institution is failing the student. Granted, the breadth of the definition speaks to the simplicity of who can be served by CLR. At face value, *underserved* includes many students. If teachers think about the underserved students in their particular classrooms, they are probably thinking of students of varying ethnicities, languages, and ability levels (low and high). The term *underserved* encompasses those students who are receiving bad customer service from the school, similar to you or me receiving subpar service at a restaurant or a department store. The difference is that we can ask to see a manager or even walk out of the establishment. Students cannot! They are stuck in a situation where the institution is failing them, so instead of asking for the manager, they simply check out mentally and emotionally. Or even worse, far too many stop attending school and are labeled *dropouts*, although in many cases they have been *pushed out*.

Who Are the Students Most Likely to Be Underserved?

Looking more specifically at which groups of students are likely to be underserved reveals why CLR is really important and shows the complexity involved in implementing the approach. Imagine that we asked all the underserved students you identified to come to the gymnasium. Research tells us who these students are most likely to be: African Americans, Mexican Americans (as opposed to the overgeneralized term *Latino*), American Indians, Samoan Americans and/or Eastern Asian immigrants, and Asian Americans (Goodwin 2011). Keep in mind that the overall intention is to better serve all students, but when we look at who is in the gymnasium now, we find these to be primarily students of color. The students are like those dissatisfied customers in a department store who need to be better served simply because of their place in the gymnasium and not endemically because of their race, nationality, ethnicity, or language. Bluntly put, we serve them because they are in the gymnasium of the underserved, not because of who they are racially, ethnically, or otherwise. In order to fully understand why students of color in particular are in the room, we need to examine the sociohistorical, sociopolitical, and sociolinguistic contexts.

Sociohistorical Context

The capstone research of John Ogbu (1978) indicates that many of these students can be described as involuntary immigrants to America. Ogbu posited that the experience in the American school was very different for an involuntary immigrant when compared to that of a voluntary immigrant or the Ellis Island immigrants. Involuntary immigrants, historically speaking, are more likely to be found in the so-called achievement gap and less likely to have post-secondary opportunities that lead to economic success. Voluntary immigrants, on the other hand, tend to perform well academically and find post-secondary opportunities that lead to economic viability and stability. The significant difference is that the involuntary immigrants' move to America comes through colonization, enslavement, conquest, or less than legal means. Simply put, these immigrants did not come through Ellis Island.

Whereas the path to success in the American school for the voluntary immigrant has come through a process of successful assimilation, the path for the involuntary immigrant and indigenous peoples has been more a process of forced or unsuccessful assimilation. The relevance of assimilation cannot be emphasized enough. In order to attain the American dream, most immigrants will have to assimilate into mainstream culture. The formula for success in academia and mainstream culture is straightforward. When offered the option of assimilating from one's indigenous (home) culture and language into that of the mainstream culture, many ethnic groups had great success in pursuing and achieving the American dream. On the contrary, those ethnic groups that were forced into the mainstream culture did not have a choice. Consequently, they did not have access to the tools that would have enabled them to become part of mainstream society. For example, the long-lasting effects of slavery, legal segregation, and institutional racism on the education of Africans in America have been well documented, and these factors still resonate in schools today (Anderson 1995; Smith 1998; Williams and Snipper 1990). Over 30 years ago, Ogbu said, "Before 1960 most societies did not provide their minorities with equal educational opportunities" (1978, 91). Howard (1988) professes that of the innumerable rights African Americans were denied during slavery, none were more important than education. The same can be said for many of the involuntary immigrant groups. According to Javier San Roman, former student advocate at the Culture and Language Academy of Success (CLAS) and now a consultant in national work for Mexican-American students, the introduction to compulsory public education began with the inferior segregated Mexican schools that operated throughout the Southwestern United States. Often, the rationale given for segregation of non-Black students at this time was that Mexican children posed potential health risks or were not redeemable outside of providing a basic level of education that was designed to prepare them for low-wage manual labor. Notable school desegregation court cases, such as *Roberto Alvarez v. Lemon Grove School District* in 1931 (the country's first successful school desegregation court victory) and *Mendez et al. v. Westminster* in 1947, dealt a significant blow to the rationale behind school segregation for all students.

For the American Indian and Hawaiian students, the process of the introduction to public education was carried forth through the boarding schools and academies that were designed to save the "native" and kill the "savage." At the Indian boarding schools, students were deliberately alienated from their language and culture and taught to value the alleged superiority of European culture and language. The early experiences of Native Hawaiian students mirrored the devaluation of their cultural and linguistic heritage in favor of European models. The collective experience of all involuntary immigrants and indigenous Americans in public education has been one of institutional neglect and a pervasive and pernicious deficit oriented toward the cultural and linguistic differences that they bring to the classroom.

Sociopolitical Context

The systematic denial of indigenous culture and language for involuntary immigrants was utilized as a means to eliminate their culture and linguistic heritages. These populations were in effect institutionally denied their own culture and, at the same time, were not given the opportunity to become part of mainstream culture. Joel Spring calls this process *deculturalization*. He defines deculturalization as the "educational process of destroying a people's culture and replacing it with a new culture. It is one of the most inhumane acts one can partake in. Culture shapes a person's beliefs, values, and morals. In the United States, historically the education system deculturalized the cultures of [American Indians], African Americans, Mexican Americans, Puerto Ricans, and immigrants from Ireland, Southern and Eastern Europe, and Asia" (1994, 7). Providing further evidence referring to American Indians, Spring notes, "Missionaries wanted to develop written

49

[American Indian] Languages not as a means of preserving [American Indian] history and religions, but so they could translate religious tracts to teach protestant Anglo-Saxon culture. In contrast, Sequoyah development of a written Cherokee language was for the purpose of preserving Cherokee culture" (1994, 28).

Angela Valenzuela terms this process of eliminating one's home culture as *subtractive schooling*. Subtractive schooling is the divestment of important social and cultural resources for students, leaving them progressively vulnerable to academic failure and the discouragement of cultural identity by presenting such characteristics as undesirable. Valenzuela says of the Mexican American student, "I came to locate 'the problem' of achievement squarely in school-based relationships and organizational structures and policies designed to erase students' culture. Over the three years in which I collected and analyzed my data, I became increasingly convinced that schooling is organized in ways that subtract resources from Mexican youth" (1999, 10). Part of being culturally and linguistically responsive requires the intentional effort to combat the long-lasting effects of deculturalization through validation and affirmation of the home language and culture. To effectively implement CLR, educators must recognize and understand the cultural and linguistic behaviors that need to be legitimized and made positive.

Sociolinguistic Context

Another commonality among students who are most likely to be underserved is their use of a nonstandard language as their home language. Historically, generations of these students' forefathers and foremothers who were in this country were denied quality formal second-language opportunities. In specific cases, as with the enslaved Africans, people were told that if they spoke their native language, their tongues would be cut out; if they congregated with more than two, they would be beaten; and if they were caught trying to learn the written language of the land, they would be punished or even killed. Here is an example of an enslavement code, written essentially as law and more commonly known as the *Black Codes* or *Slave Codes*:

> Punishment for teaching slaves or free persons of color to read:

> If any slave, Negro, or free person of color, or any white person, shall teach any other slave, Negro, or free person of color, to read or write either written or printed characters, the said free person of color or slave shall be punished by fine and whipping, or fine or whipping, at the discretion of the court

> Slave Codes of the State of Georgia, 1848
> Section II, Minor Offences

Ethnolinguists have explained that under these constraints, a second language formed that was a combination of the deep structure of the first or indigenous language and the vocabulary of the dominating language. In America, the dominant language would be Standard English, or Mainstream English. Linguists, in general, have labeled these second languages *nonstandard*. These languages have remained intact across generations to present day. For African American students, the nonstandard language is known most commonly as African American Vernacular English, or AAVE. For American Indians, there are numerous American Indian dialects. Looking at the Mexican American, particularly second or third generation, the nonstandard language is called Chicano English (Fought 2003). Lastly, Hawaiian Americans speak what is known as Hawaiian Pidgin English, or HPE. The linguistic characteristics of these nonstandard languages are described in Chapter 6.

In the context of CLR, the key is to understand that these populations share this sociolinguistic history. They share the history of nonstandard languages among racially isolated descendants who were denied the use of their indigenous languages and have traditionally performed poorly in schools (Baugh 2004). As with the cultural behaviors noted earlier, in many cases, the linguistic behaviors of these students are viewed as signs of a deficiency, laziness, or other aberration. In order to be linguistically responsive to the students in the classroom, such behaviors, therefore, have to be legitimized and made positive.

Pause to Ponder

Who are your underserved students? What data do you have to support your claim? What approaches, interventions, programs, or curricula are you using that may not be adequately meeting their needs?

Situational Appropriateness: Reason for VABBing

The processes of validating, affirming, building, and bridging move students toward being situationally appropriate—your number one reason for cultural and linguistic responsiveness. *Situational appropriateness* is the concept of determining which cultural or linguistic behaviors are most appropriate for a situation. In other words, students are allowed to make choices around cultural and linguistic behaviors dependent on the situation but without giving up or sacrificing what they consider to be their base culture or language.

Situational appropriateness is the crux of CLR. Understanding the concept will enable you to comprehend the pedagogical underpinnings or, more to the point, enrich the instructional experience for your students as well as yourself. In sum, situational appropriateness is understanding and using the most appropriate cultural or linguistic behaviors for a situation without losing who you are culturally or linguistically.

Related to situational appropriateness is the act of *codeswitching*, or what I call *cultureswitching*. Codeswitching means switching from one cultural or linguistic behavior to another for the purpose of being situationally appropriate. Note that in the linguistic literature, codeswitching has a very different meaning from that which applies in CLR. In linguistics, the term is usually associated with an action whereby one language is being utilized along with an infusion of the vocabulary of another language into the first language being spoken or written (Gardner-Chloros 2009). Codeswitching in CLR is used more literally and does not carry the pejorative association that is sometimes attached to the term. In the context of CLR, codeswitching is an *intentional* choice to skillfully and proficiently shift from one linguistic or cultural mode into another one without giving up, disavowing, or abandoning the home culture or language. You must be careful not to substitute *codeswitching* for incorrect or inappropriate language. I have found that it is harder to make those substitutions or misconstrue meaning with the terms *situational appropriateness* or *cultureswitching*, so I advocate for those in lieu of *codeswitching*.

Another way of looking at situational appropriateness is what Andy Molinsky calls *global dexterity* (2013). Molinsky defines it as learning to adapt your behavior across cultures, no matter what culture you come from, what culture you are going to, or the situation you find yourself in. Global dexterity is "fitting in without giving in" (Molinsky 2013, xi). Even though the context for this concept is the world of business and understanding how to work in different cultural spaces around the world, global dexterity as a concept aligns perfectly with situational appropriateness. We want our students, and in actuality all of us, to be "cultural chameleons," able to successfully navigate as many cultural and linguistic contexts as possible—starting with school culture.

If students who have been traditionally underserved are to overcome the barriers to achieving success in school and mainstream cultures, they must master the concept of situational appropriateness—culturally and linguistically. Situational appropriateness provides the necessary instructional experiences that form culturally and linguistically responsive pedagogy. Implementing VABB and the CLR pedagogy is the focus of the remaining chapters in this book. Each chapter describes activities that enable teachers to consistently validate, affirm, build, and bridge students to academic success in their classrooms.

Summary

In order for educators to be focused and to improve instruction for underserved students, a single term and definition of culturally responsive pedagogy must be adopted. The term I prescribe is *culturally and linguistically responsive teaching and learning*, or CLR. Four features define the key aspects of CLR: *validation*, *affirmation*, *build*, and *bridge,* or *VABBing*. CLR benefits all students but is most powerful with students who are traditionally underserved. To *validate* and to *affirm* means understanding the complexity of culture and the many forms it takes, including age, gender, and social class, using the Rings of Culture and the Iceberg Concept of Culture as references. This understanding creates opportunities for meaning-making experiences in school. Likewise, acknowledging and affirming the home language of the student as a nonstandard language speaker is another opportunity for validation and affirmation. In both cases, the general purpose is to set the framework for teaching students to be able to adjust their language and behavior as necessary to be situationally appropriate.

 **Reflection Guide**

Think back to your responses to the statements in the Anticipation Guide at the beginning of this chapter. Have your responses changed? Which parts of the chapter did you find most helpful in clarifying your understanding of culturally responsive teaching?

_____ Culturally responsive teaching is meant to help with race relations among educators and students.

_____ All students can achieve highly when given the opportunity to learn.

_____ Racial identity and cultural identity are synonymous.

_____ Nonstandard English is a simplified version of Standard English.

_____ Socioeconomic status is the most critical factor in student success.

1. From your reading of this chapter, where are you in your journey to responsiveness? Where is your school, your district?

2. What mindset changes are necessary for you to begin being more responsive to your students?

3. Which ideas in this chapter have you found to be most meaningful for your teaching situation? Share your observations with colleagues.

The Pedagogy of Cultural and Linguistic Responsiveness

Chapter 2

Anticipation Guide

What thoughts came to mind when you read the title of this chapter?

Do you agree or disagree with the following statements about the pedagogy of cultural and linguistic responsiveness?

_____ Culturally and linguistically responsive pedagogy is a curriculum.

_____ In using CLR, I should abandon what I have known to be successful with students.

_____ CLR strategies and activities can be infused into broad instructional areas.

_____ All the activities or strategies must *always* be culturally or linguistically responsive.

The Pool of Cultural and Linguistic Responsiveness

As mentioned previously, U.S. schooling is based on the sink-or-swim approach. You have some students who simply are good swimmers, meaning they "do" school well. On the other hand, you have some students who are not good swimmers or are not swimmers at all. These students don't do school "well." In order to reach those students who are not good swimmers or non-swimmers, you are going to have to jump in the pool with them and, not stand on the side of the pool. CLR is metaphorically diving into the pool and getting into the water with your students; you are meeting your students where they are, culturally and linguistically.

I use this pool analogy for the pedagogy of CLR. What separates this brand of cultural and linguistic responsiveness from other brands is a narrow focus on instructional practices, which include the why and the how of what you do instructionally. CLR bets all of its money on the fact that classroom instruction is the most impactful factor to student achievement (Dean et al. 2012). You, the classroom teacher, make the most significant difference. Therefore, in order to be culturally and linguistically responsive, you are going to have to change the way you teach for the better. Sometimes, when we hear the word change, we think "from bad to good." But this change is from better to best. Always remember that cultural responsiveness is about being "mo' betta."

This chapter is your invitation to dive into the CLR pool and start swimming so that you can be responsive to your students. Ultimately, CLR is a challenge to your existing pedagogy. Becoming culturally responsive means that your instruction changes for the better. I call this change in instruction *transformative instructional practices* or *TIPs*. CLR can renovate or overhaul your instruction, depending on where you are in your teaching and where you want to be at the end of the day. CLR is rooted in seeing and feeling the change for yourself, no different from losing weight, getting a new hairstyle, or buying a new outfit. In other words, you can see the difference without any external endorsement or research because you know that it feels right. This, however, is not to say that there is not ample research support for the effectiveness of these practices. In fact, the number of researchers providing supportive evidence is overwhelming (Dolan et al. 1993; Goodwin 2011; Johnson and Johnson 1987; Slavin 2010; Tate 2010; Zeichner 2003). Regardless, the most important evidence is seen within your students as they become more engaged and invested in their learning. The question is, are you willing to be transformed? Are you willing to participate in the journey to responsiveness?

Pause to Ponder

- What does the term *pedagogical area* suggest to you?

- In what ways do you think pedagogical areas should be designed to meet the needs of underserved students?

- In what ways do you talk to, relate to, and teach your students that are validating and affirming?

Pedagogy is defined as the "how" and "why" of teaching. Many administrators can attest to the fact that they have teachers who are strong in the "how" of teaching but weak in the content, or they have teachers strong in content but weak in the methodology. Strong pedagogy speaks to finding a balance between the "how and why" and the "what" of teaching—that is, combining appropriate methodology with knowledge of the content. CLR relies upon this pedagogical balance. In order to be successful in CLR, the practitioner has to understand the balance of the "how and why" and the "what."

The "how" of methodology comes in two parts: strategy and activity. *Strategy* means that the instructional activities must be strategically and deliberately determined. Teachers must weigh several factors, including outcome, purpose, standards-based relations, time allocation, resources, students' background knowledge, environmental space, assessment methods, and a host of other variables. Considerations of these factors will in effect determine the strategy or the activity to be used. The *activity* selected puts the strategy to action, and a wide range of activities can be chosen. Many of the activities used in CLR are familiar to teachers, but the difference lies in the strategic use of the activities to further responsiveness to the cultural and linguistic needs of the students. Many participants in my professional development programs have commented on how they have previously used the activities. What is new to them is the application within the context of a strategy or within the context of CLR.

In Chapter 1, you read about and responded to the idea of mindset shift and the concepts of VABBing and situational appropriateness. This chapter will cover the skillset of VABBing and situational appropriateness by giving you the what, why, and how. The CLR pedagogy has four components:

1. The Gatekeepers of Success

2. Methodology Continuum

3. CLR Categories and Activities: The Formula for Success

4. Re-imaging the Learning Environment

The difference between a *strategy* and an *activity* can be summed up metaphorically in a game of chess. A skilled player comes to a chess match with strategies in mind and a game plan of moves (or activities). The player then carries out the strategy through the activities. Similar to a chess game, CLR involves having a game plan (strategies) and a series of moves (activities) designed to implement that plan.

This chapter introduces and briefly describes these components. The gatekeepers of success include descriptions of classroom management, academic vocabulary, academic literacy, academic language, and learning environment. Next, you will gain an understanding of methodological practices. This understanding will be necessary because in order to be CLR, you have to be willing to teach from the different types of methodologies, as I define them. The actual pool of CLR categories and activities will be uncovered. Lastly, I will talk about why the learning environment is important to your overall CLR success. The overarching goal is for you to talk to, relate to, and teach your students differently, and the most significant difference will be how culturally and linguistically responsive you are. Part II, Building Skillsets, devotes one full chapter to each of these components of CLR pedagogy: classroom management, vocabulary instruction, academic literacy, academic language, and the learning environment. Before turning you loose to those chapters, an understanding of the primary components of CLR is necessary to enable you to progress effectively in your journey to responsive teaching.

The Gatekeepers of Success

I have identified four broad pedagogical areas and the learning environment that can be infused with CLR strategies and activities. These activity categories are identified along with the associated pedagogical areas below:

Culturally Responsive Classroom Management

- Use of attention signals
- Use of protocols for responding
- Use of protocols for discussing
- Use of movement
- Use of extended collaboration activities

Culturally Responsive Academic Vocabulary

- Use of leveled vocabulary words
- Use of Personal Thesaurus or Personal Dictionary tools
- Use of vocabulary acquisition strategies
- Use of reinforcement activities/assessments

Culturally Responsive Academic Literacy

- Use of CLR text
- Use of engaging read-alouds
- Use of effective literacy activities

Culturally Responsive Academic Language

- Use of Sentence Lifting
- Use of Role-Playing
- Use of Retellings
- Use of Revising

Culturally Responsive Learning Environment

- Use of De-Blumenbach
- Use of De-Commercialize
- Use of De-Superficialize

These pedagogical areas represent the general categories that I believe that all classrooms—regardless of grade level or content area—should have in place effectively and efficiently. In my discussion of CLR pedagogy, I include the term *responsive* in the label for each category to ensure that instruction centers on culturally and linguistically appropriate activities. These categories are the basis for instructional failure or success. CLR does not replace or shield ineffective instruction. At times, administrators will send so-called "bad" or ineffective teachers to our trainings, thinking that these teachers can be turned into "good" teachers through CLR. This is asking too much of the approach. CLR can make a difference for many inadequacies in instruction, but when the fundamentals are not effectively in place, using CLR is like putting a new suit on a dirty body. To be most effective with CLR, we have to make sure the body is clean first, meaning that educators should make sure the fundamentals are effectively in place.

Within each pedagogical area are subcategories that depict specific foci for the instruction in that area. These subcategories specify aspects for the teacher to consider when strategically determining how to do various activities. But more importantly, these areas are gatekeepers to success for students, meaning that if your students are not at least proficient or in some cases have mastery in these areas, they will not have success in school. They must be able to manage themselves in the school and classroom contexts, they must increase their academic vocabulary as they matriculate, they must improve their literacy skills, and they must be able to write and speak in academic language. If they do not do these things, they will not make it, regardless of their race or socioeconomic status. This is why I use the four areas because they affect every teacher, regardless of your grade level or content area. Listed next are more specific rationales and objectives for each of the areas. Each area will be expanded upon in its own chapter in the forthcoming section, Building Skillsets.

Responsive Classroom Management

No one can argue against the need for an effectively managed classroom (Marzano 2009). Students need to learn in a safe, secure, and positive environment that is conducive to learning and enables them to function optimally. Under the pedagogical area of classroom management, there are four subcategories: ways for responding, ways for discussing, attention signals, and movement. On the whole, these subcategories represent what *all* classrooms should have in place. Every classroom should have effective and efficient ways of having students discuss topics and respond to questions and prompts. Every classroom should have effective and efficient attention signals to indicate when the teacher needs to bring everyone back after conducting a discussion in groups. Furthermore, classroom activities should be designed to enable students to move around the room to provide opportunities for interactions with several classmates for a variety of purposes.

Pause to Ponder

How does CLR pedagogy strengthen the interrelationship between classroom management and effective learning?

Responsive Academic Vocabulary

The focus of vocabulary development is building on words that represent concepts that students bring to the classroom. Many of these words come from their cultural backgrounds and from their lives at home and in their communities. Conceptually, these words are connected to academic vocabulary, but students may not have the academic terms within their vocabulary. To promote students' acquisition of academic vocabulary, CLR teachers focus on effective common vocabulary strategies: wide and abundant reading, contextualization and conceptualization of words, knowledge of word parts, and synonyms. Using the personal thesaurus—a tool first used in the Academic English Mastery Program (AEMP) but fully developed at CLAS, teachers use activities that build on the students' words. The words selected for the personal thesaurus focus on academic words, those that Beck, McKeown, and Kucan (2002) believe teachers should target for instruction. The personal thesaurus is used to have students expand their academic vocabulary by building on words they *own* conceptually as a result of their experiences at home and in the community. Through a process of synonym development, students connect the conceptual words they have with the academic labels they are exposed to, therefore expanding their vocabulary. For teaching vocabulary terms that are in many cases specific to certain content areas, we have further developed another tool called the *personal dictionary* based on the Frayer Model (Frayer, Frederick, and Klaumeier 1969). In this activity, students create their personal dictionaries using words learned commonly in mathematics, science, social studies, and other areas.

Responsive Academic Literacy

Responsive use of fiction and nonfiction text is necessary to enhance students' success within the content areas. Strong literacy skills—reading, writing, speaking, and listening—are central to success in most content areas. Students who are strong readers and writers also tend to be strong in mathematics, science, and social studies (Krashen 2004). Think about it. Have you ever seen a student who is in both a basic reading class and in an Algebra 2 class? The answer is generally no. The effective use of literacy is a very important area for infusing CLR pedagogy. Reading aloud as a form of storytelling provides a cultural base for students in a classroom where CLR is implemented. Supplemental resources can be used to augment the core texts within the subject areas. For example, a science teacher can include supplemental articles, stories, and facts relevant to the standards-based topics from the mandated text that students are required to study. The purpose of supplementing the required text is to add a perspective that might be more culturally and linguistically relevant to the lives of students (Harris 1999). Finally, CLR proponents encourage the use of engaging literacy strategies, many of which are connected to oral and written language development.

Responsive Academic Language

The fourth pedagogical area involves the CLR teacher using the process of contrastive analysis, or codeswitching, in the students' instructional experiences. Contrastive analysis, a long-implemented second language methodology, entails having students look at linguistic forms in their home language and then translating those forms into their target language. Contrastive analysis can be used with written and oral language. In particular, when using the writing process, this type of analysis can be used during the revising and editing stages. The idea is that instead of having students "correct" their language, teachers have students "translate" to academic language. Students can practice codeswitching by participating in sentence-lifting exercises, doing situational role playing, or providing in-the-moment translations from their home language to the target language. For example, a student responds to a question in his or her home language. Let us assume the response was correct. The teacher would validate and affirm the response and then have the student translate the response from the home language into Standard English or Academic Language. Over time, having students engage in contrastive analysis on a regular basis can be empowering for them because their linguistic behaviors are validated and affirmed while they learn the benefits of speaking and writing in Standard English and Academic Language. The final subcategory in responsive academic language is situational role-playing. Having students practice situational appropriateness through role-playing is fun for them. This form of role-playing involves students in making language and behavioral choices based on the audience and the purpose of the communication.

Pause to Ponder

In what ways do you think instructional activities for vocabulary, academic literacy, and academic language overlap?

What opportunities do your students have to discuss what they are learning and be themselves, culturally and linguistically?

What is your most frequent way of having students respond to your questions in a whole-group setting?

Responsive Learning Environment

A responsive learning environment is an important aspect of CLR pedagogy. A CLR classroom environment is the key to understanding the environmental-behavior relationship that enables teachers to organize and equip the classroom so that situationally appropriate behaviors are likely to occur (Shade, Kelly, and Oberg 1997). All arranged environments can influence behavior. How spaces are organized through furniture placement, how learning materials are selected, where they are placed, and how the materials are arranged for the learners' use can have a profound impact on student achievement. These factors can send strong messages that encourage students to act in particular ways. Surrounding students with a language-rich environment rife with symbols and print that stimulate language development and literacy acquisition enables them to thrive. The arranged environment should provide the spatial context in which movement and learning activities take place. Also, the classroom environment has to provide resources rich in context, in terms of instructional materials. This includes relevant, validating, and affirming high-interest instructional resources that enhance student engagement in the learning process.

Methodology Continuum: Traditional, Responsive, and Culturally Responsive

Most instructional methodology used in the classroom falls into one of three broad categories: traditional methodology, responsive methodology, and culturally responsive methodology. Traditional instruction is teacher-centered with a higher affective filter and reliance on one-way interaction. Responsive instruction is student-centered with a lowered affective filter and reliance on two-way interaction. Therefore, culturally responsive instruction is responsive but with the addition of cultural (anthropological) elements, such as language, rhythm (music), movement, social interactions, and other aspects of culture (see Figure 1.2 and Figure 1.3). The objective is to have a balance of activities across the continuum. If this can be accomplished, then culturally responsive instruction is achieved because we know that validating and affirming activities (responsive and culturally responsive) as well as building and bridging activities (traditional) are utilized. By implementing activities across the continuum, you are meeting the needs of all students. If your instruction is heavily weighted on the traditional side of the continuum, then you need to jump into the CLR pool.

Fig. 2.1 Methodology Continuum

$$\longleftarrow\hspace{8cm}\longrightarrow$$

| Traditional Instruction | Responsive Instruction | Culturally Responsive Instruction |

How does this continuum play out in the classroom? Let's say, for example, you start your lesson with direct instruction, which most would consider traditional methodology. Then, after your brief direct instruction, you asked students to converse with an activity, such as "turn and talk." Now, you have moved to responsive methodology. Once students have engaged for about three minutes, you call them back to attention with a call and response that involves rhythm. That activity would move you to the culturally responsive side of the continuum. To close the block of instruction, you have students complete a learning log (traditional) and then have them move around the classroom to share what they have learned (responsive). As students engage with their peers, they greet them with a cultural greeting (culturally responsive).

The key point in this example is that responsive and culturally responsive instruction validates and affirms students' cultures and languages, and traditional instruction teaches and reinforces school- and mainstream-culture behaviors. Here is the hypothesis of the entire CLR approach and the point of this book in one sentence: By using the CLR recommended activities, you are inevitably being culturally responsive—*if* you have a strategic mindset as to why you are utilizing the activities. I have done the hard work for you by attaching the litany of activities to cultural behaviors defined by research and experience. Your charge, then, is to simply fill your toolbox with CLR activities.

Pause to Ponder

Consider a typical 20–30 minute block of your instructional time. Plot your activities along the methodology continuum. Are you meeting the needs of all your students?

CLR Categories and Activities: The Formula for Success

The challenge for most teachers is utilizing CLR activities strategically and intentionally. A successful culturally responsive teacher not only uses these activities but does so intentionally. There should never be random acts of teaching. Therefore, the CLR formula for success is Quantity + Quality + Strategy.

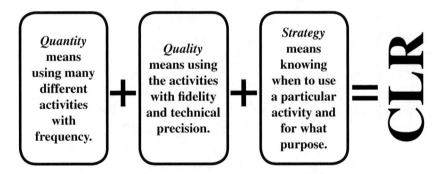

Quantity means using many different activities with frequency. **+** *Quality* means using the activities with fidelity and technical precision. **+** *Strategy* means knowing when to use a particular activity and for what purpose. **=** **CLR**

Culturally and linguistically responsive pedagogy is not a curriculum and does not come in a box. It is an approach—a way of thinking about how to instruct and how to create an instructional experience for students that validates, affirms, illuminates, inspires, and motivates them. If the general pedagogy is present, teachers must then reflect on the extent to which they are already implementing effective pedagogy and to what extent it is working. The standard agreement is this: CLR is meant to add to and to enhance what is already working, but if the existing pedagogy is not working, then the agreement is to get rid of it.

All of the recommended CLR categories and activities are research-based. For example, with the category of movement, brain-based research suggests that movement in the classroom is necessary and positive (Jensen 2005; Wolfe 2001). Providing opportunities for students to move about during class time is a factor for consideration in responsive classroom management. Having students move around the room while involved in instructional conversations provides a different way of learning that is validating and affirming. Movement takes learning from abstract to concrete (Jackson 2009). I prescribe that elementary students should be moving at least two to three times per hour and secondary students one to two times per hour.

Pause to Ponder

- Have you defined how often students should move about during class time?

- How are students' movements connected to instructional activities?

- What challenges do you anticipate as you provide opportunities for students to move about in the classroom?

Once the teacher has an established guideline of the frequency of students' movement, it is easy to check for "quantity" in the classroom. The question is straightforward. Depending on their level, how many times, on average, do students move in class? If the teacher has not planned routines and frequencies for movement, I advise that he or she do so to be more responsive to the needs of students. After establishing the quantity, check for the quality of the activities.

The question now becomes this: If the teacher is having students move two to three times per hour, what is it that he or she is having them do and, most importantly, is it working? For example, in a professional development session in which I asked participants to describe movement activities, a teacher described a question-answer relay game. The teacher used the game to review for a test. Individual students came up to the board, and the teacher gave them a question. If the student gave the correct answer, he or she could then relay the answer to a teammate, and that student would come up to the board. Although the students are moving, the quality of this movement would not be seen as responsive. Simply having one student move to the front of the room to answer questions is not considered instructional movement. The quality of the movement is poor in this example. Examples of higher-quality movement activities include *Give One, Get One*; *Think-Pair-Share*; or *Corners*. Effective instructional movement activities engage all of the students in mobility and instructional conversations while moving.

When working with CLR, identify quality pedagogy and build on it with frequency and CLR strategy. It is also important to identify where quality pedagogy is lacking, get rid of the activity, and replace it with a CLR strategy.

The Strategy of CLR: Focus on Intent and Purpose

There are two important questions to focus on regarding the strategy of the CLR pedagogy:

- What specific activities are to be infused into the general lesson? (This question speaks to intent.)

- What makes the lesson culturally and linguistically responsive? (This question speaks to purpose.)

Thinking back to the earlier example of movement, the following four steps speak to how the activity is broken down in terms of strategic use:

1. The first thing that students must do when they move and talk to one another is to greet one another in culture-specific ways. We acknowledge firsthand that greetings are cultural. This greeting comes through a cultural orientation that has been learned at home or in the community and that has been passed down from one generation to the next. For example, in Black culture, the greeting might be the "soul shake," or what is known as the "Black Man's hug." In a Middle Eastern culture, it might be a kiss on the cheek. Whatever the case, students are asked to culturally greet one another. The purpose is to validate and affirm the superficial behavior of cultural greetings.

2. Move! Every student has to be in and out of his or her desk. Unless physical limitations or challenges are at play, the expectation is that all students will be out of their seats. The purpose is to validate and affirm kinesthetic and social interactions.

3. Do the task. The task changes, depending on the activity. For example, in the activity *Give One, Get One*, students have a response that they have to give to another classmate (give one); in turn, they receive a piece of information (get one) from a classmate. The intent is structure and accountability.

4. Students may not talk to the individuals in their own row or group or in the group or row adjacent to them. The purpose of this step is to increase interaction among the students in the class and to ensure that they are not always talking to the same classmates. The intent is structure and accountability.

These steps represent CLR movement, but they also provide the intent and purpose, which speak to their strategic use.

Planning for Quantity, Quality, and Strategy

In Appendix G, I have provided several templates that are useful for planning lessons or thinking about how to infuse CLR into your teaching. Mainly, though, the templates give you a way to process how to think about CLR in the context of any lesson. For teachers embracing CLR pedagogy, two distinct aspects have to be realized:

1. A change in mindset about students' cultural and linguistic behaviors

2. Intentional incorporation of the strategies into daily teaching

Figure 2.2 shows a three-step template for how the CLR formula works.

- Step One—Quantity: What CLR activities am I using, and how frequently?

- Step Two—Quality: What is my accuracy and fidelity with the use of CLR activities?

- Step Three—Strategy: What is my intent and purpose with the use of CLR activities?

Fig. 2.2 Sample Three-step Template for CLR Lesson Planning

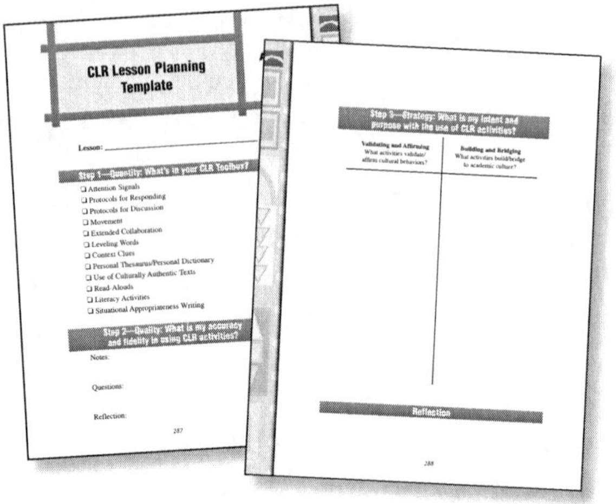

Step 1—Quantity: What's in your CLR Toolbox?

This step is the proverbial "activity" toolbox. It is here that you want to list the CLR activities that you feel you have conquered. This is your *quantity*. The activity would be listed in the box and in parenthesis is the CLR category that you are pulling from. Two examples show a use of call and response (attention signals) and a discussion protocol, Think-Pair-Share (protocols for discussion).

Step 2—Quality: What is my accuracy and fidelity in using CLR activities?

In this step, you assess the *quality* of your use of the activities. Do you have the accurate directions? Have you established the necessary procedures to enact the activity with your students? Have you allowed for practice with your students? Do you have all the necessary resources? Is your room environment conducive to doing the activity? Answering all these questions beforehand will ensure that the CLR activities are done with accuracy and fidelity.

Step 3—Strategy: What is my intent and purpose with use of CLR Activities?

This step gets to the heart of the matter with your CLR planning because now you have to specify which of the activities in the lesson are validating and affirming (VA) and which activities are building and bridging (BB). Remember that when you VA, you are consequently being responsive to your students' cultural and linguistic behaviors, and when you BB, you are teaching and reinforcing school culture behavior. Even though it is not explicitly stated here, know that the use of the activity goes with specific cultural behaviors. The thought is that over time, you know the behaviors because of your frequent use of the activities. As you can see in Figure 2.2, sticking with our movement example, there are two VA activities listed and two BB activities. The way they are listed is not by accident, as the next section will explain.

The Art of Juxtaposition

Prescribing that teachers use the responsive strategies with all students ensures that they will have ample opportunity to learn how to switch between languages or cultures and how to be situationally appropriate. To achieve success, students must have multiple instructional experiences in which they practice cultureswitching for situational appropriateness. This learning *must* occur through instruction. Lectures from guest speakers, movies, field trips, ethnic food days, ethnic dress days, or anything that superficially addresses multiculturalism or appreciating diversity will *not* produce the desired results. To avoid these surface attempts at achieving situational appropriateness, an action known as *instructional juxtaposition* is necessary. An instructional juxtaposition is intentionally pairing a VA activity right next to a BB activity to simulate situational appropriateness for the students. By doing so, you are giving students practice in determining which cultural and/or linguistic behaviors are necessary for the instructional context. Your goal is to create as many juxtapositions of VA and BB during instruction as possible.

Traditional strategies or activities can, by default, be defined as teacher centered, having medium-to-high affective filter, and limiting student choice. These activities include what I call *random urgency*. Random urgency is the situation in which any student can be called on at any time, and students do not resist being called upon because they believe the process is fair and random. In contrast, teachers can use instructional juxtaposition to allow students to give verbal responses spontaneously. In the activity *Give a Shout Out*, students can "shout out" their responses, but their responses have to be one-word responses done in chorus. For example, the teacher might ask, "What is the answer for the problem *two times three minus four*?" The teacher would then say, "Shout out," and the class, in unison, would respond with the answer "two." *Give a Shout Out* can be juxtaposed with *Back It Up*, an activity in which the teacher calls on students. The former activity is culturally and linguistically responsive, and the latter is more traditional. By experiencing both activities in proximity, students get to practice cultureswitching and situational appropriateness through the teaching and learning. With ample practice over time, students can begin to decide for themselves which way of responding is most appropriate for them to use, depending on the situation. A series of these types of juxtapositions are empowering not only for students but for the teacher as well. "When I give activities that are responsive to my students, I seem to get more out of it than they do. It is liberating. It is empowering," a St. Louis teacher commented after using juxtapositions in her teaching. These and other CLR activities are described in the appendices section of the text. Figure 2.3 shows how juxtapositions would be displayed in the VA/BB Strategy Box. Each arrow represents a juxtaposition.

Fig. 2.3 Instructional Juxtapositions

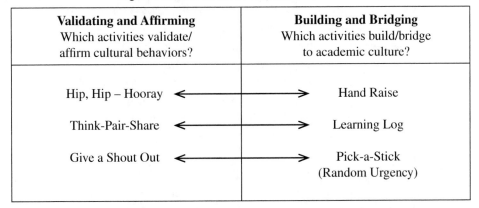

Validating and Affirming Which activities validate/ affirm cultural behaviors?	Building and Bridging Which activities build/bridge to academic culture?
Hip, Hip – Hooray ⟷	Hand Raise
Think-Pair-Share ⟷	Learning Log
Give a Shout Out ⟷	Pick-a-Stick (Random Urgency)

Pause to Ponder

Select a day or two of lessons across at least two content areas. Reflect on the lessons in terms of instructional juxtapositioning.

- To what extent did you consciously employ instructional juxtapositioning as you planned the lessons?

- Were the opportunities for juxtapositioning the same for each subject area?

- Where do you think your strengths were in planning the lessons? In VA activities? In BB activities? In ensuring that you VABBed the lessons?

Moving from Theory to Practice

If you were to take all the books, research articles, and presentations on culturally relevant teaching and put them in one area, you could probably fill up an average-size hotel room from the floor to the ceiling. If you were then to take all the books, research articles, and presentations on the classroom practices for culturally relevant teaching, you would be lucky to fill up the bathroom. The literature on the theory of CLR far outpaces the research on the instructional practice. Because of the lack of information on actual practice, the approach overall has suffered. CLR has remained too abstract for some practitioners who view it as a good idea in concept but not realistic for use in the classroom. For others, CLR is not sufficiently results based, difficult to construct in the classroom context, and not student focused. Guaranteed attacks on CLR come in the form of questions about achievement data and exemplary classroom models.

A great part of my inspiration to become engaged in the study of CLR was to defend it against such attacks. Initially, I observed that some attacks were warranted, particularly in the lack of exemplary classroom models. I thought the best way to address such criticisms was to create a school centered on the concept of culturally and linguistically responsive pedagogy. Consequently, I along with my colleagues Janis Bucknor and Anthony Jackson and a team of outstanding teachers, started the Culture and Language Academy of Success (CLAS), a nonaffiliated kindergarten-through-eighth-grade charter school in Los Angeles, which operated from 2003 through 2013. Centered on a positive mindset about students' culture and language, CLAS became one of the few models in the nation to demonstrate what CLR looks like in practice and in which instruction has been transformed by the use of strategies and the activities prescribed by the approach. The positive impact of CLR pedagogy is revealed in the school's test results. According to the California Standards Test and the Academic Performance Index, CLAS maintained high achievement results specifically in English language arts when compared to the local district and the state. The Academic Performance Index (API), the California state report card on schools, showed that for 2010, CLAS had a score of 822 in its elementary school and 728 for the middle school. Figure 2.4 shows a comparison between CLAS and the Los Angeles Unified School District over five years. Similarly, according to the Federal Annual Yearly Progress (AYP) report card, nearly 60 percent of CLAS students were advanced or proficient in reading/English language arts. These impressive results serve to inform those who have criticized the value and effectiveness of CLR pedagogy.

Fig. 2.4 Academic Performance Index (API) Comparison of CLAS and LAUSD from 2005–2010

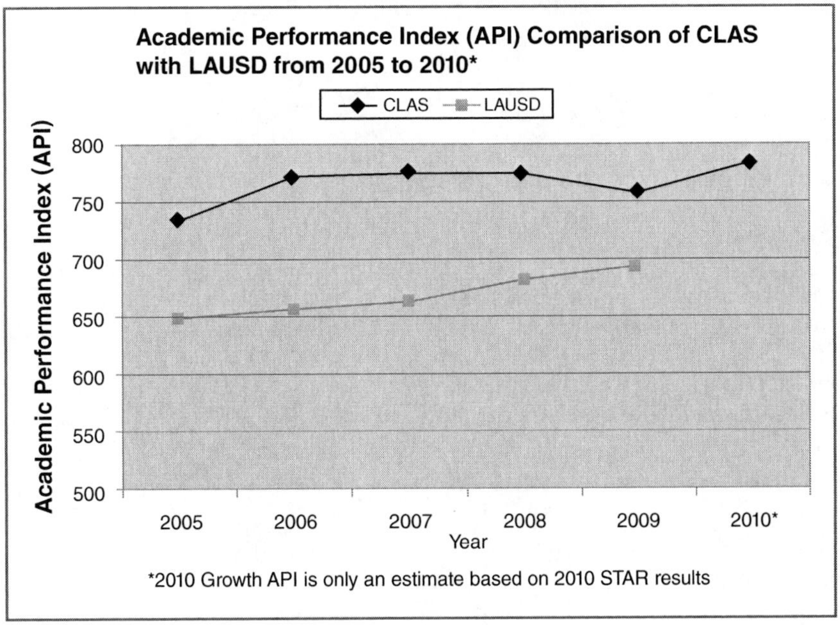

Academic Performance Index (API) Comparison of CLAS with LAUSD from 2005 to 2010*

*2010 Growth API is only an estimate based on 2010 STAR results

Summary

Pedagogy plays a critical role in the CLR formula. First, there has to be an agreement on common elements that must function effectively and efficiently in any classroom. These elements are summed up in four broad areas called *CLR pedagogies* or *focus instructional categories*. Second, there has to be a measurement of the quantity of the agreed-upon pedagogy. Does the pedagogy exist, and to what frequency or depth? After measuring for quantity, we check for quality, or very simply, is the pedagogy working? If it is not, the teacher agrees to let it go. Now we are ready to infuse CLR—or, as we say in our professional development, make it "funky"—through strategic activities, meaning intentionally and purposefully validating and affirming, and then building and bridging. Transforming traditional activities into CLR means involving responsive cultural and linguistic elements, using a variety of activities, and creating many instructional juxtapositions. When this is done, we accomplish teaching our students differently and see the results, like we saw at CLAS and that hundreds of teachers see across the country.

Reflection Guide

Think back to your responses to the statements in the Anticipation Guide at the beginning of this chapter. Have your responses changed? Which parts of the chapter did you find most helpful in clarifying your understanding of the pedagogy of cultural and linguistic responsiveness?

_____ Culturally and linguistically responsive pedagogy is a curriculum.

_____ In using CLR, I should abandon what I have known to be successful with students.

_____ CLR strategies and activities can be infused into broad instructional areas.

_____ All the activities or strategies must *always* be culturally or linguistically responsive.

1. What activities do you currently use that could be described as culturally and linguistically responsive? Do you think these activities are effective? Why or why not?

2. How could you use the activities *Give a Shout Out* and *Back It Up* with your students? What would you do to help them become familiar with the expected behaviors for each activity?

3. For CLR to be implemented successfully, the strategies and activities are prescribed for the teachers. What is your reaction to the prescriptive requirement for using CLR?

Building Skillsets

Part
2

Is My Classroom Management Culturally Responsive?

Anticipation Guide

What immediately comes to mind when you see the term *culturally responsive classroom management*? Do you agree or disagree with the following statements about the concept? Indicate *A* for agree and *D* for disagree.

_____ Effective lesson planning is the key to responsive classroom management.

_____ Students' cultural behaviors must *always* be considered in the context of classroom management.

_____ You consider your current classroom management system to be culturally responsive.

_____ Students should become accustomed to adjusting their behavior to meet the requirements of the classroom.

_____ The teacher's beliefs about systems of classroom management can affect the nature and quality of interactions with students.

_____ A permissive classroom atmosphere creates a welcoming environment for underserved students.

_____ No matter what the circumstances are, teachers should "love" their students.

The Why and How of Responsive Classroom Management

Effective classroom management has always been a staple of any teacher's recipe for success. It is a timeless truth of teaching and learning. Research on classroom management consistently indicates that skilled classroom management is a crucial element of effective teaching (Dolan et al. 1993; Fan 2014; Griffin, Hughes, and Martin 1982; Kane et al. 2011). For students to have success as they matriculate through school, they must be able to understand and to accept the school's institutional culture, the varied classroom expectations and procedures, and the ever-changing unspoken rules. For maximum learning to occur, both students and teachers need to value a well-managed classroom.

How then does cultural responsiveness apply? It relates to classroom management in two ways. The first way is to support increased student engagement (Marzano 2010). CLR pinpoints the existence of increased student engagement to highlight the positive classroom management that exists. The objective of CLR as it applies to classroom management is to increase student engagement and decrease management issues with responsive strategies and activities. The second way cultural responsiveness applies to effective classroom management is in the issue of race and equity. Typically, there is a disproportionate number of African American and Latino males given referrals, suspensions, and expulsions (Gregory, Skiba, and Noguera 2010). By becoming culturally responsive in classroom management, student engagement will increase, and referrals, suspensions, and expulsions, especially among the aforementioned groups, will decrease.

While the adage that an engaging lesson plan is the best resource for classroom management is true, the need for an effective positive classroom management culture will always exist. An effective management system may seem mundane and simple; however, it is in fact filled with complexities and intangibles that factor into successful infusion of culturally and linguistically responsive teaching. Before infusing CLR into the management system, teachers first need to assess the quantity and the quality of the current classroom management system. This assessment will lead to in-depth understandings of the strengths and limitations of the current system.

Chapter 3 is comprised of two main sections that provide opportunities for reflection. The first section enables you to examine your classroom management system: your management philosophy and its alignment with CLR; the extent to which you have the *Three Rs* (rapport, relationship, respect) in place; and how the *Three Ps* (positive, proactive, preventive) approach works for you. The second part looks at separating culturally inappropriate behaviors from unacceptable behaviors and how to use the CLR activities to validate, affirm, build, and bridge those behaviors toward the situationally appropriate.

Pause to Ponder

Think about your classroom management system. To assess the status of your system, answer *True* or *False* to the following statements.

1. Your students respect you, meaning that they have confidence that they will learn in your class.

2. You feel that you can comfortably communicate with your students in multiple ways, and they "get you."

3. You know your students, who they are personality-wise, where they are from, and what makes them tick and thrive.

4. You have a positive, affirming, caring classroom energy and vibe.

5. Most times, you are proactive with students who could be troublesome.

6. Your classroom environment is arranged in a way to prevent potential classroom management problems.

7. Your classroom management philosophy is collaborative and democratic but authoritarian when necessary.

Answering *true* to all these statements means your classroom management system is CLR ready.

What Is Your Classroom Management School of Thought?

The first step in assessing the current classroom management system requires teachers to examine their beliefs about management practices. This assessment calls on teachers to know the general management school of thought they aspire to as compared to what actually occurs during the course of the school day, week, and year. Emmer, Evertson, and Worsham (2003) describe the three most common schools of thought as *authoritarian*, *permissive*, and *democratic* (or *collaborative*, as it is sometimes called).

- *Authoritarian* speaks to the most traditional philosophy, whereby the primary control of the classroom rests with the teacher. The teacher is always in charge.

- *Permissive* is on the opposite end of the continuum. Students are not only in control, but they are in control in a way that tends to be negative, confrontational, and tension inducing in the environment of a traditional public school setting. In general, students do not like these classrooms, and administratively, they cannot be tolerated. Permissive classrooms are lose-lose situations. However, it should be noted that there are situations where the permissive stance does work, notably in some Montessori schools.

- The *democratic* or *collaborative* school of thought best aligns with the CLR approach. Democratic management is a collaborative process whereby a safe, comfortable environment that is conducive to learning is present. The adult facilitates that process for the class, and students participate in that process.

Of the three classroom management schools of thought described previously, which one do you aspire to demonstrate in your classroom?

CLR fits best with the collaborative approach because it lends itself to student choice, collaboration, and eventual independence. Students need to understand those factors, but they also need to recognize that the teacher is the final voice of authority in the classroom. CLR goes so well with the democratic approach because the approach not only garners control of the classroom but also provides students with opportunities to develop a love of learning. For CLR teachers, the one caveat is knowing when it is appropriate to be authoritarian. This caveat speaks to the art of teaching—that is, the meshing of intuition and skill. Often, this type of "knowing" in teaching cannot be taught, trained, or put in a manual. In reality, there are some teachers who intuitively just know when students need to be directed authoritatively and when they need more collaborative guidance. Interestingly, students will respond more positively to the democratic approach infused with CLR when there is an established respect for the teacher, an understood rapport between the student and the teacher, and a developing bonding relationship. When the Three Rs are present, then "going there," or becoming authoritarian, is more doable. Teachers who practice cultural and linguistic responsiveness tend to be collaborative in their philosophy, but they also know when to be authoritarian and how to be artful about it.

Do You Have the Three Rs: Rapport, Relationship, Respect?

The next step in reflecting on your classroom management system is recognizing that CLR does *not* replace ineffective classroom management. Many times, administrators will send teachers to my professional development sessions in hopes that what they learn will change these "poor and ineffective" classroom managers into effective educators. Isolated CLR training cannot solve the problems of teachers who are unable to manage their classrooms. To some extent, CLR strategies can bolster or enhance the situation in some struggling classroom management systems that, over time, can lead to improvement. However, what I have realized in working with thousands of teachers over nearly 20 years is that there are undeniable intangibles that have to be present to have an effective system. I have dubbed these intangibles the *Three Rs: Rapport, Relationship, Respect*. These three elements are inclusive of CLR, but the extent and depth of that inclusivity remains relative to the context. The three elements are described in the following table.

Fig. 3.1 The Three Rs: Rapport, Relationship, Respect

The Three Rs	Definition
Rapport	Rapport speaks to a special connection between the teacher and the student that leads to an understanding based on concern and care for one another. Rapport is the condition that allows one teacher to be able to banter with students while another teacher with the same students is not able to do so.
Relationship	Building relationships is another intangible but essential component. Teachers who have built relationships with their students are trusted. Trust will liberate the teacher and the student to be what they need to be at given moments. The implication is that there are times when the teacher may not like what a student is doing but has the freedom to manage the behavior because of the trust that exists between them.

The Three Rs	Definition
Respect	Mutual respect between the students and the teacher has to be in place. The respect for the teacher is very simple. The student has to have the confidence that the teacher can teach. Over time, underserved students lose confidence in the ability of teachers to teach. For these students, the first criterion for respect is based on the teacher's ability to convey knowledge with understanding and sensitivity to the audience. With respect in place, the other two *R*s are made possible.

As teachers reflect on the management issues in their classrooms, they need to be fully aware of the nature of their relationships with their students. The advantage of validating and affirming your students regularly is that doing so supports building rapport and developing relationships with them. You will eventually, then, earn their respect. Culturally speaking, respect is not given on general principle; it is earned over time.

Pause to Ponder

Survey your students to find out how the *Three Rs* are operating in your classroom.

- Do they feel like they have a good relationship with you?

- Do they feel like you know them culturally and linguistically?

- Do they respect you? If so, do they respect you for how you teach and treat them or because you are the authority figure in the room?

What evidence do you have that your management style supports the Three Rs?

Do You Use the Three Ps Approach: Positive, Proactive, and Procedures?

The third step of the reflection is what I call the *Three Ps* approach. Teachers who are intent on incorporating CLR into their classroom management system should subscribe to the *Three Ps* approach: being *positive*, being *proactive*, and using *procedures*. The first *P*, being *positive*, is the most pertinent to the CLR approach. Showing love to students for who they are might be the most basic principle for any CLR teacher. By default, to show love, an educator must be positive in vibe and in energy. What does it mean to be positive? It means having a set of uncomplicated and intangible characteristics that are demonstrated consistently to students, such as care, empathy, sensitivity, kindness, calmness, humor, forgiveness, and patience (Gay 2000). Being positive means that students' behaviors do not negatively impact the educator, which could result in such situations in which the teacher is visibly unhappy, is not enjoying coming to work, and is not finding the spark that matters so much in teaching. In other words, the teacher has become a negative source in the classroom because of the students' behaviors. A positive stance is best shown in CLR through the consistent use of affirmations—positive sayings, poems, verses, and words of praise.

The second *P*, *proactive*, is being ahead of the curve in the classroom management game. To stem disruptions in the classroom, CLR educators have to be able to predict potential problems and know where and when trouble can arise. Being proactive entails knowing who the students are and recognizing when occurrences on the schoolyard or happenings in their personal lives have preceded (and likely contributed to) what happens in the classroom. Without the teacher being proactive, reactions will rule, keeping the teacher backpedaling and putting out fires. Functioning reactively takes time away from instruction. Proactive behavior beats reactive behavior every time.

Typically, proactivity can be accomplished through changes in the classroom environment. For example, a teacher wants her students to enter through one door and exit out the other door. A student refuses to do so and enters and exits through both doors. The proactive teacher simply locks the exit door until its intended use at the end of the period. Here is another example that I sometimes joke about in my presentations. If a teacher knows that there is a student with "sticky fingers" in class, rather than constantly observing the student, the teacher can simply clear his or her desk of anything that can be lifted during the time that student is in the class. Do not fight that battle. Proactivity saves time and energy in the long run.

The final *P* is for using *procedures*. In classroom management terms, procedures are the engine to any classroom management system. Depending on a list of rules is ineffective. Ultimately, it will be the unwritten procedures that will determine your success. I liken your classroom procedures to the various ways of doing in your household, where there are no written rules. Your procedure for what happens after you wake up in the morning is on automation. Everyone in the household, including your pet(s), smoothly falls into place with when to go to the restroom, when to get dressed, and when it is time to leave for the day. Your classroom procedures have to be the same. Your students must do them automatically, with as little direction as possible. Your entire classroom management system hinges on the effectiveness of your procedures. Many times, teachers, especially new ones, underestimate the importance of procedures and begin focusing on the students as the problem. This situation moves them into a deficit orientation, which we discussed in chapter one—a big no-no for CLR.

You will find plenty of recommended procedures for effective classroom management in books written on that topic and on education websites. Routines should be established by the teacher before school begins and explicitly taught to the students and reviewed periodically to ensure that students understand them and participate effectively. Use the table on the next page to evaluate your effectiveness in implementing procedures. For each item, put a (+) if the procedure is working (meaning your students follow it without reminding), put a (−) if the procedure is not working and you have to repeatedly remind students to implement it, and put a 0 if you do not have a procedure in place. This list of procedures is by no means exhaustive. But every answer of – or 0 indicates a potential classroom management issue that needs to be addressed before you can focus on cultural responsiveness.

Type of Procedure	+ 0 –
How class officially begins	
What students do when work is complete	
What students do when they do not have supplies or need to sharpen a pencil	
Use of cell phones, headphones, or other technologies	
Late assignments	
Emergency drills	
Getting the teacher's attention during independent work	
Entering/exiting the classroom	

Pause to Ponder

For every – or 0 indicated on the chart above, try to find a colleague with a + in that particular procedure. Ask your colleague to share his or her procedure and how it was taught and practiced with students.

Once you have reflected upon your classroom management system and recognize that your philosophy is democratic, the Three Rs are in place, and the Three Ps approach is in effect, the steps to culturally responsive classroom management can be fully enacted. Don't miss the point of the previous section. Before you can dive into CLR and effective classroom management, you have to ensure that the fundamentals are first in place.

Understanding Behavior

The crux of culturally responsive classroom management is distinguishing culturally inappropriate behavior from unacceptable behavior and being committed, when necessary, to validating, affirming, building and bridging your students to culturally appropriate behaviors. In other words, you support them in being situationally appropriate. The next section discusses how to separate culturally inappropriate behaviors from unacceptable behaviors. Then, I go more in-depth on how to validate and affirm (VA) and build and bridge (BB) through the CLR categories and activities discussed in Chapter 2.

Separating Culturally Inappropriate Behavior from Unacceptable Behavior

Students coming from a culture—particularly one influenced by ethnicity, religion, or socioeconomics—that does not match the culture of school can find it challenging to conduct positive interactions and build positive relationships with teachers when their cultural behaviors are not recognized. Cultural norms and mores that emanate from students' home, community, and heritage lead to what I term *cultural misunderstandings* and *miscommunications* in classrooms every day. The way people interact with one another—for example in the use of call and response, whether they take turns to talk, how they use eye contact and proximity, and their conceptual measurements of time or space—are all culturally determined and machinated by how these functions are conducted in the home, within the family, and in the community (Villegas and Lucas 2007). Sometimes, these ways of communicating and interacting are not congruent with the expected cultural behaviors of the school. The clash between these cultural determinations and the expected cultural behaviors of a school (which are largely based in the White Anglo-Saxon or mainstream culture) all too often results in failure for teachers and students alike.

Since these misunderstandings and miscommunications occur for the most part unintentionally, students need to be taught situational appropriateness—the intentional use of the appropriate cultural and linguistic norms for the situation. But first, you, the teacher, have to learn how to validate and affirm your students in how you talk to them, how you relate to them, and how you teach them. Through teaching situational appropriateness, no judgment is passed or value assessed on any culture, in terms of bad versus good, high versus low, or standard versus substandard. The *appropriate* behavior is determined solely by the situation. In order to have success, CLR teachers must be able to deliberate and to decipher *unacceptable* behavior from *culturally inappropriate* behavior. Teachers, therefore, need to understand what these cultural behaviors are and why they exist.

Focus on Cultural Behaviors, Focus on Your Belief System

Being CLR is a constant challenge to your belief system around the cultural behaviors of your students. Understanding—and believing in—your students' cultural and linguistic behaviors is the essence of cultural and linguistic responsiveness. Focusing on cultural and linguistic behaviors builds on the proactive approach of utilizing validating and affirming engagement activities to culturally appeal to students. When these engagement activities are used, you are validating and affirming students' behaviors like sociocentrism, kinesthetic learning, communalism, and verbal expression. When examining cultural behaviors, I turn directly and specifically to the research in anthropology. *Keep in mind that our focus is not on race because it does not apply to behavior.* We look at cultural behaviors in a very broad sense, including the Rings of Culture, to avoid pigeonholing students. The best source for a general perspective of cultural behaviors is The Iceberg Concept of Culture (see Figure 1.3).

The Iceberg Concept of Culture is invaluable when looking at culture broadly because it provides us a way to talk about culture without stereotyping. The behaviors presented in the CLR framework are prototypical, not stereotypical. Molinsky says that when cultural differences are prototypes, they are presented as "on average or typical differences" within a given population (2013, xvi). This means that a behavior would not occur in every instance, and it is expected that there will be variations. In short, stereotypes generalize with assumptions; prototypes generalize without assumptions. In order to learn how to recognize cultural behaviors, you have to review the Iceberg to first recognize these behaviors as cultural versus fictitious or random. Note that there is a superficial perspective of culture in the figure, which is not the essence of cultural responsiveness. For example, having an annual International Food Day in your classroom where you serve foods from various ethnic groups does not truly validate and affirm your students' culture or make your teaching culturally responsive. While the students may enjoy tasting various ethnic foods, this type of activity does not actually help students achieve academic success by building and bridging to the culture of academia and mainstream culture. Thus, your focus should be on the behaviors below the line in the Iceberg Concept of Culture, for it is these behaviors that you are going to ultimately link to your classroom management practices. For example, these behaviors include such elements as courtesy, concept of time, patterns of handling emotions, or preferences for competition or cooperation.

The most common cultural behaviors exhibited in the classroom are described in Figure 3.2. These are the behaviors that you are going to have to check your belief system against what is culturally inappropriate and what is unacceptable. This is not to say that they are the only behaviors of focus, since culture is very nuanced and complex. Using a cultural lens to view students' behavior allows you to see your students differently in many ways, which is the end goal. When you acknowledge that your students are being culturally inappropriate, what you are then conceding is that your students are not being disrespectful, disruptive, insubordinate, or any other negative adjectives with which the institution of schooling has labeled them.

Fig. 3.2 Common Cultural Behaviors: What Do You Believe?

Behavior	Definition	Example
Communalism	"We" is more important than "me." Culturally, students are more invested in the success of the whole class or their group than individual accomplishments. In the classroom, students practicing communalism are sometimes thought to be unfocused or "worrying about everybody else."	Viewing the classroom as a community rather than a group of individual students
Eye Contact	We communicate with our eyes. In some cultures, maintaining eye contact demonstrates respect, focus, and intrigue. In other cultures, *not* maintaining eye contact actually demonstrates these characteristics. When students who are not part of an eye-contact-maintaining culture are told to focus by looking at the teacher, it sends a message that their cultural norm is unacceptable.	Students from many Latin American and Asian cultures show respect by avoiding eye contact with authority figures. On the contrary, in mainstream American culture, avoiding eye contact is often viewed as disrespectful.
Realness	How truth and authenticity are communicated to others can be culturally-based. In some cultures, directness is considered polite and expected, while in others, indirectness is more appropriate. In school culture, being direct is typically not preferred.	A student from a direct-communication culture tells the teacher that a lesson is boring. The student gets attention redirected by having the teacher ask the student what he or she is supposed to be doing at that moment instead of commenting on the lesson.

Behavior	Definition	Example
Orality and Verbal Expressiveness	It is not *what* you say but *how* you say it. For some cultures, nonverbal communication is more important than verbal communication. Reliance on nonverbal communication is known as *verbal expressiveness* and is sometimes viewed as being too dramatic or emotional in the context of school.	In mainstream American culture, the ability to express oneself verbally is considered very important. In other cultures, such as East Asian cultures, verbal expression is used cautiously and silence is often valued over speech.
Proximity	The distance between two people who are interacting is culturally dependent. Some cultures prefer more than a foot between speakers while for others the norm is less than a foot. It is important to understand the proximal space of your students and to teach them what is appropriate for school in different circumstances.	When conversing, specific cultures have different concepts of proximity. While some cultures are comfortable standing close together, other cultures prefer to maintain greater distance between people while talking. Whether a person is asking a question, seeking information, or simply wanting to relate through conversation all affect proximity.

Behavior	Definition	Example
Concept of Time	In some cultures, time is seen conceptually as precise, meaning the clock controls the beginning and end of an event. In other cultures, time is seen as relative, and the event is controlled by human interaction (what is going on at the moment), not the clock. Students who embrace the relativity of time can be seen as disrespectful when tardy or viewed as lazy when not finishing assignments on time. **Note:** Students should be on time and finish assignments promptly. However, understanding why they may be late and not immediately assuming it is out of disrespect goes a long way.	Some cultures, such as mainstream American culture, view time as limited and therefore place a high value on punctuality. Other cultures, such as Latino cultures, place a higher value on the human transactions that occur during a given time rather than the specific time itself, and therefore do not value punctuality as highly as mainstream American culture.
Conversational Patterns	In some cultures, interrupting or jumping in while someone is talking is acceptable or even expected. The timing of the jump-in is culturally or linguistically based. Clearly, in the school culture, it is not seen that way. Students who come from "jump-in" cultures are confused when they are chastised for interrupting frequently, given that their understanding of conversations at home with family are comprised of regular jump-ins.	In mainstream American conversation, participants are expected to jump into conversations in order to express their views and opinions. Japanese conversations follow a more orderly system where everyone takes turns expressing his or her opinion in an effort to reach a common goal.

Consider common cultural behaviors and see if you can culturally align them to some of your students. As a reminder, think about culture, not race.

The Context of Culturally Inappropriate Behavior

Imagine that you are attending a spiritual service of any type. You are a visitor and not a subscriber to the faith. As the service begins, you immediately notice the differences between your usual spiritual service and the service you are attending. Your home service starts with a boisterous praise and worship. People are on their feet, singing and clapping. This service starts with a silent prayer and a calming hymn. Your home service allows for expected interactions with the pulpit through a process known as call-and-response. This service does not. In fact, you have the feeling that if you shout out "Amen," you might be asked to leave. Now, as an observer to this experience, the question becomes, *Would it be wrong or simply inappropriate culturally if you were to shout "Amen" during the sermon in the context of this service?* The answer to that question is the understanding of how to infuse CLR into any classroom management system.

Sticking with the example, most would say that shouting out "Amen" during a spiritual service is inappropriate given the situation but not wrong given the spirituality. Clearly, the "Amen" is the right thought and feeling, but the response in this situation is inappropriate. My contention is that many students are being punished or dealing with negative consequences because their cultural behaviors are seen as wrong rather than inappropriate. Many times, underserved students are shouting out "Amen" in the classroom, but the teacher sees it as defiant, disruptive, or disrespectful.

In order to change this dynamic, teachers must understand cultural behaviors and be able to recognize them as such. This awareness will provide the opportunity for students to practice situational appropriateness. Instead of being sent out of the room, given a time-out, or being embarrassed in front of their peers, students can be taught how to switch to the culturally appropriate behavior. This process starts, however, with a validation and affirmation of the base behavior. Notably, the teacher has to know what is cultural and what is not. Fortunately, research provides ample data and support to help educators learn about the commonly accepted cultural behaviors of many underserved students. Figure 3.3 shows the traditional cultural behaviors of underserved students contrasted with the expected cultural behaviors of school, which, for the most part, are directly aligned with the mainstream or White Anglo-Saxon culture (Shade, Kelly, and Oberg 1997).

Fig. 3.3 General Commonly Accepted Cultural Behaviors

Cultural Behavior of Underserved Students	School Culture Behavioral Expectations
Sociocentric: The act of social interaction is more valued than the content being discussed; expectation of nonlinear discourse patterns	Egocentric: More of a focus on the individual than the group dynamic and the intended outcome of the interaction; nonlinear discourse discouraged
Cooperative: Working together and sharing responsibility is seen as a positive contribution to overall performance.	Competitive: Focused on the individual performance in relation to others; working alone and independent
Subjective: Essential understanding of a topic or concept lies in the relativity, perspective, granularity, and not just right and wrong; qualifiable	Objective: A more black/white, right/wrong, correct/incorrect lens, where perspective is based in fact, quantifiable and measurable
Relational: Thought processes based on multiple directions and ways to attain	Linear: A process of thinking rooted in the step-by-step movement through prerequisites

Cultural Behavior of Underserved Students	School Culture Behavioral Expectations
Dynamic attention span: Demonstration of varied ways to show focus and task orientation	Static attention span: Only one way to show focus and task orientation, mostly evidenced externally
Immediacy: Actions that all at once communicate warmth, acceptance, closeness, and availability	Distance: When activities communicate hierarchy, less directness, lack of emotion or connectedness
Spontaneous: Comfort level found in environments and contexts that are marked by impulse and improvisation	Prompted: Value based in cued, timed, and structured environments and contexts

While beneficial in describing a range of cultural behaviors, the research has been detrimental by presenting the behaviors in a dichotomous fashion, keeping the thinking about them divided and binary. My perspective allows for looking at the broad cultural categories in a relative, nuanced, and mundane manner. Rather than looking at the behaviors as one or the other, we can examine them on a continuum that determines their relativity in comparison to general categories that are applicable to all cultures. Molinsky's concept of global dexterity referenced in Chapter 1 shows the range of appropriate behavior, with each behavior best described as the *zone of appropriateness*. He says, "When adapting our behavior across cultures, we often mistakenly believe that there is one very specific way of acting in that new setting. But that's simply not true. Instead there is a zone of appropriate behavior" (2013, 17).

In other words, the common research presented in Figure 3.3 is too broad, even though it is on target in terms of identifying some of these behaviors. For an examination similar to the continuum I describe, I turn to the work of Wade Nobles (1987), an expert on African American psychology and Afrocentric perspectives. Nobles posits by implication in his examination of Black culture that all cultures are represented by five general categories: themes, values, customs, laws, and prerequisites. A series of descriptors under each topic comprises the topic and is thus representative of the cultural behavior. Figure 3.4 is an adaptation of Nobles's cultural matrix.

Fig. 3.4 Cultural Relativity Matrix and Continuum

Themes	Values	Customs	Laws (Precepts)	Prerequisites
• Spirituality • Resilience • Humanism • Communalism • Verbal expressiveness • Personal style and uniqueness • Emotional vitality • Musicality/ rhythm	• Respect (elders) • Self-mastery thought/behavior • Patience • Race pride • Collective responsibility • Restraint • Devotion • Cognitive flexibility • Persistency • Reciprocity • Productivity • Courageousness • Resiliency • Defiance • Integrity	• Belief in God (moral character) • Hard work • Sense of excellence • Sense of appropriateness • Importance of history	• Consubstantiation • Interdependence • Egalitarianism • Collectivism • Transformation • Cooperation • Humanness • Synergy	• Sense of family • Sense of history • Language orientation • Significance of names/naming • Importance of signs and symbols (music and rhythm; dance) • Dietary habits

Each descriptor associated with a general category represents a continuum with a zone of appropriateness to be discussed in terms of its relativity to a culture. For example, under the topic of customs, *hard work* is listed as one of the descriptors. First, looking through the anthropological lens of culture, we can make the safe assumption that all cultures have customs, and under customs there is the concept of hard work. The scale of relativity, however, says that hard work has more relevance or pertinence in some cultures than in others. Some might hypothesize that in White Anglo-Saxon culture, hard work is highly relevant. However, if one is to go on the generalized and stereotyped mainstream media perspective of the underserved when looking at Black culture, some would argue that hard work is not seen as very important. Of course, a deep and accurate understanding of Black culture reveals that this perception is not true. In fact, hard work is seen as very important in Black culture. The overall point is that one could take any of the cultural concepts posited by Nobles's matrix and examine them according to the scale of relativity, depending on the culture and the person's knowledge of that culture.

Foremost, the CLR teacher has to recognize that all these concepts apply to every culture in some capacity or another, and that from an anthropological standpoint, no value is placed on them. Consequently, the CLR educator must have a keen awareness of these descriptors as cultural behaviors and how they play out behaviorally in the culture of school. A detailed accounting of each of these concepts is beyond the scope of this book. To learn more about the specific cultural behaviors of underserved students, I encourage you to go to the work of Hale-Benson (1986), Nobles (1987), and Shade, Kelly, and Oberg (1997), to name a few. What is germane to this book, however, is the knowledge of how to be responsive to the cultural behavior once it is recognized as a cultural behavior and not an unacceptable behavior.

The next step in this process is probably the most important one of all. Once CLR educators have opened up to the possibility of recognizing some behavior as culturally inappropriate instead of unacceptable, they have to be able to quickly distinguish between the two options and make split-second decisions about how to manage the behavior. If the behavior is determined to be unacceptable as opposed to culturally inappropriate, then the response must follow the teacher's classroom management system. The point to internalize is that the decision is the difference between a negative exchange or a positive exchange, an escalation or a diffusion, or a student being redirected to on-task behavior or ending up out of class and missing valuable instruction.

Pause to Ponder

Belief System Quiz:
Is It Cultural or Not?

Are the following common classroom occurrences cultural or not?

1. A student is talking while the teacher is talking but is affirming what the teacher is saying.

2. A student is tapping on the desk while other students are working quietly.

3. A student is bullying another student.

4. A student calls the teacher a degrading name.

5. Students in one collaborative group are talking with students in another collaborative group.

6. A student is stealing.

7. A student is assertively (as opposed to aggressively) "talking back" to the teacher, trying to make a point.

Consistent with the research on cultural and psychological behaviors as well as the responses of thousands of teachers in my trainings, most educators agree that items 1, 2, 5, and 7 can be culturally related, therefore calling for responses that validate, affirm, build, and bridge. The other items (3, 4, and 6) are considered unacceptable behaviors and should be dealt with accordingly through the classroom management system in place. When it comes to being responsive to culturally inappropriate behaviors, the response is for the most part addressed proactively through instruction. There is no prescription for what to offer instructionally. Determining the appropriate instruction is a descriptive process. The appendices provide examples of effective instructional practices that are culturally and linguistically responsive. The next section gives context for VABBing when culturally inappropriate behaviors occur.

Validating and Affirming Cultural Behavior through Talking, Relating, and Teaching

Students need daily opportunities and ample practice with situational appropriateness to become conversant with the cultural behaviors of school and mainstream society. When students use behavior that you recognize as culturally inappropriate, you must validate and affirm (VA) the student with your words by using the behavior to build a relationship and/or by using an activity that validates and affirms the student. Imagine one of your students—a male African American seventh grader—comes into your classroom loudly, greeting his classmates with high-fives and soul shakes. Your first thought may be to say, "Go back out and come back the right way," or, "Sit down." Remember our CLR mantra: *My first thought will not be my last thought.* This reaction is normal and to be expected, but it is not responsive because the way the boy came into your room was cultural. The question is, do you recognize that behavior in the moment? What culture is this? you ask. There are three cultures at play here: *youth culture*, because young people typically greet one another in this way; *gender culture,* because while not exclusive to boys, they are the most likely to be boisterous about greetings; and *ethnic culture,* because we find that Black and Mexican American (Chicano) cultures are demonstrative in this way. Now that you see that the behavior is indeed cultural, you must validate and affirm the student. While the behavior is culturally inappropriate for the context of the school, you are acknowledging that the student was not being "bad."

There are three ways in which you can address this behavior:

1. **Talk differently**. Instead of saying "sit down," say, "I love how enthusiastically you come into my classroom" or "I respect how you are culturally greeting your classmates, showing them some love." These are called VA statements and they are followed by a BB statement, without using a word that is contrasting. So, for this example, the BB statement would be: "Now, show me the school culture way to greet your classmates." And if the student knows how to be situationally appropriate, he will do so.

2. **Relate differently**. Offer your students opportunities to greet you in a cultural way on some days. Choose other days when they have to demonstrate more situationally appropriate greetings.

3. **Teach differently**. Incorporate greetings from both home and school cultures into movement activities during instruction.

This example illustrates the VA process for classroom management. When it comes to cultural behaviors, you will need to be skilled at recognizing them as inappropriate for school culture (rather than inappropriate in general), validating, affirming, building, and bridging the students to the situationally appropriate behavior. Your process must be one of changing your mindset and your language from deficit or neutral to validating and affirming.

Figure 3.5 shows words and phrases that move from a negative orientation to a "positive plus"—another way of saying a validation and affirmation orientation. Imagine that I am standing at your classroom door listening to you speak to your students. What words would I hear you say to your students? Or put another way, when was the last time you told your students that you honor and value their cultural and linguistic behaviors?

Fig. 3.5 Vocabulary for Responding to Student Behaviors

Deficit Terms	Neutral Terms	Validating Terms
should	understand	appreciate
ought to	tolerate	honor
wrong	allow	value
value-based terms	another chance	love
fix it	consequence-based terms	respect
correctly		inspired
right way	this time	moved
our way	next time	affirm
your way		connect
the only way		empathize
		can relate
		grateful

Linking the Use of CLR Activities to Classroom Management

Students need daily opportunities and ample practice with situational appropriateness to become conversant with the cultural behaviors of school and mainstream society. Teachers can offer students these rehearsals in the following ways:

- systematically using forms for responding and discussing

- strategically incorporating movement activities

- effective attention signals for procedural movements
- consistent collaborative group work

Ways of Responding and Discussing

Forms for responding and discussing define how some cultural behaviors are conducted within a culture or a community, even in terms of school and the society in general. Cultural behaviors, such as when to start talking when someone else is talking, how long to talk, and what tone to use while talking, can be relative and different for students depending on their home culture. Many of these behaviors are culturally and linguistically determined. For instance, the tone used can differ greatly between the home culture and the school culture. For schools, many protocols are schoolwide (macro-level), while some are classroom specific (micro-level). Some examples of schoolwide protocols include where and how to stand in line on the schoolyard when recess ends, how to move through common areas in the school, and how and where to sit in the cafeteria. Classroom-level protocols relate to the structure of the classroom. Some classroom-specific protocols include when and how to sharpen your pencil, where to place learning materials, who passes out papers, and which learning tools are needed at specific times.

In classroom-management terms, many protocols are considered procedures or routines. Effective teachers are well aware that they need to be clear and explicit with instructions for these routines. There is no expectation that the students know how to do all of these things without first explaining and practicing them. Effective teachers also know that there will be some students who will continue to struggle with the procedures and that reteaching and revisiting the procedures on a consistent basis is necessary.

Giving students multiple ways of responding and discussing in class is part of responsive classroom management (Kagan and Kagan 2009). The key is making explicit how to respond in class and how to conduct discussions so that students know what protocol is most appropriate for the response and/or for the discussion. This explicit instruction also enables students to learn why these routines are necessary. These protocols teach situational appropriateness—the types of behavior or participation that are appropriate for a particular situation. In addition, the consistent use of the protocols provides for variation in the types of responses and discussion in the classroom, leading to increased engagement overall.

Protocols for responding are used to *explicitly* communicate to students how the facilitator or teacher wants them to respond to questioning or instruction as a *whole group*. In other words, the teacher knows the purpose of the question being asked (e.g., checking for understanding, assessing prior knowledge, checking for engagement, sharing of personal experiences) and clearly communicates how the students should respond to the question. The involuntary ways of responding also encourage accountability and engagement on the part of the learner and provide more accurate feedback to the teacher about students' understanding as a whole group, demonstrated by their need for random participation.

The use of such ways of responding, for example, *Roll 'Em* or *Pick-a-Stick* (see Figure 3.6), establishes a learning environment in which everyone plays a critical role and is validated in the process. These activities are effective in that they convey to students that:

- Their attention and participation are required during whole-group instruction and questioning so that they learn.

- They are all integral members of the classroom community.

- Everyone's thoughts, ideas, and attention are necessary for an effective learning environment.

In addition, the teacher's use of a variety of explicit ways of responding further enables students to be more aware of the need to correlate their participation and behavior with the given needs for a particular setting (i.e., to be situationally appropriate). Various ways of responding should be used throughout the entire day.

During all of these times, the teacher already has an expectation of how he or she wants students to participate, whether it is simply listening, silently taking an assessment, answering questions one at a time, or shouting out an answer. Truly, there is never a time when students are not participating in the classroom whether as a whole group (through responding) or in small groups (through discussion). Protocols for increasing student engagement are provided in Appendix E. Amy Coventry, a founding CLAS teacher and current consultant, developed a resource that summarizes successful protocols we have used in hundreds of schools across the country.

In a CLR classroom, the activities are designed to validate and affirm cultural behaviors. Figure 3.6 demonstrates matches between cultural behaviors and CLR infusion activities. Several of the infusion activities are those described in Appendix E. By identifying the cultural behavior, the teacher is able to select those activities that are most responsive to student needs.

Fig. 3.6 Cultural Behaviors Matched with Effective CLR Infusion Activities

Cultural Behaviors	CLR Infusion Activities
Sociocentric	morning song (while they socialize and prepare for the day); nonvolunteer (equity and inclusiveness)
High movement	Give One, Get One; Tea Party; Silent Appointment; Musical Shares; Inner-Outer Circle
Cooperative/Communal	Numbered Heads Together; Put Your Two Cents In; Three-Step Interview; Jigsaw; Team-Pair-Solo; Partners; Send-a-Problem; Roundtable; Round Robin Brainstorming; Whip Around; Train Reading; Give a Shout Out; Call and Response; nonvolunteer participation protocols (equity and inclusiveness)

Cultural Behaviors	CLR Infusion Activities
Relational	Corners; Roll 'Em; Train (Pass It On); Pick-a-Stick; Circle the Sage; Numbered Heads Together; Whip Around; role plays; poetry slam; speeches
Musical	Call and Response; Musical Shares; Give a Shout Out; chants; rhymes
Conversation Patterns	Give a Shout Out; Numbered Heads Together; Corners; Tea Party (some greetings)
Purpose-driven	Participation protocols; visual organizers depicting unit activities; Thinking Maps; explicit direct instruction; Morning Report/ Daily Agenda; real-world connections and applications
Inductive	Visual organizers; Thinking Maps; frontloading
Field dependent	Visual organizers; Thinking Maps; frontloading; accessing prior knowledge; personal connections; culturally and linguistically responsive literature/text/content; Personal Thesaurus; Personal Dictionary. thematic instruction

Effective Attention Signals

Effective classroom managers are able to get the attention of their students at a moment's notice. The attention signal is designed to intrigue the students and to motivate them to listen attentively as the teacher gives further directions, transitions to a new activity, or winds down the class. I promote responsive attention signals as a way of creating what Hooks (2003) calls *cultural resonance* with the students. This provides students with something that they can relate to while at the same time brings them to attention. If the teacher has effective attention signals, then adding responsive signals to the repertoire and using them strategically can make a big difference.

Attention signals are primarily used when students are working in collaboration or having a discussion. I have found that many teachers will not use collaborative groups or are less likely to have students engage in discussion simply because they know they will not be able to regain control once the students are "let loose." However, with an effective attention signal system in place, teachers are *more likely* to use collaborative groups and allow students to conduct discussions. I think that this creative opportunity speaks directly to the power of CLR and how it can make a difference in instruction. The caution is that attention signals can be tricky in terms of when to use, timing, or overuse. Attention signals are specific to getting students back during and after an activity but not necessarily for getting students to be quiet. There is a fundamental difference in the two purposes. Lack of understanding of this difference leads to overuse. Wolfe (2001) says that none of these attention signals will prove useful over time because of habituation. Hammond (2015) makes a compelling case for how call-and-response in particular is connected to brain-based teaching and its effectiveness with students. Flicking the light switch to get students' attention may work well the first few times, but with extended use, students often will fail to notice or respond to this signal. Kiechelle Russell, one of the founding teachers at CLAS and a national consultant for CLR training, compiled examples of successful attention signals that have been widely used with great success (see Appendix E).

Pause to Ponder

Think about how many times a day the whole class is engaged with you or another designated speaker or is responding to your prompts or questions.

- How do you engage students and maintain their attention?

- What are your expectations for students' behavior during whole-class activities?

Movement Activities

Adding movement activities to instructional activities provides additional sensory input to the brain and probably enhances the learning (Wolfe 2001). Jensen (2005) reports that brain researchers have verified that sensory motor integration is fundamental to school readiness. Indeed, other research has shown that there may be a link between violence and lack of movement (Kotulak 1996). What is the point? Students need to move while learning. Put another way, movement should be an integral part of instruction, which is why it has to be a part of responsive management.

The lesson for educators in this particular pedagogical area is that having students move frequently and with purpose can actually *decrease* management issues in the classroom. This result is due primarily to the factor of increased engagement overall based on the simple truth that when students are engaged, they are less likely to disrupt the class or stray off task. Fortunately, many of the activities and concepts mentioned in this chapter involve movement and can be easily infused into everyday teaching.

Summary

To say effective classroom management is a necessary and required component of the classroom is to say what we already know. CLR is a way to bolster and to enhance any system by first assessing the classroom management system, then determining the cultural behaviors as such, and finally, using effective CLR activities strategically. While I offer no prescriptions, an artful teacher can find the balance between being responsive, validating and affirming, and teaching the necessary behaviors to be successful in school and mainstream society.

Reflection Guide

Think back to your responses to the statements in the Anticipation Guide at the beginning of the chapter. Have your responses changed? Which parts of the chapter did you find most helpful in clarifying your understanding of responsive classroom management?

_____ Effective lesson planning is the key to responsive classroom management.

_____ Students' cultural behaviors must *always* be considered in the context of classroom management.

_____ You consider your current classroom management system to be responsive.

_____ Students should become accustomed to adjusting their behavior to meet the requirements of the classroom.

_____ The teacher's beliefs about systems of classroom management can affect the nature and quality of interactions with students.

_____ A permissive classroom atmosphere creates a welcoming environment for underserved students.

_____ No matter what the circumstances are, teachers should "love" their students.

1. What are the most difficult situations you encounter with classroom management? How have you attempted to address these situations? What advice would you offer a novice teacher about effective classroom management?

2. What experiences have you had with student behaviors that are culturally based but inappropriate in the culture of the classroom or school? How are these issues resolved in your school?

3. In what ways do the school administration and individual teachers communicate with the school community (e.g., parents, caregivers, interested members of the public) about the distinction between cultural behaviors and unacceptable behaviors? What information from this chapter can you use for such communications?

4. Protocols for Increasing Student Engagement and examples of Effective Attention Signals (Appendix E) provide many practical activities that enhance students' engagement in learning activities. Which of these activities do you plan to incorporate into your instruction?

Is My Vocabulary Instruction Culturally Responsive?

Anticipation Guide

What do you think of when you encounter the term *academic vocabulary*? Do you agree or disagree with the following statements about vocabulary development? Record *A* for *agree* and *D* for *disagree* on each line.

_____ Effective vocabulary instruction relies on students memorizing definitions.

_____ The purpose of culturally responsive vocabulary instruction is to enable students to recognize relationships between their personal vocabularies for concepts and the academic terms for those concepts.

_____ Students acquire new vocabulary primarily through indirect approaches, such as reading widely.

_____ Teachers should focus primarily on explicit teaching of vocabulary rather than relying on incidental approaches.

_____ The contexts in which students encounter words affect their interest in words and their motivation to expand their vocabularies.

Contexts for Vocabulary Instruction

There are not many topics in education that find general agreement among educators. The importance of students increasing their academic vocabulary skills is one of the few. I consider vocabulary another gatekeeper area for a specific instructional purpose in cultural responsiveness. Without increasing their academic vocabulary as they matriculate through school, students will struggle to achieve academic success (Marzano and Pickering 2005). As educators—especially as practitioners—we bear a responsibility for how students learn to "own words" by increasing their reading, writing, and speaking skills along with other opportunities in all school situations. Even though there is general agreement about the importance of vocabulary, I have discovered (albeit unscientifically) that the majority of teachers do not have a systematic way of teaching vocabulary. Further, those who do resort to the traditional methodology of—you guessed it—dictionary work. The point is that before we can discuss how to make your vocabulary instruction culturally responsive, we have to ensure that vocabulary instruction is occurring in the first place.

To an extent, any vocabulary teaching is better than nothing at all. Fortunately, today's college- and career-readiness standards require students to interpret words and phrases as they are used in a text, including how specific sentences, paragraphs, and larger portions of the text relate to each other and the whole. I strongly recommend that you have a baseline of vocabulary teaching in order to infuse CLR. In other words, if you are not teaching vocabulary on a regular basis, it may be difficult to practice cultural responsiveness. This chapter is about how to make your vocabulary instruction responsive in three ways.

1. Understand the overall validating and affirming aspect of the culturally responsive approach, which is to honor the words that students bring from home and recognize that students are not blank slates when it comes to their word knowledge.

2. Equip students with the necessary skills for success, using research-based strategies students need to attack unfamiliar words.

3. Utilize developed tools for success—the Personal Thesaurus and Personal Dictionary—that help support validation, affirmation, building, and bridging.

Before we begin, think about how you learned vocabulary in elementary and middle school. Your acquisition of new words probably involved one or all of the following tasks: studying a list of 20 teacher-selected words connected to an upcoming text in a certain content area; looking up the words in the dictionary; attempting to use those words in a sentence or a story; and taking a quiz on Friday. On the surface, this traditional approach to vocabulary learning makes sense. Students are exposed to words weekly, practice and reinforcement are provided through a variety of formats, and a weekly assessment is conducted for monitoring and support. However, from what is known about vocabulary development today, an argument is easily made about the ineffectiveness of the traditional approach (Graves 2006). The time for this approach to teaching vocabulary has long come and gone. I liken the traditional approach to vocabulary instruction to someone bringing an eight-track cassette to a party that is playing MP3 files only and the sinking feeling that comes once the individual realizes there are no eight-track players anywhere in sight. The MP3 files of today's vocabulary instruction focus students on acquisition tasks that are robust and authentic.

Establishing the Pedagogy

A survey of the literature clearly indicates several principles of vocabulary instruction that should be included in any program or approach (Beck, McKeown, and Kucan 2002; Graves 2006; Stahl 1999). These principles include:

- Providing definitional and contextual information about the word's meaning

- Actively involving students in word learning through talking about, comparing, analyzing, and using the target words

- Providing multiple exposures to meaningful information about each word

- Teaching word analysis

When working with students, especially underserved students, teachers must consider these time- and research-proven concepts. Activating prior knowledge, making schematic connections, and building on the words that students already know are central to any basic vocabulary instruction. Teaching vocabulary in a culturally responsive way acknowledges that students have a comprehensive, conceptual knowledge base rooted in their culture, community, and life experiences that can be used to build academic vocabulary. Plainly put, students come to school with some knowledge already in place. Through their rich out-of-school experiences, students have a multitude of thoughts, opinions, and concepts about the communities they live in and the world around them. More importantly, they have given their own labels, names, and words to these concepts. Students have vast conceptual vocabularies upon which strategic vocabulary instruction can be built.

Culturally responsive vocabulary instruction is based on the following four premises:

1. Students come to school with conceptual meanings of words intact and need to expand their home vocabularies with academic vocabulary.

2. Teachers must focus on recommended key vocabulary strategies for word acquisition, not simple word memorization.

3. Synonymous usage of words needs to be developed, particularly for unaccepted language speakers or second-language learners.

4. Slang, profanity, and racially charged terms can become sources of academic vocabulary expansion, influencing students' word choice and awareness of situational appropriateness.

Linking VABB to Building Academic Vocabulary

Students bring to school their home and community vocabularies that are based in real-world concepts. The intention of expanding academic vocabulary as a pedagogical approach involves bridging the students' worlds of words to the academic world of words. This bridging takes into account that the concepts are generally the same in both worlds even though the terminology may differ. Therefore, the first step, as always, is the validation and affirmation.

Acquiring an understanding of the concepts that words represent is different from simply knowing the meaning of the words. Although some teachers have their students use the dictionary to find definitions, this activity is not particularly useful for building students' vocabulary or validating and affirming their home vocabularies. The dictionary is a reference source to be used judiciously to help students confirm meanings after they have had opportunities to engage in other more productive vocabulary acquisition activities. Expanding academic vocabulary through an approach that is validating and affirming differs from traditional instruction in that it assumes that the students already have

Graves (2006) provides another way of thinking about how we know words. He defines four vocabularies:

- **Receptive-oral:** words we understand when we hear them
- **Receptive-written:** words we can read
- **Productive-oral:** words we use in our speech
- **Productive-written:** words we use in our writing

the concepts but lack the academic words or labels. Culturally responsive vocabulary instruction is an approach that validates and affirms the words students bring from home.

The building and bridging aspect of the approach is illustrated in the idea of the dimensions of knowing a word (Cronbach 1942). Notably, the overarching goal of vocabulary instruction is for the student to *own* the word, not merely to memorize a definition for it. Figure 4.1 shows the dimensions of knowing a word. The words you want your students to know are the academic ones; therefore, you will need to build and bridge as well as validate and affirm.

Fig. 4.1 Cronbach's Dimensions of Knowing a Word

Dimension	Description
Generalization	Ability to define a word
Application	Ability to select or recognize a situation appropriately
Breadth	Ability to apply multiple meanings
Precision	Ability to apply a term correctly to all situations and to recognize inappropriate use
Availability	Ability to actually use the word

Pause to Ponder

Which dimension of knowing a word do you usually aim for in your instruction? Which dimension do you think your students usually achieve?

After presenting and discussing the dimensions in my workshops, I ask participants which dimension they typically implement most in their classrooms. The almost unanimous response is *generalization*. Keep in mind that this response is in the context of traditional vocabulary teaching in most situations where there is no uniform vocabulary program in place. In contrast, culturally responsive vocabulary, which validates and affirms first and then builds and bridges, pushes the instruction beyond simple generalization to the other dimensions. The ultimate goal in culturally responsive vocabulary instruction is to lead students to the dimension of availability—the level at which students *own* the words.

Vocabulary Instruction Focuses on Acquisition

A common question that is asked in vocabulary instruction is *What do proficient readers do when they come across a word they do not know?* (Krashen 2004). The point of the question is to show that proficient readers use what I call *acquisition strategies* rather than the dictionary to figure out what a word means (Stahl 1999). Ironically, many times, struggling readers are told to go to the dictionary when they come across an unfamiliar word. Such a directive is not an acquisition strategy. According to research on vocabulary development (Bromley 2007; Graves and Watts-Taffe 2002; Yopp and Yopp 2007), vocabulary acquisition strategies include:

- Wide and abundant reading

- Contextualization and conceptualization of words

- Knowledge of word parts

- Utilization of synonyms

Ample practice with these strategies is integral to students' approach to expanding academic vocabulary.

Krashen (2004) has made the assertion that reading often and widely is the best way to acquire vocabulary. This notion is not new, but it is hotly debated in terms of implicit instruction as opposed to explicit instruction (National Reading Panel 2000). My position is that reading cannot hurt and that both types of instruction are necessary for increasing vocabulary. One does not negate the other.

Using Synonyms to Expand Vocabulary Knowledge

How we think about word usage can be related to our linguistic background or home language. In particular, our use of synonyms can be traced to linguistic origins. In some unaccepted languages, synonymy (that is, using multiple linguistic forms to express one meaning) is not commonplace; rather, a single word or phrase may have more meanings and be more broadly used than it typically is in Standard English. For example, in African American Vernacular English (AAVE), terms like *bad* and *get* remain constant in usage with an increasing number of evolving meanings. In AAVE, *bad* has essentially three uses. There is the *bad* bad, meaning "not good." There is the good or awesome *bad*, as in "That is a *bad* car you have there." Lastly, there is the now commonly said *my bad*, which is an offer of contrition. *Get* has numerous meanings as well; for example, "get down," "get out of here," "get real," "get me a soda," "get on my nerves," "get it straight," "get your groove on," and so on. Standard English speakers, in contrast, are more likely to employ synonymous usage by choosing different terms to convey the variety of expressions above.

Culturally responsive teaching recognizes this linguistic dynamic and uses it as an opportunity to validate and affirm the home language while building and bridging to academic language. Several of the strategies described later in this chapter, in particular the personal thesaurus, help students build their knowledge of synonyms and consequently expand their vocabularies.

Assessing the Quantity and Quality of Vocabulary Instruction

What vocabulary program or approach is already in place in your classroom or school? This question is central to determining the pedagogy teachers will use to help students develop academic vocabulary. Building academic vocabulary as presented here is not a program but a way of thinking about how vocabulary works. Often, when I ask this question in workshops, many teachers surprisingly indicate that they do not have a program in their schools. When they do indicate a program, it is usually part of a basal program. I cannot emphasize enough the importance of having a quality vocabulary program in place and augmenting the activities with those I describe in this chapter.

Whether there is a system in place for vocabulary instruction or one has not yet been established, the next factor to consider is how the words for instructional focus are selected. Is the teacher using the words based on a basal text? In other words, were they determined by the authors of a program? Or does the teacher have a selection process based on what students are studying? Other variables for choosing vocabulary might include content area and grade-level specificity. The way the words are selected is key because the responsive approach requires teachers to make a second selection. I have found through my research that teachers are more likely to do this second selection if they are choosing the words for instruction themselves. When the words are preselected, there is often a reluctance to choose additional words. This situation, unless addressed, can lead to weak implementation of strategies for developing vocabulary. These two questions represent the assessment of the quantity and the quality of what is currently in place. Once these conditions are identified, it is possible to move to the five steps of responsive vocabulary instruction.

Five Steps to Responsive Academic Vocabulary Instruction

Wilhelm observes, "When we teach a subject, or any topic or text within that subject, we must teach the *academic vocabulary* necessary for dealing with it—not just the words, but also the linguistic processes and patterns for delving deeply into and operating upon that content" (2007, 44). To ensure that students have ample opportunities to acquire academic vocabulary, teachers should follow five steps to plan their instruction. These steps are:

1. Contextualize the word selection or "tier" words according to frequency and relevance for the topic or selection (Beck, McKeown, and Kucan 2002).

2. Teach the Tier Two, or what we will call academic words, as concepts, not memorized words (Beck, McKeown, and Kucan 2002).

3. Develop synonyms and antonyms using the Personal Thesaurus.

4. Utilize common vocabulary strategies for meaning development and richer representation as well as for multiple assessments.

5. Develop Tier Three words, or content-specific words (Beck, McKeown, and Kucan 2002) using the Personal Dictionary.

- What vocabulary development strategies do you use with your students successfully?

- How do your strategies compare to the ones mentioned in this book?

- What is your favorite professional source for ideas about teaching vocabulary? In what ways have you found it helpful? In what ways does the source support concepts in culturally and linguistically responsive teaching?

Step 1: Leveling Words

The value of Beck, McKeown, and Kucan's *Bringing Words to Life* (2002) is that the teacher has the creative but informed license to determine which words students should acquire for a given lesson or text. Given that the teacher knows his or her students better than the authors of the text, the selection of words can be customized to the specific needs of the students as maturing language users. Beck defines three tiers for words:

- Tier One words are those that students already know, or common everyday words.

- Tier Two words are those that students should know as mature language users.

- Tier Three words are those that students should be familiar with but will rarely encounter in print or in speech.

For our purposes in CLR, I rename these levels as *everyday*, *academic*, and *content-specific*.

The academic words are the ones that should be the focus for vocabulary acquisition in general and also in particular for second-language learners and unaccepted language users. According to Beck, McKeown, and Kucan, academic words have importance, utility, and instructional potential. *Instructional potential* refers to words that can be taught in a variety of ways so that students can build rich representations of them and their connections to other words and concepts. These are words for which students understand the general concept but also provide precision and specificity in describing the concept.

Most basal anthologies provide a list of words that the students should know for each unit, chapter, or selection. These words usually are ones that students are likely unfamiliar with, and the teacher should cover them through vocabulary instruction so that they will be able to navigate the text successfully. What Beck, McKeown, and Kucan (2002) recommend is taking the list provided by the anthology and categorizing the terms by the three tiers. For academic words, there should be five to seven words that will become the focus of the vocabulary acquisition and instruction. These words should be strategically selected based on the criteria that they will give students the most mileage in usage as readers, writers, and speakers of Standard English, beyond the context of the specific unit of study in which they are introduced.

Step 2: Using Vocabulary Acquisition Strategies

In this step, teachers use the three key vocabulary strategies that are recommended consistently by research (Graves 2006):

- Using context clues
- Memorizing the meanings of word parts
- Developing synonyms and antonyms

Using *context clues* is an important skill that enables students to guess the meanings of words from details surrounding the word in the text. The teacher can prepare sentences or a brief paragraph with the academic words embedded. Students are called upon to use context clues to guess at the meanings conceptually. Since the teacher is more interested in the conceptual meanings rather than the technical meanings, the students initially are going to provide words that they *own* from their vocabularies. In this activity, at this point, teachers have to keep in mind that the meanings will not be an exact match to dictionary definitions. If there is doubt about the accuracy of the student's guess, the teacher can help the student determine if the estimated meaning is adequate to move the reader along in the text. If the answer is yes, the student can continue reading. If the answer is no, the teacher should probe students to examine the text further. Figure 4.2 shows a sample context clue exercise.

Fig. 4.2 Context Clue Exercise

Target Word in Context	This is what I think the word means…	What were the clues in the sentence that helped you guess?	My new word for the target word
The assignment was so **tedious** that he started to fall asleep.	boring	started to fall asleep	boring

Using *word parts,* or morphological analysis, is a second vocabulary acquisition strategy important for students to learn and apply. "By separating and analyzing the meaning of a prefix, suffix, or other word root, students can often unlock the meaning of an unknown word" (Rasinski et al. 2007, 21). As a strategy for determining word meaning, teaching students to use an understanding of word parts is effective in that it allows them to use their inductive reasoning skills. Simultaneously, they build their deductive reasoning ability. Again, teachers must keep in mind that deduction skills are being developed as a result of this process and that exact meanings may not result right away. It is more important that students understand the value of using word parts as a strategy to assist them in determining word meaning than in hitting on a precise definition of a word.

Step 3: Using the Personal Thesaurus to Develop Tier Two (Academic) Vocabulary

The Personal Thesaurus (PT) is a tool my colleagues and I at CLAS developed from our work with AEMP to help students build knowledge of synonyms and antonyms. Here is the description of the process:

1. Students are introduced to an academic vocabulary term.

2. Students brainstorm synonyms (of words they own) for the target word from their own vocabulary bank, indicating that they understand a concept. (It does not have to be the exact meaning.)

3. Students make a list of synonyms for the vocabulary term.

4. Students place and highlight one of their owned words (from the synonyms generated in Step 3) at the top of the chart.

5. The vocabulary term is added on the line beneath the owned word.

6. Any other academic (Tier Two) synonyms are added on the following lines thereafter.

7. An antonym (academic, owned, or both) goes in the last box.

Students should be encouraged to utilize their own Personal Thesaurus during writing and speaking activities.

Figure 4.3 illustrates an example of a Personal Thesaurus chart. The figure shows both synonyms and antonyms that the student generated for the vocabulary term *ingenuous*.

Fig. 4.3 Sample Personal Thesaurus Chart

Owned Word	basic
Vocabulary Term	ingenuous
Tier Two Synonym	unsophisticated
Tier Two Synonym	artless
Tier Two Antonym	urbane

Step 4: Using Common Vocabulary Strategies and Multiple Assessments

Teachers are well aware that there are too many words to be taught to students one by one. Furthermore, there is too much to be learned about each word to be covered by having students memorize definitions. Consequently, a variety of methods must be used to develop students' vocabulary knowledge. In this step, students are given multiple opportunities to engage with and interact with new words and to practice the new vocabulary acquisition strategies that they are learning. Reinforcement and practice are essential because students are internalizing new words by making connections and expanding their conceptual understandings. After students have been introduced to the words and worked through direct instruction for vocabulary-acquisition strategies, the teacher provides reinforcement and practice opportunities. Teachers should keep in mind that the goal of reinforcement and practice activities is to make students' word knowledge flexible so that they can both understand the word and apply the word to a variety of contexts. Each activity for reinforcement and review gives the teacher an opportunity to informally assess students and engage in discussions that help students explore the facets of word meaning and consider relationships among words. This interaction will build students' confidence and move them toward assessment readiness.

Assessing what students have learned is the second part of this step for teaching vocabulary. As Beck, McKeown, and Kucan (2002) assert, it is important at the outset to consider the type of learning that is the goal, which will determine the type of assessment given. Vocabulary assessment should always be looked at as an opportunity to develop standardized test-taking skills, which means multiple-choice assessments are appropriate. (Although today's standardized tests utilize multiple question types, multiple-choice questions remain the most commonly used for assessing vocabulary.) Multiple-choice assessments give students a chance to practice using context clues and word parts to determine word meaning as well as to explicitly practice test-taking strategies. Multiple-choice assessments, however, do not adequately assess students' deeper levels of word knowledge. There are a variety of activities and assessments that the teacher should utilize to give students the opportunity to demonstrate their knowledge.

For more on common and effective vocabulary strategies, I recommend the work of Allen (2008), Blachowicz and Fisher (2006), and Feldman and Kinsella (2003).

Step 5: Using the Personal Dictionary to Develop Tier Three (Content Area) Vocabulary

Within the content areas, vocabulary instruction differs from that provided for academic vocabulary. Recall that Tier Three words are those that students will rarely encounter in speech or print. These words are not to be used with the Personal Thesaurus because, typically, students will not have their own concepts for these words. Therefore, it would be much more difficult to generate synonyms. For this reason, I recommend using the Personal Dictionary, a tool based on the Frayer model (Frayer, Frederick, and Klaumeier 1969). Figure 4.4 is a diagram that illustrates the model for an English language arts Tier Three vocabulary term, *personification*. Unlike in the Personal Thesaurus, a technical definition is supplied for the term and the student has to create an illustration and a personal connection. The illustration and connection are the features that provide the schemata as suggested by Frayer. Similar to the Personal Thesaurus, students are able to build their own collections of vocabulary terms by completing the Frayer four-square model for their Tier Three words on index cards, in a journal, or as digital notes.

Fig. 4.4 Sample Personal Dictionary Card Based on the Frayer Model

Content-specific Term	Personal Illustration
personification	
Technical Definition	**Personal Connection**
A representation, usually of an inanimate object made animate	The clock spoke to me directly, saying, "You are late for the show."

The directions for using the Personal Dictionary are as follows:

1. Students can use the Personal Dictionary after building conceptual knowledge. In the first step, students:

   a. Record the Tier Three (content-specific) term.

   b. Record the technical definition, as provided by the teacher or a (text) source.

c. Describe their personal connection(s) to the term.

d. Add a personal illustration of the term that is associated with either their personal connection or the technical definition.

2. Teachers can supply students with personal connection starters. For example: *It is a thing that... It was a time when... It is a place where...*.

3. Students can add, revise, and edit their definitions as they continue to build their knowledge of the term through other experiences and activities.

Two additional examples of the Personal Dictionary are shown in Figure 4.5 and Figure 4.6.

Fig. 4.5 Example of a Mathematical Personal Dictionary

Content-specific Term	Personal Illustration
adjacent	
Personal Connection	**Personal Definition**
I am adjacent to my friend when I sit next to her in class.	It is a word that means being directly next to something or someone.

Fig. 4.6 Example of a Science Personal Dictionary

Content-specific Term	Personal Illustration
atmosphere	

Personal Connection	Personal Definition
I see the atmosphere when I look up at the sky.	It is a word that means the part of the sky that starts from the ground and goes far above Earth.

Slang as a Source of Academic Vocabulary Expansion

Many mistakenly see slang as completely representative of what an unaccepted language is rather than recognizing that slang is simply part of the vocabulary of any language. In general, vocabulary or semantics is one of the six language dimensions (including phonics, morphosyntax, syntax, vocabulary, nonverbal languages, and discourse style) that comprise any linguistic entity (Levine 2002). Slang is evident in most languages and is not to be confused with certain jargons or technology talk (e.g., texting or legalese).

A second aspect of slang, for the most part, is that it's the language of young people. While *young* is a relative term, broadly speaking, teenagers and young adults are the primary users of slang terms rather than older adults. In this context, I consider slang to be a part of youth culture; therefore, teachers must respond to it in validating and affirming ways so that students' use of these words can be bridged to academic language appropriate to the context of school. In order to do this, though, educators must see slang usage as a positive to be expanded upon, not as a negative to be degraded. If done skillfully, teachers can capitalize on students' use of slang as another opportunity to expand their academic vocabulary.

To help you validate and affirm your students' natural use of slang terms, I promote an activity called *academization*. Through "academizing" their slang, teachers build and bridge students to the use of academic vocabulary. Academization works like this: first, you must listen to your students; hear what they are saying. Similar to being culturally aware, you need to be a linguistic detective in your classroom. When you hear slang, rather than going ballistic, getting preachy, or "turning old," inquire as to what students mean by the words they are using. Your students will be excited to tell you—to teach you. Once you understand what a slang term means, then you take that concept and academize it for them by providing an academic word to use when situationally appropriate. The last step is that the slang words and their academic counterparts are entered into students' personal thesauruses. Figure 4.7 shows examples of academizations.

Fig. 4.7 Academization of Slang

Slang Term	Academic Term
on fleek	sophisticated
throw shade	saboteur
call me out	critique

Profanity and racially charged terms can also provide opportunities for academization. Visit www.culturallyresponsive.org for information on addressing these topics.

Summary

When it comes to literacy development, the acquisition of academic vocabulary is directly related to larger success in reading, writing, and speaking. Culturally responsive vocabulary offers an opportunity to expand on what the research says about quality vocabulary instruction by adding three enhancements:

- leveling words (i.e., categorizing them as Tier One, Tier Two, or Tier Three)

- focusing on leveraging strategies

- using a variety of activities and assessments

Similar to what has been presented thus far, the responsive teaching of vocabulary does not supplant the "good teaching" that has been established in a classroom. By validating and affirming the words students bring from their cultures, the intention is to enhance, enable, and empower teaching and learning, as seen with expansion of the vocabulary approach.

 Reflection Guide

Think back to your responses to the statements in the Anticipation Guide at the beginning of the chapter. Have your responses changed as a result of what you read in the chapter? What new insights did you gain from the chapter?

_____ Effective vocabulary instruction relies on students memorizing definitions.

_____ The purpose of responsive vocabulary instruction is to enable students to recognize relationships between their personal vocabularies for concepts and the academic terms for those concepts.

_____ Students acquire new vocabulary primarily through indirect approaches, such as reading widely.

_____ Teachers should focus primarily on explicit teaching of vocabulary rather than relying on incidental approaches.

_____ The contexts in which students encounter words affect their interest in words and their motivation to expand their vocabularies.

1. What are your preferred strategies for helping underserved students acquire academic vocabulary? What evidence of these strategies is present in your classroom?

2. Fostering a love of words in students is an essential goal of vocabulary instruction. How successful are you in helping your students become "verbivores"? If that word is unfamiliar to you, what strategies are you using to determine its meaning?

3. Which part(s) of this chapter have given you new insights into responsive vocabulary instruction? How do you plan to incorporate these insights into your instructional program?

Is My Academic Literacy Instruction Culturally Responsive?

Anticipation Guide

What do you think of when you encounter the term *academic literacy*? Do you agree or disagree with the following statements about the concept? Record *A* for agree and *D* for disagree on each line.

_____ The majority of texts mandated for use in schools lack effective examples of culturally appropriate content.

_____ Typically, anthologies of literary selections include the more traditional and well-established authors of culture-based topics.

_____ Read-aloud activities are most appropriately used with younger students and those who struggle with reading.

_____ Culturally and linguistically responsive activities are substitutes for established literacy practices.

_____ People who are unfamiliar with the purposes and nature of CLR instruction may be susceptible to myths surrounding the approach.

The Context of Academic Literacy

The number one determinant of a student's academic success is the ability to read and write proficiently in Standard English using academic language. Having strong literacy skills—reading, writing, listening, and speaking—is the gatekeeper to success in almost all content areas. Students who are proficient and advanced in reading and writing tend to be in the accelerated mathematics courses, while students who struggle with reading and communication find themselves in the less advanced mathematics courses. The discouraging statistics around reading achievement that we have become accustomed to in our schools tell only half the story. Not only are many underserved students doing poorly in reading, but teachers also know that they are doing just as badly in mathematics and other subject areas. With increased literacy skills being key to these students' overall academic success, CLR provides a particular focus on building literacy skills.

Consider, for example, that boys have the lowest scores on standardized measures of reading and verbal ability (National Center for Educational Statistics 2008) and that boys are more likely to be in remedial reading classes (Lietz 2006). Slade and Trent (2000) link these results for reading with boys being the larger group of dropouts and at-risk youth. Being academically literate makes all the difference. Even so, the main challenge is getting all educators to accept that it is everyone's responsibility to develop students' strong academic literacy skills. Across the board, today's standards raise the bar for what students are expected to do to be considered academically literate. Alvermann and Xu (2003) have said for many years that texts are important in our daily lives for reading and writing and for developing the skills to comprehend authorial intent. But it is equally crucial to understand how texts function as social practices that show identities, values, beliefs, and social networks. What is the overall point? We have every reason to be focused on all students' increased academic literacy.

CLR addresses the development of literacy skills by focusing on two specific areas: academic literacy, which is discussed in this chapter, and academic language, which is discussed in Chapter 6. The focus of academic literacy is through the lens of the use of text, a focus on using read-alouds culturally, and infusing effective literacy practices across all content areas. The following three objectives define the use of text in CLR instruction:

- To engage students with culturally and linguistically responsive texts/media

- To use engaging read-alouds in the oral tradition of cultural storytelling

- To purposefully use effective literacy strategies responsively

These objectives are designed to give students more opportunities to understand the relationships that exist between their experiences and the language and concepts they encounter in school. As students become aware of these relationships, they are better able to deal with the demands of the mandated texts. In addressing these objectives, students develop stronger academic literacy skills.

Pause to Ponder

In your classroom, what types of culturally relevant texts are your students being exposed to?

Engaging Students with Culturally and Linguistically Authentic Texts

The task sounds simple. Find texts that are representative of who your students are, culturally and linguistically. But what sounds simple often is not. Educators who practice cultural responsiveness frequently encounter difficulty in finding appropriate instructional resources. This challenge is threefold. In general, there is a lack of culturally specific and authentic resources available to the consumer (students, parents, teachers, and administrators). The Cooperative Children's Book Center at the University of Wisconsin-Madison (2014) reports a steady decrease in books about people of color even though there has been a consistent increase in the number of books published each year. For instance, in 2010, out of 3,400 books the Center received to review, 308 books were about people of color. In 2012, out of 3,600 books the Center reviewed, approximately 280 of them were about people of color. That figure is less than 10 percent of the total books reviewed. In both cases, the numbers are dismal and appalling. Furthermore, the chances of finding numerous pieces of culturally authentic texts in mandated curricula, commercial basal programs, or the standard content-area textbooks are very slim. While the number of culturally responsive texts in publication may be sadly limited, the chances of these types of texts appearing in materials are even worse (Ball and Tyson 2011; Gay 2000; Peterson 2008). Finally, the problem of scarcity worsens exponentially when we consider whether the texts are culturally—and not just racially—based. If books are cultural, are they specific and authentic? Not every book or piece of text featuring characters of color is culturally responsive.

Expanding Culturally Relevant Texts to Culturally Authentic Texts

In general, textbook publishers are doing a better job of representing more cultures in an accessible manner in their books, but these attempts are still largely tokenistic and arrayed with the known authors of the past. Recently, I asked a publisher to send me a selection of "culturally responsive" literature highlighted in their anthology so that I could prepare for a presentation at a reading conference. Not to my surprise, what they sent were the classic Langston Hughes (1951; 1990) and Gwendolyn Brooks (1966; 1973) selections. Yes, you guessed it—*Montage of a Dream Deferred* and "We Real Cool," respectively. True, these texts are certainly culturally responsive, but they are overused in anthologies. Usually, these texts span several grade levels with the result that over the years, the selections have lost their punch. What underserved students face today is a dearth of culturally relevant texts.

The CLR educator cannot expect the state-mandated textbooks to be genuinely authentic in nature because they are primarily representative of the institutional hegemony. From evidence presented in the previous chapters, we know that the institution—in this case, the textbook—unintentionally recycles the cultural hegemony; consequently, the choice of selections continues to be limited. The only option for CLR educators is to actively *plan to supplement* the state-mandated anthologies with culturally responsive texts.

Supplementing mainstream text with culturally responsive resources hinges completely on the selection process. Books with African Americans and Latinos on the cover are not necessarily texts that deal with Black and Chicano culture (Harris 1999). CLR educators must be aware of three types of culturally responsive texts and resources when deciding on which materials would be the most appropriate ones to use with their students. The three types of texts are *culturally authentic (CA)*, *culturally generic (CG)*, and *culturally neutral (CN)*.

- *Culturally authentic* is the preferred type of text for the culturally responsive educator. A culturally authentic text is a piece of fiction or nonfiction that illuminates the authentic cultural experiences of a particular cultural group—whether it addresses religion, socioeconomic status, gender, ethnicity, nationality, orientation, age, or geographic location. The language, situations, and illustrations have to depict culture in an authentic manner as well. (Refer to Figure 1.2 Rings of Culture and the related discussion.) Again, race is not one of the rings of culture.

- *Culturally generic texts* feature characters of various racial identities but contain few and/or superficial details to define the characters or storylines in an authentic cultural manner. The book *Corduroy* by Don Freeman (1976) prominently features characters of color, but the substance of the book does not include culturally relevant information.

- *Culturally neutral texts* feature characters of "color" but the stories are drenched with a traditional or mainstream theme, plot, and/or characterization. For example, in the popular series *Katie Kazoo, Switcheroo* by Nancy E. Krulik, the main character, Katie, is white, while her best friend, Suzanne, is African American. However, the reader only knows that Suzanne represents an underserved population by looking at the limited number of illustrations in the chapter book; the text itself does not contain any reference—authentic or otherwise—to culture or race. Any racial group could be substituted for Suzanne's character, and it would not change the story. Culturally neutral texts are the least preferred texts and should be avoided when possible by the culturally responsive educator. (Note that there are always exceptions, as there are many quality texts that build literacy but are culturally neutral.) What we are trying to avoid at all costs is the cardinal sin of using a culturally neutral text thinking that it is culturally authentic. The teacher's understanding of the type of text selected is crucial.

Dots Survey for Culturally Appropriate Texts

How can you then gauge a type of text? There is no black or white answer to this question (no pun intended). In some ways, determining the cultural authenticity of a text is in the eye of the beholder because the assessment of texts is quite subjective. When evaluating the cultural authenticity of texts, the focus is on reflecting on what you are selecting for your students and stimulating discussion with your colleagues and students as to why representation in texts matters. Fortunately, though, you do not have to rely on putting your finger in the wind to determine a type of text. At the nudging of many CLR teachers, I created a scale of sorts to guide you in your selection process. *Responsive Dots* is a survey that helps educators analyze the cultural authenticity of texts. Figure 5.1 and Appendix D show the *Responsive Dots* survey. Each question that can be answered affirmatively receives a dot (i.e., a filled-in bubble). The more dots a text has, the more authentic it is. A scale for assessing the type of text is given at the end of the survey.

Fig. 5.1 Culturally Responsive Dots Survey Criteria

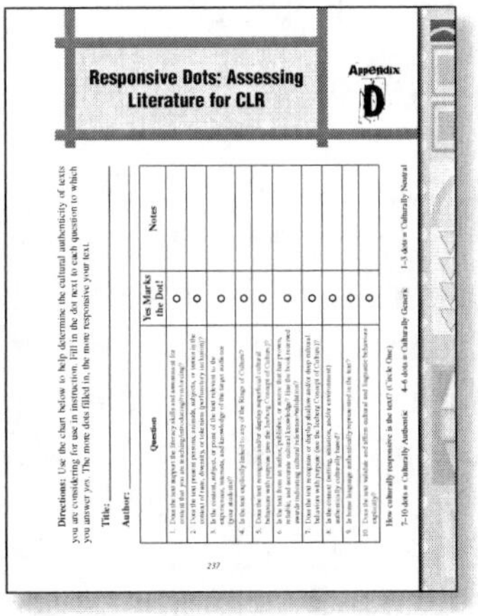

Based on feedback from a number of folks who have used the *Responsive Dots* survey, it at least accomplishes the goal of stimulating discussion and debate. I know that there is a strong desire to have a concrete answer as to what type of text a book is, but I believe that defeats a key theme of CLR overall: it's all about how you get there—the journey. To paraphrase Nick Saban, championship head coach of the Alabama Crimson Tide, "Trust the process." (And to be clear as to my loyalties, Go Trojans!)

To avoid the pitfalls of selecting texts that are culturally neutral, LeMoine (1999) offers the following tips:

147

- Choose well-known authors, illustrators, publishers, and vendors who have developed solid reputations for producing culturally relevant materials.

- Critically analyze how the characters are portrayed in the story, how the facts are presented, and in what context they are presented.

- Evaluate factual information for accuracy.

- When applicable, analyze the author's use of nonstandard language for authenticity and thoroughness.

- Carefully examine the illustrations for appeal, ethnic sensitivity, and authenticity.

The overall goal in the selection process is to choose culturally authentic texts of all types that are consistent with the themes, standards, and/or the content-specific topics represented in the mainstream titles. I *prescribe* at least one reading or interaction with a piece of culturally responsive text to go along with every mainstream title, state standard, or topic covered in the course of a lesson or unit. At times, it is incumbent upon the teacher to seek stories, poems, essays, articles, songs, or any texts that the students can relate to culturally and linguistically. Teachers should beware of two challenges they will encounter in meeting this requirement: time and resources. At first, it takes a great amount of time to seek out appropriate supplemental novels, short stories, and other texts for units of study or themes in the various content areas. If feasible, this type of preparation is best done in the summer months. To address the resource challenge, CLR educators from around the country have already done significant work in curating materials. Lydia McClanahan, the culturally authentic text guru at the Center for Culturally Responsive Teaching and Learning, has compiled over 200 titles that are all culturally authentic or generic (see Appendix F). In no way is her list exhaustive; it is simply a nudge for you to begin the work of collecting titles with the trust that you will continue the process based on the particular needs of your students and their cultures. Visit the Responsive Reads link at culturallyresponsive.org for additional text reviews.

Pause to Ponder

- What titles have you selected to supplement the mandated texts in the subject area(s) you teach?

- What challenges have you faced in finding suitable resources to use with your underserved students?

Using Read-Alouds in the Oral Tradition of Cultural Storytelling

The focus on culturally responsive academic literacy is meant to engage students who might be otherwise disengaged, unmotivated, or turned off to the idea of reading as a source of pleasure and entertainment as well as information and knowledge. The strategies covered in this chapter enable necessary levels of engagement to lead to increased achievement in literacy and compel students to a stronger desire to read. Reading aloud is the cultural complement to storytelling for many students, including those in the middle and secondary grades. It is a reminder of the elementary years when everyone came to the rug to hear a story from the teacher. While reading aloud has taken some knocks in current research, I still see it as a powerful way to connect to students culturally and build their literacy skills in ways that Harris (1999) and others describe.

In *Issues and Trends in Literacy Education*, Kindle supports the academic benefit of reading aloud when she says, "The read-aloud context has proven to [be] an effective vehicle for vocabulary instruction, but teachers need to recognize the practices that optimize word learning and determine the most effective manner for adding elaborations and explanations during the story reading without detracting from the pleasure of reading itself" (2012, 101). Without mentioning the term cultural responsiveness, reading aloud has two advantages: improving literacy skills and promoting the pleasure of reading. The dual benefits of reading aloud cannot be underestimated. Using read-alouds strategically can have a meaningful impact on the skill levels of students in the areas of vocabulary, fluency, and comprehension. Torgesen and Hudson (2006) advise that the most productive and research-based approach to the prosody-comprehension connection is for teachers to model prosody regularly when reading aloud to students and to always expect students to read with prosody. These reasons illustrate the positive impact of reading aloud on students' literacy skills. In CLR, these factors serve to support the build and bridge aspect of the strategy. But there is an even more important benefit related to the validation and affirmation of students: storytelling.

When using engaging read-alouds, the culturally responsive teacher is also validating and affirming students by simulating the oral tradition of storytelling. When you read aloud to your students, you are responding to the cultures in your classroom that have oral language and storytelling as important norms and traditions.

In summary, the evidence is overwhelmingly in favor of using engaging read-alouds. Some say that reading is a silent activity and that when we focus too much on reading aloud, we could be doing students a disservice (Garan and DeVoogd 2008; Reutzel, Fawson, and Smith 2008). Let us say that this assertion is true, but this point does not outweigh the clear advantages of using engaging read-alouds. Rarely does research look at cultural advantages. However, those studies that address culture find that reading aloud has a positive effect on cultural competence (May, Bingham, and Pendergast 2014).

"Many people within certain cultures, namely Native American, consider storytelling an art form because it combines the talents of the speakers, who use their hands, bodies, and voices to express emotion, spirit, and style. Storytelling produces strong responses in both the teller and the listeners. It can be used to entertain or to educate" (Torgesen and Hudson 2006, 126).

Effective Read-Alouds

According to the National Reading Panel (2000), fluency is the ability to read text with speed, accuracy, and proper expression. Fluent readers recognize words automatically, read aloud effortlessly with expression, and do not have to concentrate on decoding while comprehending what they are reading. Fluency has three components: *accuracy*, *rate*, and *prosody*. In order to implement fluency into reading instruction, teachers need to be aware of the three components.

Reading aloud to students helps them develop and improve literacy skills, such as reading, writing, speaking, and listening (Trelease 2001). Research indicates that listening to skilled readers stimulates growth and understanding of vocabulary and language patterns. Reading aloud benefits children for whom Standard English is not their first language. Students need daily opportunities and consistent practice with reading to improve their fluency. Reading aloud can help students become more fluent, competent readers. However, it is important not to put new English learners or nonproficient readers on the spot in read-aloud sessions. English learners and nonproficient readers need plenty of time to experience receptive language (listening) while they are becoming more confident with expressive language (speaking and reading aloud). I have included a collection of read-aloud activities in Appendix E. These can be used to model fluent reading, guide oral reading, and give students opportunities to practice. Each read-aloud is described along with the pros and cons of the activity and an explanation of its cultural responsiveness. The collection includes activities that are familiar to many teachers, for example, *Fade In, Fade Out*; *Echo Reading*; *Buddy Reading*; and *Choral Reading*. Consistent with the CLR pedagogy, the read-aloud activities have to be examined in the context of the VABB frame. For example, one of the more popular read-aloud activities that teachers try immediately is *Jump-In Reading*. This particular read-aloud activity is meant to validate and affirm verbal overlap, spontaneity, and community (culturally speaking). It would then be juxtaposed to *Fade-In, Fade Out*, which is a BB because it reinforces taking turns and being prompted. Additional read-aloud activities are offered in *Strategies for Culturally and Linguistically Responsive Teaching and Learning* (Hollie 2015). When using read-aloud activities, remember to recognize and sort them as validating and affirming or building and bridging.

Pause to Ponder

- How have you used read-aloud activities with your students?

- What instructional purposes do your read-aloud activities serve?

- How do your students respond to read-aloud activities?

Using Effective Literacy Strategies Responsively

A common myth about CLR is that the strategies and activities are meant to replace effective practices. I urge teachers to take heed of this caution. The observation is not true in general, and it is not true about effective literacy strategies. Infusing CLR does not mean throwing the baby out with the bathwater, as the saying goes. When it comes to literacy practices, teachers must continue to do what they know works for students. The key is to infuse CLR into effective literacy practices.

Now that you have learned what culturally responsive literacy looks like, it is time to fill your toolbox with general language and writing activities to use. These activities are used throughout literacy instruction to provide students with an even deeper culturally and linguistically responsive classroom experience. All of these activities are intended to increase engagement and give you different ways to support your students' literacy development.

These activities are appropriate for instruction across the curriculum. Content-area teachers who do not normally incorporate reading and writing into their lesson plans will find models that enable them to enhance content learning through effective literacy strategies. Many of the activities can be considered validating and affirming, or at least responsive. By utilizing these activities, you are able to strike a balance between coverage of your content and your methodology. With a new focus on text complexity, critical thinking, and discussion, today's standards require teachers to teach differently. In discussing these changes, a 2006 study by ACT, the company that creates the well-known college-readiness tests of the same name, concluded that "a pedagogy focused only on 'higher-order' or 'critical' thinking was insufficient to ensure that students were ready for college and careers: what students could read, in terms of complexity, was at least as important as what they could do with what they read" (CCSS 2010c, 2).

My colleagues and I have culled the literacy research and have identified effective literacy strategies that are well matched with CLR activities. These strategies are particularly well suited to the CLR classroom because they offer a source of motivation and interest to students for the purposes of increased engagement. I have included a collection of Culturally Responsive Literacy Strategy Activities in Appendix E, which includes descriptions and recommendations for their use. The activities are described and recommendations for their use are provided. I am confident that there are many familiar activities; however, I hope that the descriptions and suggestions for use will provide new insights about how to use these activities with underserved students. The resource includes activities such as *Hink-Pinks*, *Thinking Maps*, *Reader's Theater*, *Reciprocal Teaching*, and *Anticipation/Reaction Guide*. This collection is not meant to be exhaustive by any measure. What CLR teachers must do is find the "right" fit for their students and strategize about how to effectively implement activities into their instruction. Remember, the purpose of CLR infusion is increased engagement.

Summary

As students advance in school, the materials they encounter in language arts and the content areas present new demands on their literacy skills. CLR activities are designed to enable students to become proficient with the use of text. To enhance their students' learning, the primed CLR teachers must accomplish the following three tasks:

- Consistently and appropriately select culturally responsive texts that supplement the core instructional program.

- Effectively use read-aloud activities, which validate and affirm the cultural norm of storytelling for many students.

- Continue to use effective literacy strategies with the strategic infusion of CLR activities.

Above all, the teacher cannot lose sight of the fact that strong literacy is the gatekeeper to overall academic success.

Reflection Guide

Think back to your responses to the statements in the Anticipation Guide at the beginning of this chapter. Have your responses changed as a result of what you read in the chapter? If so, what new insights did you gain from the chapter?

_____ The majority of texts mandated for use in schools lack effective examples of culturally appropriate content.

_____ Typically, anthologies of literary selections include the more traditional and well-established authors of culture-based topics.

_____ Read-aloud activities are most appropriately used with younger students and those who struggle with reading.

_____ Culturally and linguistically responsive activities are substitutes for established literacy practices.

_____ People who are unfamiliar with the purposes and nature of CLR instruction may be susceptible to myths surrounding the approach.

1. What sources have you used to expand your access to materials that are culturally and linguistically appropriate for students in your classes?

2. How do you plan to use the list of Culturally Authentic Texts (Appendix F)?

3. Compare the activities you use for reading aloud with those presented in Culturally Responsive Read-Aloud Activities (Appendix E). Which activities are new to you? How do you plan to incorporate these into your instruction?

4. Which of the Culturally Responsive Literacy Activities (Appendix E) do you use most often with your students? To what extent do you think the activities are effective with your students? What new activities from this resource do you plan to use?

Is My Academic Language Instruction Culturally Responsive?

Anticipation Guide

What do you think of when you encounter the term *academic language*? Do you agree or disagree with the following statements about language forms students bring to school and the development of academic language? Write *A* for *agree* or *D* for *disagree* on each line.

_____ The needs of students who use unaccepted languages have been ill served by educational policies that have contributed to institutionalized linguistic prejudice.

_____ Lack of linguistic knowledge among educators and the public is a major contributor to controversies surrounding the use of unaccepted languages in school.

_____ Teachers have an obligation to accommodate students' home languages in the classroom.

_____ CLR is singular in its recognition of the value of unaccepted languages in enabling students to achieve success in school.

_____ Characterizing an unaccepted language as "bad" negates the principles of structure and pattern that apply to all languages.

The Context of Unaccepted Languages

Of the myriad of topics I cover in my professional development programs, the validation and affirmation of nonstandard languages, or what I call *unaccepted languages*, remains the most controversial and provocative. It stands to reason that controversy occurs because language is arguably the most central and integral aspect of an individual's cultural base and heritage. With that centrality can come hypersensitivity that causes some people to become what I define as *offensive*; that is, having a combination of emotions that causes one to become defensive, offended, and overly sensitive all at once.

Moreover, discussions about language seem to be coupled with ignorance, misinformation, and entrenched negative beliefs about unaccepted languages. Validating and affirming home language requires the developing CLR educator to have more extensive background knowledge about language. This knowledge is meant to undo the damage of institutional linguistic racism and institutional ignorance about unaccepted languages and language use in general. Notably, *language deficit* is a perspective commonly held about the home languages of students who have been identified as the most likely to be underserved. CLR is designed to overcome the barriers that this perspective presents not only for students but also for teachers, administrators, and policymakers. Specifically, CLR educators must accomplish three objectives in order to be responsive to the home languages of their students. These objectives are:

1. Recognize the linguistic rules of the unaccepted languages.

2. Give students ample opportunities to practice codeswitching.

3. Infuse writing activities into everyday teaching.

In achieving these objectives, educators must realize that deficit terminology is unacceptable in the CLR world. Such terms as *fix it*, *correct it*, *make it better*, and *wrong* are frequently used in the context of language deficiency. In CLR, these terms are replaced with such validating and affirming words and phrases such as *translate*, *put another way*, *switch*, *give in school/academic language*.

In previous chapters, I have defined terms that are central to understanding the concepts of culturally and linguistically responsive teaching. Similarly, I want to clarify the terminology used in this chapter by recognizing that there are many labels for unaccepted languages. To reiterate, I think the disagreement about the terminology used and the ongoing debates about the legitimacy of these linguistic entities contribute to resistance toward and divisiveness about CLR as it applies to implementing the approach to make it part of the school culture. These arguments are futile and become barriers to actual CLR classroom implementation. In order to keep the discussion and progression moving forward, it is best to have clarity, if not agreement, on the terms used. I recommend these terms and definitions be used in CLR discussions. These terms and their definitions are delineated in Figure 6.1.

Fig. 6.1 Terms Central to Understanding Culturally and Linguistically Responsive Teaching

Term	Definition
Language	A legitimate linguistic entity defined around the parameters of phonics, markers, grammar, vocabulary, nonverbal uses, and discourse styles.
Home Language	The language utilized by family members in the home and others in the community that is different enough from the parameters defined by language from Standard English.
School Language	The language utilized in the context of school; commonly associated with Standard English.

Term	Definition
Unaccepted (Nonstandard) Languages	Not the opposite of *standard language*; only used in the generic context of the term *language*; speaks to the non-acceptance of these languages, not to their lack of legitimacy, and linguistically speaking are seen as just as legitimate as the so-called standard languages.
Academic Language	The language used in textbooks, in classrooms, and on tests; different in structure (e.g., heavier on compound, complex, and compound-complex sentences) and vocabulary (e.g., technical terms and common words with specialized meanings) from Standard English.
African American Language, African American Vernacular, or Black English	The systematic, rule-governed language that represents an infusion of the grammatical substrata of West African languages and the vocabulary of English.
American Indian Language	The language of American Indians used at home, on the job, in the classroom, and in other areas of daily experience. It shows extensive influence from the speaker's native language tradition and differs accordingly from nonnative notions of standard grammar and appropriate speech (Leap 1993).
Chicano or Mexican American Language	The systematic, rule-governed language spoken by the Chicano and/or Mexican American community united by common ancestry in the Southwestern United States and/or Mexico.
Hawaiian American Language or Hawaiian Pidgin English	A native speech that evolved as a result of Hawaii's diverse background. It is also called *Da Kine* or, more commonly, *Pidgin,* when it really is not a pidgin anymore but actually a creole, or Hawaii Creole English, as termed by the Ethnologue Database. Unlike other English-based pidgin, Hawaiian Pidgin is founded within several different languages, with the Hawaiian language contributing the most words. Still, the term *Pidgin* remains.

- What is the policy for unaccepted languages in your school or district?

- What mandates are provided to ensure that the policy is implemented?

- Are sufficient resources available to allow for effective implementation of the policy?

- How do you validate and affirm your students' home languages?

Authenticity of Unaccepted Languages

Surprised is the word that I hear most frequently from educators when discussing the veracity and authenticity of nonstandard languages. Like the general public, educators often exhibit great ignorance about the historical and present-day context of these linguistic entities that linguists have studied for decades.

Corson (1997) revealed that formal educational policies for the treatment of nonstandard languages in schools are conspicuous in their absence in most educational systems. This research aptly points out, however, that these varieties are one way or another brought into the work of the school. Educators have to recognize that students coming from these backgrounds often possess two or more languages that they use in the home. But because of the lack of a formal policy recommendation, often the result is that students are penalized for having a language variety that is different from the linguistic capital that has high status in the school (Corson 1997). William Labov (1972), the grandfather of research on Black English in the United States, argued that there is no real basis for attributing poor performance to the grammatical and phonological characteristics of any nonstandard language. So, why is educational policy lacking in support for nonstandard languages? According to Corson (1997), this absence exists mainly because of simple ignorance about the range of varieties that can and do coexist in a single linguistic space. The point not to be missed here is that any language policy that excludes support for nonstandard languages creates a paradox for nonstandard language users and the teachers who teach them.

The Unaccepted Languages of the Underserved

Most people view nonstandard languages to be dialects or, even worse, just slang. The research on these languages, which has been a source of vigorous academic debate for decades, strongly refutes that limited perspective. While there is disagreement about the historical derivation of the noted unaccepted languages, there is clarity about the differing views. The views fall into the following four broad linguistic categories:

- Enthnolinguistic perspective

- Creolist perspective

- Dialect perspective

- Deficit perspective

These views represent a continuum of perspectives from most responsive to least responsive, as shown in Figure 6.2. This continuum has particular relevance for culturally and linguistically responsive instruction.

Fig. 6.2 Language Perspective Continuum

Most Responsive			Least Responsive
Ethnolinguistic	Creolist	Dialect	Deficit

Each of these categories has a body of research in and of itself with numerous books, articles, and studies readily available. The following summaries do not do justice to the complexity and depth of each argument or to the historical context and the relevance to present-day CLR. The *ethnolinguistic* and *dialect* perspectives will be discussed primarily because the ethnolinguistic view is aligned more directly with the concept of validating and affirming home languages; however, the dialect view is the perspective most accepted by educators. The *creolist* perspective offers a worldview, while the *deficit* view is seen as racist today.

Ethnolinguistic Perspective

The ethnolinguistic perspective holds that derivation of the unaccepted languages is rooted in the social, historical, and linguistic development of the people and that any understanding of the language has to be inclusive of these aspects. Essentially, the language was developed through a linguistic process termed *relexification*, which produces a hybrid language consisting of the grammatical structure of the indigenous language meshed with the vocabulary of the dominant language.

Numerous studies acknowledge that African American students, as well as the other previously mentioned research-identified populations, come to school speaking a language that is dissimilar to but no less valuable than the language of instruction (Standard English). Dillard (1972) estimated that at least 80 percent of all African Americans speak some aspect of African American Language. Smitherman (1998) figured the estimate to be as high as 95 percent. Robert L. Williams (1975), affectionately known as the Father of Ebonics, defines Ebonics as the linguistic and paralinguistic features that on a concentric continuum represent the communicative competence of West African, Caribbean, and United States slave descendants of African origin. Ebonics does include the various idioms, patois, argots, idiolects, and social dialects of Black people, especially those who have been forced to adapt to colonial circumstances. As a term, *Ebonics* derives its form from *ebony* (black) and *phonics* (sound) and refers to the study of the language of Black people. This term was coined in 1973 at a conference of Black psycholinguists and sociolinguists. It was not invented during the 1996 Oakland Ebonics controversy. Ebonics refers to the "language family" spoken by Africans throughout the diaspora, which includes Black people in Jamaica (Jamaican Patois) and the Caribbean (Caribbean dialects), South America, Mexico (Black Spanish), and Europe (Black Portuguese). In other words, wherever the enslaved Africans were taken throughout the world, some form of Ebonics exists today.

Ernie Smith (1992) views African American language from an Afrocentric perspective. His view is that African Americans, as descendants of enslaved Africans, are not native language speakers of English. They are descendants of the West and Niger-Congo regions of Africa, where a variety of African languages were spoken—Fula, Mandinka, Ewe, and Umbundu, to name a few. According to Smith (1992), research since the 1930s has argued that African American speech is an African Language System—the linguistic continuation of Africa in Black America. Smith says, "African Americans have, in fact, retained a West and Niger-Congo African thought process which is manifested in the substratum phonology, morphosyntax, and semantic lexical structure of their speech. African Americans' native language is Ebonics, a linguistic continuation of Africa in America" (1992, 40). Smith goes on to say that Ebonics is not "genetically" related to English. Ebonics is not a synonym for Black English. In fact, it has nothing to do with the grammatical structure of English. The quote from Melville Herskovits (1941, 143) best sums up the ethnolinguistic perspective:

> This being the case, and since grammar and idiom are the last aspects of a new language to be learned, the Negroes who reached the New World acquired as much of the vocabulary of their masters as they initially needed or was later taught to them, pronounced these words as best as they were able, but organized them into aboriginal speech patterns.

Thus arose the various forms of Negro English, Negro French, Negro Spanish, and Negro Portuguese spoken in the New World, their peculiarities being due to the fact that they comprise European words cast into African grammatical mold.

The ethnolinguists' view forges the belief that the unaccepted languages developed without the benefit of American educational institutions. For the purposes of validating and affirming, as will be shown later, the ethnolinguistic perspective has the greatest potential for impact because it calls for the educator to explicitly acknowledge and affirm the home language as a means to achieving Standard American English proficiency.

Dialect Perspective

The *dialect* perspective represents another point on the continuum of language responsiveness. Nieto (1999) defines a dialect as a variety that is spoken because one belongs to a particular region, social class, caste, age, group, or other relevant grouping. Dialects are identified on the basis of the systematic co-occurrence of particular linguistic features among groups of people. For Mexican Americans who are English dominant, for example, this means that their language has rules similar to those of English but manifests some surface variations of the Spanish rules, especially within the phonological component. Varying from the ethnolinguistic view, the dialectologists present what many consider to be a Eurocentric view. Because the rules of the unaccepted language features are always explained in juxtaposition to the English language, the dialect focus is representative of a deficit perspective.

Therefore, terms such as *-lessness, weakening, omission*, and *reduction* appear in the dialect research. This opposes the ethnolinguistic view, which links linguistic differences to a systematic, rule-governed language with linguistic roots. In the context of school, underserved students who speak a different home language come to the classroom with a dialect that can be *corrected*. Students just need to be taught the appropriate referencing and manner of articulation when it comes to Standard English sounds (reading and speaking) and the correct Standard English syntactical structures when it comes to grammar (writing). In other words, these students can be "corrected" out of their home language. Bilingual education calls this type of instruction *subtractive bilingualism*.

An example of how this view plays out in a structured school situation comes from programs in Hawaii that focus on the home language of Hawaiian Pidgin English (HPE). These programs are bolstered by linguistic research that studies language in a social context in which linguistic differences between HPE and Standard English (SE) are identified. The well-researched Kamehameha Early Education Program has shown marked achievement with this population. These researchers concluded that the culturally congruent style of discourse management was more effective, as it led to more productive achievement-related behavior by the students on a variety of measures (Jordan 1984). Similarly, the researchers determined that culturally congruent participation structures in the classroom not only foster reading achievement but also facilitate the development of spoken Standard English as well (Nieto 1999). The dialectologist view is the mostly widely held perspective by linguists, educators, and the general public. For example, in terms of the current stage of research concerning the linguistic variety most commonly known as Chicano English, the dialectologist view categorizes this linguistic variety as a contact "dialect" because it emerges in the linguistic setting where there is contact between Mexican Spanish and American English. Fought (2003), a prominent researcher of Chicano English, maintains that while Chicano English is a contact dialect, it is not truly a creole, since creoles generally emerge from a setting where multiple languages are involved.

Creolist and Deficit Perspectives

The other two views—*creolist* and *deficit*—do not need extensive summaries. The creolist position is very similar to that of the ethnolinguists, with the difference being that creolists do not necessarily attribute the grammatical base to the indigenous language. They see it more as a pidgin that over two generations creolized into a solidified linguistic entity. The deficit perspective simply holds that nonstandard languages are nothing but bad or improper English and the speakers of the nonstandard languages are incapable cognitively of mastering Standard English. On the surface, this view is easily refuted and today is seen as blatantly racist. At a deeper level, the reality is that up until the 1940s, this perspective was commonly held and had become institutionalized knowledge. Gonzales (1922), a noted deficit linguist, theorized that the development of a hegemonic perspective around language is not surprising, for it is a linguistic axiom that when two groups of people who have different languages come into contact—the one on a relatively high, the other on a relatively low cultural level—the latter adapts itself freely to the speech of former, whereas the group on the higher cultural plane borrows little or nothing from that on the lower.

Linguistic Absolutes

Regardless of the differing perspectives in the linguistic research, the following three agreed-upon linguistic absolutes are evident:

1. All language is good. Conceptually and linguistically speaking, there is no such thing as a *bad* language. Languages are not inherently bad, improper, wrong, or incorrect. In CLR, these terms are considered deficit in nature and useless with an affirmative position on language.

2. All linguistic forms are rule governed and patterned. They are not haphazard, made up, randomized, or created by rappers. The range of these rules covers all dimensions of language—phonics, morphemes, syntax, semantics, pragmatics, and discourse. Indeed, the fact that there are rules in each of these dimensions speaks to the veracity of the linguistic entity.

3. We acquire the language that is spoken by the primary caregivers at home, beginning at prebirth and continuing up to prekindergarten. In fact, the language that is spoken at home will be the language the student uses at school. The student comes to school with all the rules of that language intact and, most importantly, with a positive view of the language. Unfortunately, the beginning of school chips away at that positive view as, all of a sudden, students are told that the way their grandparents, uncles, siblings, and parents speak is wrong.

To be CLR, the educator has to subscribe to these absolutes, as they are the first steps to being able to validate and affirm students' home languages.

Rules of Unaccepted Language

With the shift in mindset about unaccepted languages and acceptance of the three absolutes in place, the process of validation and affirmation can begin for the CLR educator. Similar to the examination of culture presented in Chapter 1, what exactly the teacher must validate and affirm needs to be made clear in the context of nonstandard languages. Therefore, CLR educators need to become aware of the researched-based linguistic rules or features of the nonstandard languages spoken in their classrooms so as to know what is worth validating and affirming. The rules are based on a formula of understanding that has three parts.

- **Part 1: Lose the hegemonic view of Standard English.**
  Just because Standard English has certain usage or structure
  as a rule does not mean that all languages have the same
  rule.

- **Part 2: Understand the derivation of the rule in the
  context of the indigenous language.** In other words, it
  must be recognized how the rule came into existence,
  especially in comparison to Standard English rules.

- **Part 3: Codeswitch appropriately.** Translate from the
  home language to the target language (or in some cases,
  make reverse translations).

These aspects of understanding linguistic absolutes are clarified
in two examples based on features of African American Vernacular
English (AAVE): the habitual form of the verb *be* and multiple
negation, shown in Figure 6.3 and Figure 6.4, respectively.

Fig. 6.3 Habitual *Be* Form

Example 1

Name and Explanation of Rule in AAVE: Habitual BE (commonly made fun of or ridiculed by mainstream media when discussing Ebonics). The BE form is typically formed with

- Be + verb ending in –ing
- Be + adjective

Examples: *I be late to work* or *She be playing Bingo a lot at the casino.*

Standard English Rule: The use of *be* in this form does not exist.

Standard English Equivalent: Appropriate tense of the verb "to be" in Standard English in addition to an adverb that describes time frequency (e.g., always, usually, normally, often, frequently).

Translation: I *am always* late to work. She *frequently plays* Bingo at the casino.

Fig. 6.4 Multiple Negation

Example 2

Name and Explanation of Rule in AAVE: Multiple Negation

- Multiple negation refers to the use of multiple negative words in a sentence.

- With multiple negation, the more negative words in a sentence, the greater the negative sentiment being expressed by the speaker.

- The negative words act as intensifiers, words like *any*, *none*, *no*, *either*, and *some*.

- An intensifier heightens or lowers the intensity of meaning of an item.

Examples: *I do not have no pencil for you* and *She won't never share her snacks.*

Standard English Rule: Multiple negatives are not allowed. In Standard English, the rule is called *double negative*. Standard English grammar rules dictate that a sentence can only have one negative word. Two negative words, double negatives, cancel each other out; therefore, expressing a positive sentiment. Intensifiers are considered adverbs and adjectives.

Translation: I *do not* have any pencils for you. She *never* ever shares any of her snacks.

Teachers should familiarize themselves with language rules that apply to the languages that their students use. For reference and awareness, language rules as they apply to African American Language (AAVE) and Mexican American Language (Chicano English) are presented in Figure 6.5 and Figure 6.6, respectively.

Fig. 6.5 African American Language (AAVE) Common Rules List

Categories	Examples
Sounds	**Sounds**
/th/ Sound (digraphs)	<u>Dis</u> is my <u>mouf</u>.
Consonant Clusters	I put my <u>tes'</u> on your <u>des'</u>.
Vowels Short /ĕ/ and Short /ĭ/	I am <u>tin</u> years old.
Reflexive /r/ Sound or /er/ Sound	<u>Yo sista</u> is Ca'ol. Did you <u>caw</u> me?
Markers (Morphemes)	**Markers (Morphemes)**
Past Tense Marker "ed"	He <u>visit</u> us yesterday.
Possessive Marker	That is my <u>sister</u> bike.
Plural Marker	I have 25 <u>cent</u>.
Syntax	**Syntax**
Multiple Negation	He <u>don't</u> have <u>none</u>.
Habitual *Be*	She <u>be</u> mean.
Topicalization	That <u>boy he</u> funny.
Present Tense Copula Verb	She pretty.
Regularized Patterns	**Regularized Patterns**
Reflexive Pronoun	He hurt <u>hisself</u>.
Present Tense Singular Verb	He <u>run</u> fast.
Past Tense Singular Verb	We <u>was</u> here.

Fig. 6.6 Mexican-American (Chicano English) Common Rules List

Categories	Examples
Sounds	**Sounds**
/th/ Sound (digraphs)	<u>Dis</u> teecher is mean.
Final Consonant Clusters and Medial Consonant Clusters	I <u>lef</u> my game over there. My dad went to da <u>harware</u> store.
Vowels Short /ĕ/ and Short /ĭ/	I don't got a <u>pin</u>.
/z/ and /v/ Sounds	The firemen <u>safed</u> many <u>lifes</u>. He won da <u>price</u> at the fair.
Circumflex Intonation (Nahuatl influenced)	<u>Doon't</u> bee <u>baaad</u>!
Breath H (Nahuatl influenced)	My hair was all <u>hwite</u>, so I dyed it.
Stress Patterns	I get paid <u>tooday</u>.
Markers (Morphemes) Phonologically Influenced	**Markers (Morphemes) Phonologically Influenced**
Past Tense Marker *ed*	She <u>move</u> to San Diego.
Morphological Sensitive Rule (*thuh* before consonant/*thee* before a vowel)	We saw <u>thuh</u> ocean over there.
Plural Marker (dropped when forming a separate syllable)	He always <u>ditch</u> school.
Syntax	**Syntax**
Multiple Negation	She <u>don't</u> like <u>nobody</u>.
Intensifiers	Mom was <u>all</u> lost on the way to my Tia's. This DVD <u>barely</u> came out.
Topicalization	My <u>brother he's</u> going to the movies.
Present Tense Copula Verb	<u>This…</u>a school.
Prepositional Variation	He was sitting <u>in</u> the couch.
Regularized Patterns	**Regularized Patterns**
Indefinite Article	Do you want <u>a</u> ice cream?
Present Tense Singular Verb	He <u>jump</u> rope to get in shape.
Pronoun	Now they can do it by <u>theirselves</u>.

Effective Instructional Practices

Familiarity with common rules in unaccepted languages enables CLR educators to know what to validate and affirm in their students' languages. Furthermore, such knowledge ensures that the teachers do *not* react negatively to students' use of home language. The positive steps teachers take to help students build and bridge to the language of school negate the deficit view of an unaccepted language. Such terms as *fix it*, *correct it*, *speak correctly*, or *say it like you make sense*, which are examples of deficit terminology, should not be used in CLR. These terms must be replaced with affirmative expressions, such as *translate*, *put another way*, *switch*, or *say in school (or academic) language*. CLR instruction enables students to learn how to switch from their home language to the language of school, or academic language. However, that instruction has to first consider whether the student has the skill set to switch. Many students lack the necessary skills, which is a failure on the part of the school. Although many students, particularly older ones, quickly conceptualize what is needed to switch to the appropriate language for the situation, this awareness does not mean that they will actually be able to switch. Providing students with explicit instruction and ample practice in contrastive analysis is necessary to ensure students build this skillset.

Pause to Ponder

- In what ways do you validate and affirm your students' unaccepted languages?

- How do you build your students' skills and confidence in switching to situationally appropriate language?

Contrastive Analysis

Language codeswitching, known academically as *contrastive analysis*, is the practice of comparing and contrasting the linguistic structure of two languages. This strategy facilitates acquisition of Standard English by increasing students' awareness of the differences (rules) between the languages they bring from home and the language of school. Research shows three benefits of contrastive analysis for students:

1. It increases a student's ability to recognize the differences between Standard English and his or her home language.

2. Students become more proficient at editing and revising the grammar, vocabulary, and syntax in their work.

3. Students gain greater facility in the use of Standard English in both oral and written expression.

Many of the instructional activities in Figure 6.7 are based in contrastive analysis and vary as necessary for the content and/or grade level. Reading/language arts and social studies provide more opportunities for sentence lifting and retellings, while other content areas (including mathematics and science) are more geared toward role-playing and teachable moments.

Fig. 6.7 Language Switching Activities

Activity	Definition
Sentence Lifting	*Sentence lifting* is the use of literature, poetry, songs, plays, student-elicited sentences, or prepared story scripts that incorporate specific contrasts of home- and Standard English-rule forms. The student performs the contrastive analysis translations to determine the underlying rules that distinguish the two language forms. For example, teachers commonly take lines of rap music and ask students to change those lines into Standard English and then analyze the sound difference, effect on audience, or focus on grammar structure.
Retellings	Students first listen to a selection presented in Standard English. Then, they use their home languages to retell the story or piece of text. The students' retellings are taped so that they can be compared and contrasted with the language of the text.
Role-playing	Role-playing gives students opportunities to practice situations through acting and writing in Standard English. The emphasis is on situational appropriateness, which calls on students to weigh the language most suited to the environment, audience, purpose, and function.
Teachable Moments	Teachable moments are a form of contrastive analysis in which the teacher elicits spontaneous verbal responses from the students about material read or presented, creating on-the-spot opportunities for situational appropriateness in the classroom.

Dr. Jamila Gillenwaters uses role-playing contrastive-analysis exercises with students in the upper-elementary grades. The scenario that follows (Figure 6.8) is an example of such an exercise that provides an opportunity for students to practice, making choices for which statement is most appropriate given the situation. The activity is based on the AAVE *Habitual Be* rule described in Figure 6.3.

Fig. 6.8 Situational Appropriateness Example

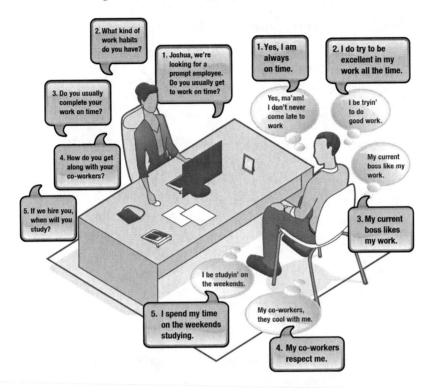

Another example of a contrastive analysis exercise is presented in Figure 6.9. Based on the AAVE *multiple negation* rule described in Figure 6.4, this activity requires students to categorize the expressions according to home language or school language.

Fig. 6.9 Example of Multiple Negation Rule

School Language or Home Language?

Directions: Read each of the following sentences with a partner. Decide if the sentence is written in School Language or Home Language.

- José never ever messes with anybody.

- We don't never go nowhere on the weekend.

- I didn't go anywhere this weekend.

- Girls won't never play fair!

- You don't ever have any money!

- Why won't boys ever play fair?

- You don't never have no money!

- Nobody better not mess with José!

These kinds of exercises are usually presented in the form of worksheets, which are often criticized as another type of "drill and kill" activity. Although this may be a fair criticism, the value of such exercises cannot be overlooked. As students work to complete the activities, they are gaining experience in analyzing language forms as well as interacting with one another. Obviously, it is the nature and purpose of the activity that is important, not the format.

Sentence lifting, retelling, role-playing, and teachable-moment activities are effective in helping students recognize the similarities and differences between their home language and that of school. I recommend that teachers routinely use such activities, varying them according to subject area or grade level. Importantly, the choice of activity should be based on the instructional needs of the students. When CLR teachers observe opportunities for students to build on their home language to learn Standard English, they should provide lessons that capitalize on the situation. Beginning with validation and affirmation of their students' home languages, teachers can best meet the learning needs of underserved students.

Using Effective Writing Strategies

Writing activities are another way to provide students with opportunities to develop their skills in language switching. Once CLR teachers are familiar with the linguistic features of their students' home languages, they are equipped to develop lessons that accommodate these features in the context of standards-based instruction. The writing activities that I describe are examples of those that my colleagues and I have culled from research and have used successfully at our laboratory school. These activities are described in Appendix E of this book.

Summary

Responsive academic language instruction is designed to enable students to learn how to move from their home language to the language of school. To develop appropriate instructional activities, CLR teachers have to be informed about the nature of nonstandard language and subscribe to a belief system that validates and affirms the use of such language. In doing so, teachers play a pivotal role in eliminating institutional rejection of nonstandard languages that has resulted from the hegemony of Standard English in schools.

Reflection Guide

Think back to your responses to the statements in the Anticipation Guide at the beginning of the chapter. Have your responses changed as a result of what you read in the chapter? What new insights did you gain from the chapter?

_____ The needs of students who use unaccepted languages have been ill served by educational policies that have contributed to institutionalized linguistic prejudice.

_____ Lack of linguistic knowledge among educators and the public is a major contributor to controversies surrounding the use of unaccepted languages in school.

_____ Teachers have an obligation to accommodate students' home languages in the classroom.

_____ CLR is singular in its recognition of the value of unaccepted languages in enabling students to achieve success in school.

_____ Characterizing unaccepted language as "bad" negates the principles of structure and pattern that apply to all languages.

1. What have you observed about your students' use of nonstandard language forms? How have you incorporated information from your observations into your lesson planning?

2. Which section of this chapter has had the most dramatic effect on your thinking about responsive academic language instruction? How will you use the insights you have gained to strengthen your teaching?

Is My Learning Environment Culturally Responsive?

Anticipation Guide

What do you think of when you encounter the expression *culturally responsive learning environment*? Do you agree or disagree with the following statements about the classroom learning environment? Write *A* for *agree* or *D* for *disagree* on each line.

_____ The traditional classroom structure with students sitting in rows is most effective in maintaining discipline with underserved students.

_____ Excessive use of decorative materials in the classroom can be distracting for underserved students.

_____ An inviting classroom environment encourages students to interact positively with one another and the teacher.

_____ Learning centers are necessary in primary-grade classrooms but are not essential for students in the upper grades, notably middle and secondary levels.

_____ Fair and clear procedures for classroom behaviors contribute to a sense of community in the classroom.

_____ A combination of teacher-directed and student-centered activities is needed to maintain a responsive learning environment.

The Contexts of Classroom Environments

Creating a positive learning environment is actually the first step teachers should take as they strive to create a classroom that is culturally and linguistically responsive. Given the importance of this factor, teachers may be wondering why I have left this topic for the end of the book. My reasoning is that the concepts underlying a culturally responsive learning environment are implicit in every aspect of CLR pedagogy described in previous chapters. The absence of a positive climate in the classroom makes it impractical, or more likely impossible, for teachers to implement the strategies that foster and enhance learning for underserved students. A culturally responsive learning environment is one that conveys respect for every student, notably respect for the knowledge, experiences, and language students bring to the classroom. Such a context is central to validating and affirming students' home language as well as building and bridging their efforts to use school language.

Understanding the relationship between the environment and behavior enables teachers to organize and to equip the classroom so that optimal learning is more likely to occur. According to Shade, Kelly, and Oberg (1997), an inviting learning environment establishes a pleasant physical and psychological atmosphere that welcomes students. How the students function within the particular environment depends on their comfort level. Moos (1979) said that for students of color and families of immigrants, their initial assessment of their acceptance into the school environment depends on whether they perceive pictures, symbols, and other visual representations that remind them of their homes, communities, and values.

Organization of physical space can influence behavior and learning. Conspicuous features, including furniture placement, learning materials, bulletin boards, use of technology, and spatial/viewing capacity, can have a profound impact on students by sending strong messages for powerful learning.

All learners, but especially underserved learners, thrive in environments that stimulate language development and literacy acquisition and surround them with language-rich visuals rife with symbols and print. The strategically arranged environment creates the spatial context in which movement and learning activities can take place. Also, the optimal environment provides resources that are rich in context and instructional materials, which include relevant high-interest instructional resources to enhance student engagement in the learning process.

There is no right answer for your room environment. A consideration that you have to make is what I call the Three Ds: De-Blumenbaching, De-Commercializing, and De-Superficializing. These Three Ds are assessed in order to help you uncover the ways in which your mindset affects your classroom's learning environment.

De-Blumenbaching

Johann Friedrich Blumenbach was a German anthropologist in the late 18th and early 19th century who developed a system of racial classification that divided the human species into five races based on physical features and perceived beauty (Caucasian, Mongolian, Malayan, Ethiopian, and American). Blumenbach's work upheld the common belief that Caucasians were the superior race because they were directly descended from the biblical figures Adam and Eve. While Blumenbach's theories about racial classification were discarded long ago, the underlying concept of the superiority of the Caucasian race persists in many subconscious and less explicit ways. As discussed in Chapter 5, texts rarely include authentic descriptions and representations of cultures outside mainstream culture. Furthermore, the media overwhelmingly focuses on individuals of the Caucasian race; consumer products, including those made for classroom use, are often dominated by images of Caucasians. Thus, as culturally responsive educators, it is necessary to "de-Blumenbach" ourselves, especially in the context of schooling and classroom learning environments. This means making deliberate decisions about the images you display in your classroom and seeking out materials that represent your students' cultures, rather than the mainstream White Anglo-Saxon culture. Research has demonstrated how seeing or not seeing one's culture reflected in media and literature can impact one's identity. As a result, it is important that you critically examine your learning environments, textbooks, and the images around your school in order to make the necessary changes to move toward a more representative and culturally responsive environment. The bottom line is to critically examine your learning environments, textbooks, and the images around your school to see how they have been "Blumenbached" and then—more importantly—how to change it to more accurately reflect the students in your school.

De-Commercializing

Perhaps the best way to ensure that your classroom environment is representative of your student population is to display students' work, rather than commercial products, in your classroom. By developing your classroom environment around work created by students, you are automatically making it more culturally responsive. When students see their own work on classroom walls and bulletin boards, they immediately see themselves as an integral part of the classroom and school. By creating a classroom community that is built by students rather than with commercial materials, you are validating and affirming both students' talents and their own personal perceptions of cultural identity.

De-Superficializing

As seen in the Iceberg Concept of Culture (Figure 1.3), there are many different layers and levels of culture. When you are working to make your classroom environment more culturally responsive, it is important to go beyond the superficial images of cultural diversity and strive for authentic and genuine representations of your students' cultures. For example, simply displaying a woven

African basket in the corner of your classroom does not make your classroom environment more culturally responsive. Most students, even if they are from an African American background, will probably not notice, let alone identify, with this type of cultural artifact without intentional instruction. However, the purposeful use of bright and culturally meaningful colors to make a classroom environment more inviting and conducive to learning is an authentic and effective way to make your classroom more responsive.

Evidence of a Culturally Responsive Learning Environment

My experience with working in numerous classrooms across the country as well as evidence from research (Murphy 2009) provides the context for describing features of a responsive learning environment. *Responsive* here means that which validates and affirms students in the environment—*not* what remediates them. Through the work of my colleagues at our laboratory school and my professional development work with thousands of teachers, we have developed a formula for creating a responsive learning environment. In general, we strive to provide a welcoming environment that has evidence of students' perspectives and lives.

The many visitors who have come to CLAS have noted and been awed by the exemplary learning environment. Dr. Rebecca Powell, professor at Georgetown University in Kentucky, acknowledged:

> Throughout the building and in all of the classrooms, there was affirmation of the African American community. Pictures on walls reflected their culture and community. In one hallway, we saw a chart that compared Ebonics structures with Standard English structures, clearly the result of a lesson (or perhaps even a series of lessons) that validated their language while comparing it to the language of power. In a first grade classroom we visited, the class had developed brainstorm webs of "My Community

Place" that examined students' special places in the community. The classrooms had what we would call a 'print rich' environment, with hundreds of books of various genres, all of which had Black protagonists (Powell and Rightmyer 2011).

Dr. Powell's observations are a tribute to the extensive efforts of CLAS faculty to create and sustain a responsive learning environment.

As witnessed by Dr. Powell and other visitors, the CLR recipe for a culturally responsive learning environment is framed around eight elements:

1. **Print-rich Environment:** 70 percent authentic and 30 percent commercially produced

2. **Learning Centers:** reading, writing, listening, math, science, and cultural

3. **Culturally Colorful:** ethnic textiles, prints, artwork, and artifacts

4. **Arranged Optimally:** allowing for presentations, movement, and teacher and student space

5. **Multiple Libraries:** culture-specific, multicultural, content-specific, reading level, and signature literature

6. **Use of Technology:** utilized and prominently displayed

7. **Relevant Bulletin Boards:** cultural, student work, current unit, current events, and content-area oriented

8. **Displayed Student Work and Images of Students:** current, ample, and unit-related

These ingredients are to serve as they would for an actual recipe—meaning that in order to create the dish, the chef absolutely needs these ingredients. However, the exact amount and mixture of the ingredients are left up to the chef's creativity, intuition, and experience. This intentional flexibility supports the customization of the learning environment for the unique students in each classroom. In other words, the responsive environment should not be cookie-cutter or branded. Even though the components are prescriptive and defined, how the environment will ultimately look is descriptive, dependent, and highly reliant on the CLR teacher to think out of the box. The teachers at our laboratory school in Los Angeles used these components in their own ways with the result that each classroom looked completely different. In the next sections, I describe the features of a responsive learning environment along with photos from CLAS classrooms. These photos will help you appreciate how a responsive environment is put together.

Pause to Ponder

Which of the eight elements of a culturally responsive learning environment are you currently applying in your classroom?

In what ways could you adjust your classroom environment to incorporate more of these elements?

Print-rich Environment

The importance of a print-rich environment has been well documented (Roskos and Neuman 2011). Students need the exposure to letters and words that is provided in a word-rich environment. For content-area classrooms, the environment should be deluged with print representations of the specific content. Students should walk into the room and immediately know the content area or see the various subjects represented in an elementary classroom. Traditional markers such as signs, symbols, characters, and word walls make significant differences for both early readers and struggling readers.

Learning Centers

Learning centers are commonly recommended for creating an effective room environment. Thinking beyond the traditional centers, such as reading, writing, or science, is key for this ingredient. Centers that feature culturally-related speaking and listening activities are welcome additions to traditional centers. A litany of research has demonstrated how audio—namely music—helps to stimulate the brain (Hammond 2015). Cultural music, ranging from the American Indian flute to American Jazz, can set the tone and assist in learning. Cultural centers featuring items students have brought from their home and community are strongly encouraged. In these centers, students have opportunities to write about the artifacts and, of course, *show and tell* on a frequent basis. The center acts as a living museum for the class and becomes a source of unity as all students, regardless of their culture, are expected to contribute. Here, it is important to think broadly beyond ethnicity in developing resources for the center. That breadth of the culture center should include youth, socioeconomic, gender, and religious representations.

Culturally Colorful

What colors come to mind when you think of a school? Are you thinking drab, dark, gray, plain, solid? Culturally responsive classrooms are just the opposite of what the traditional colors of a school may be. Bright, dynamic, lively, and inviting colors are characteristic in CLR classrooms. These colors exude fun, student friendliness, and excitement about learning. An inviting classroom focuses on the use of color, lighting, and sound. Here, it is well thought to steal a page from the business world, where the manner in which the environment can actually facilitate employee productivity has been well documented (Raziq and Maulabakhsh 2015).

This can be the case for classrooms as well. For example, according to Shade, Kelly, and Oberg (1997), American Indian cultures seem to prefer earth-tone colors and in some cases bright yellows and pastels. All these colors denote activity and vibrancy. Some CLR teachers have been known to request new colors in their classrooms or even offer to paint their own rooms during the summer months, with permission. The point, in this case, is that color does make a difference.

Arranged Optimally

How to arrange the desks, tables, and/or chairs is one of the toughest decisions for teachers to make. Many teachers probably go through several iterations of room configurations during the course of a year before actually deciding on one or two that are optimal. In truth, there is no one configuration that can be prescribed. Whatever the arrangement, it should promote movement, viewing capability, and space (as in breathing room) for the students and teacher alike. The arrangement of desks and tables speaks to the importance of interpersonal relationships in the class among students as well as between the students and the teacher.

Research suggests that, in addition to the spatial accommodation for collaborative groups, it is just as important to have space whereby students can connect individually with the teacher. Both of these components allow for a feeling of community, connectivity, and collaboration. Student proximity can affect the reception of verbal and nonverbal cues, which then influence positive or negative classroom behaviors (Good and Brophy 1977). For instance, Mexican American students often view one another as strong sources of support in accomplishing tasks, and they readily offer assistance to peers. The room arrangement has a great impact on students' ability to engage in this cultural collaboration.

Multiple Libraries

In addition to a print-rich environment, CLR classrooms should first and foremost have large quantities of books organized in multiple libraries. The multiple libraries can be curated in a variety of ways, focused on genres, themes, or reading levels. How the books are displayed is important as well. Similar to the idea behind culturally colorful classrooms, libraries that are set up in ways that are inviting and enticing to students can make a huge impact. The appeal of the display can bring a student to the library, whereas a disorganized collection may actually keep students away. The more books the better, and the greater the variety of books, the better—especially for underserved students who may struggle with reading. Again, with variety in mind, I am insistent that teachers think beyond race and ethnic identity. Include books that address the many Rings of Culture, including gender, socioeconomic status, and youth relevance. Appendix F offers a list of culturally authentic texts that can be included in a CLR classroom library. Figure 7.1 shows a CLR library with baskets of books labeled with culturally responsive categories.

Fig. 7.1 Example of a Culturally Responsive Classroom Library

Digital and Media Resources

According to Renee Hobbs, "children and young people are growing up in a world with more choices for information and entertainment than at any point in human history. Most Americans now live in 'constantly connected' homes with broadband Internet access, 500+ channels of TV and on-demand movies, and with mobile phones offering on-screen interactive activities with the touch of a fingertip" (2010, 13). The use of technology has changed, and cultural responsiveness is about being able to keep up with these rapid changes. Our students need exposure to anytime, anywhere technology, where the device is less important than the actual use, purpose, and platform. In 2009, the Knight Commission on the Information Needs of Communities in a Democracy made these four recommendations for digital and media literacy:

1. Analyze messages in a variety of forms by identifying the author, purpose, and point of view, and evaluating the quality and credibility of the content.

2. Create content in a variety of forms, making use of language, images, sound, and new digital tools and technologies.

3. Reflect on one's own conduct and communication behavior by applying social responsibility and ethical principles.

4. Take social action by working individually and collaboratively to share knowledge and solve problems in the family, workplace and community, and by participating as a member of a community.

All of these recommendations are in alignment with CLR and the new emphasis on digital and media literacy.

In Figure 7.2, a student at Liberty Elementary in Baltimore is engaged with an interactive eBook.

Fig. 7.2 Effective Use of Technology in the Classroom

Relevant Bulletin Boards and Displayed Student Work

The prescription of the bulletin board is typically twofold. One is to have a bulletin board that is connected to the lesson or content that is currently being covered. The other is to have a bulletin board that relates to the overall theme of the lesson. After those two, the range of bulletin boards is wide and open. Youth culture is an important responsive key here and an easy way to draw in students.

CLR promotes student work everywhere. Displayed student work should be updated every three weeks. The work should be exemplary in nature but not exclusionary. We all recall the warm feeling that goes with seeing your work displayed; it is the classroom's version of having your name in lights. We want all students to have that feeling, so the best efforts of every student in the classroom should be validated and affirmed by having their work periodically presented for view, as shown in Figure 7.3.

Fig. 7.3 Displaying Student Work

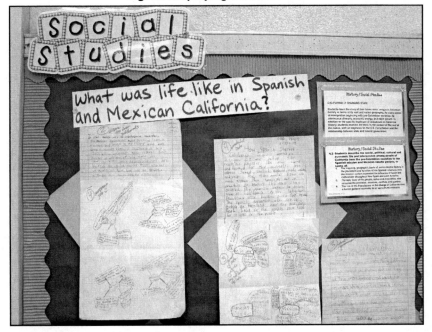

Examining the Learning Environment

Classroom walk-throughs are intended to provide a picture of learning in schools. They are "powerful tools that educators can use to stimulate conversations around improving teaching and learning" (Perry, cited in Richardson 2006, 2). I encourage walkthroughs so that teachers can gain feedback from their colleagues.

Supporting that obvious purpose, teachers gain ideas about how to make their classrooms more culturally responsive as they visit other classrooms. We use the CLR Learning Environment Survey, a tool that helps us to focus our observations and follow-up conversations with colleagues. The survey topics include print-rich environment, learning centers, culturally colorful design, optimally arranged rooms, multiple libraries, technology, and relevant bulletin boards. Each topic is accompanied by a five-point rating scale ranging from very responsive to least responsive. The survey is provided in Appendix H.

Fig. 7.4 Example of an Effective Learning Environment

Summary

As you see from the principles presented in this chapter, a culturally relevant learning environment can have a great impact, beginning with a positive first impression for students when they walk into the room on the first day of school. Several elements constitute an exemplary CLR learning environment, or what I call the *recipe of success*. What must be remembered is that there is always room for teacher innovation in creating a learning environment that is responsive to students' cultural and linguistic needs and expectations. Creating a responsive learning environment takes into consideration both physical and social factors. The physical factors include elements that make the classroom intellectually attractive and stimulating to students: furnishings and their arrangement, learning resources and their organization, displays of student work, and displays of items that reflect who the students are.

Reflection Guide

Think back to your responses to the statements in the Anticipation Guide at the beginning of the chapter. Have your responses changed as a result of what you read in the chapter? What new insights did you gain from the chapter?

_____ The traditional classroom structure with students sitting in rows is most effective in maintaining discipline with underserved students.

_____ Excessive use of decorative materials in the classroom can be distracting for underserved students.

_____ An inviting classroom environment encourages students to interact positively with one another and the teacher.

_____ Learning centers are necessary in primary-grade classrooms but are not essential for students in the upper grades, notably middle and secondary levels.

_____ Fair and clear procedures for classroom behaviors contribute to a sense of community in the classroom.

_____ A combination of teacher-directed and student-centered activities is needed to maintain a responsive learning environment.

1. Review the photographs showing features of culturally responsive classrooms. Compare the features of your classroom to those presented in the photographs. What do you observe about similarities and differences?

2. Sometimes it is difficult for teachers to make changes in the physical arrangement of the classroom. What difficulties, if any, have you encountered when you attempted to make such changes? How have you dealt with those problems?

3. With a colleague, use the CLR Learning Environment Survey (Appendix H) to examine your classrooms. Where are the strengths and limitations of your learning environments? What changes are necessary? What is your plan for making those changes?

A Personal Coda

Are You Capable of and Willing to Love Outrageously?

Chapter 8

In recent years, I have come to realize more and more that what is truly essential for cultural and linguistic responsiveness is love. I have traveled enough now (accumulating an abundance of frequent flyer miles), been in enough classrooms (over 2,000), and talked with enough educators (hundreds) to see that oftentimes the missing ingredient for many underserved students is *love*. These students do not need more stuff—not more books, more technology, more teachers and support staff, more programs, more grants, and not even more professional development for their teachers. Sometimes they just need more love. But not just any love.

I assume that if you are reading this book or have participated in my professional development programs at some point, you love your students and you love what you do regardless of your position. You remind yourself every day as to why you became whatever role you play. I know for a fact that you love who you serve. So, the love I am talking about is beyond your ordinary love. It is *more love*. It is when you are loving in the best way that you can, and yet the situation, the students, the parents, your staff, a colleague, or the institution says to you, "But I need more."

This "more" is defined as *outrageous love*, which is cultural and linguistic responsiveness. For those of you in the classroom, you have a student right now who is looking at you, pleading for more love. For those of you in leadership positions, there is a staff member or a colleague who is begging you to love him or her outrageously. For those of you who cook, clean, answer phones, yard supervise, drive the bus, or, in other words, do the dirty work, there is something that you need to do which is calling on you to stretch your love. I never thought I would be quoting Fred Rogers of the renowned Mister Rogers' Neighborhood television show of the late 20th century, but here I go: "Love isn't a state of perfect caring. It is an active noun like 'struggle.' To love someone is to strive to accept that person exactly the way he or she is, right here and now" (Rogers 2003).

Now, in this last chapter, I need to ask the most difficult question: Are you capable of and willing to love outrageously? Are you willing to give more love to those who need it the most but are the least likely to receive it? I need to know. Of course, it will take your heart and mind (mindset) to be in the right place—the topic I addressed in Chapter 1. It will take your skillset as well, because you will need to develop your skills to be the best you can be at giving outrageous love. For teachers, I have spent the previous five chapters explaining how you can do that responsively. For leaders, I have, along with my esteemed colleague Anthony Muhammad, challenged you to have the courage, the will, and the skill to give outrageous love (Muhammad and Hollie 2011). As a final thought, then, I want to nudge you to love outrageously. First, I will give you the official invitation to dive into the pool of CLR activities and a criteria chart to evaluate your current level of "swimming proficiency." Then, I want to give you some tips for relating the idea of cultural responsiveness to your students. Last, I will provide you with how to look for results and the best references for success.

Jump into the CLR Pool and Start Swimming

I use the metaphor of a pool because I liken the process of becoming culturally responsive to learning how to swim. (I was inspired by the swim lessons of my twin daughters, Biko and Zora.) At the swim school, there are six swim levels with a set of very discrete skills under each level. The pre-beginner level is an *Emerger*, a swimmer standing on the side of the pool, daring oneself to get in. The top level is a *Free Styler*, a swimmer ready for Olympic competition. (Keep in mind that this is all being interpreted by a non-swimmer, me.) I think that these swimming levels are a perfect way to look at the infusion of culturally and linguistically responsive pedagogy in your instruction. Thus, as shown in Figure 8.1, I borrowed the labels from the swim school and created six infusion levels for becoming CLR.

Fig. 8.1 Continuum of Infusion Levels to being CLR

Emerger	Use of 0–1 CLR activities in an instructional block
Splasher	Use of 2–3 different CLR activities in an instructional block
Floater	Use of 4–5 different CLR activities in at least two instructional areas in an instructional block
Kicker	Use of 5–7 different CLR activities in at least three instructional areas in an instructional block
Streamliner	Use of 6–8 different CLR activities in at least three instructional areas in an instructional block
Free Styler	Use of 9 different CLR activities in at least three more instructional areas in an instructional block

While these levels are meant to quantify CLR practices, they are not black and white. Yes, numbers are attached, but the quality of how the activities are done and the intention and purpose of using them outweighs any quantitative analysis. That said, an activity counts as anything done in one of the CLR categories, such as attention signals or read-alouds. (See Appendix E, or *Strategies for Culturally and Linguistically Responsive Teaching and Learning* [Hollie 2015].) An instructional area refers to classroom management, academic vocabulary, academic literacy, academic language, and learning environment, which make up the chapters in Part II: Building Skillsets. The instructional block is any determined chunk of instructional time (e.g., 15, 30, or 45 minutes). Therefore, the number of activities will vary depending on the time allocation (obviously), but also depending on the quality and strategy of the activity. In short, CLR is a moving target instructionally, and it will fluctuate within a targeted range. The key variable for the fluctuation will be your *mindset*.

The end goal of becoming culturally and linguistically responsive is to be at the Kicker level or above. A Kicker is a teacher who uses five to seven CLR activities throughout the lesson, in different categories and instructional areas. Therefore, upon completion of this book, you can expect to be at least kicking in your culturally and linguistically responsive pool and your classroom, with the hope that over time you will be a Free Styler. Each infusion level increases your instructional activity in cultural and linguistic responsiveness. Most times, teachers enter into the pool splashing and then move toward kicking. Some teachers enter emerging. Regardless of where you begin, it is where you end that counts. For more on the CLR infusion levels, please refer to *Strategies for Culturally and Linguistically Responsive Teaching and Learning* (Hollie 2015).

Pause to Ponder

As of right now, where are you in the CLR Pool?

Which activities have you infused successfully into your instruction?

Which activities did you initially encounter difficulty using? How did you address the difficulties?

Three Steps to Start

If you go back to Chapter 2, which focused on the CLR pedagogy, the three steps to your official CLR start are couched in the CLR Formula for Success: Quantity, Quality, and Strategy.

Recall that *Quantity* speaks to filling your instruction toolbox with the necessary CLR activities to start swimming. The number one inhibitor to starting infusion of CLR into your daily practice is not a mindset orientation but actually a skillset issue. The first step will be to fill your toolbox. *Quality*, the second step, involves doing the strategy accurately and with fidelity. Many times, teachers new to CLR will try something and find that it does not work the first time. They may give up. Given that teaching is, to some extent, trial and error, it is to be expected that when trying new activities the first or second time, you may not have 100 percent success. Keep trying. The Quality step focuses your attention on the effectiveness of your implementation. *Strategy* is the third as well as an ongoing step that asks two questions: Why am I doing this particular activity at this particular time? What do I intend to accomplish? Therefore, using the CLR activities must accompany a strategy. Think of strategy here as a plan of action or a method for accomplishing a goal. You must plan your CLR use with intention and purpose each and every time.

In the CLR professional development program, we educators who have success in this work "personally train" other educators in becoming culturally and linguistically responsive. One key aspect of this training is infusing CLR activities into daily teaching. When a teacher is working with me, we use five steps for planning, shown in Figure 8.2, as a guide for how to infuse specific activities into what the teacher is already doing. A *CLR Lesson Planning Template* is provided in Appendix G.

Fig. 8.2 CLR Lesson Planning

Lesson: In fewer than five sentences, describe the content of your lesson and what your students will be learning.

Step 1: Quantity: What am I using from My CLR Toolbox in this lesson? List the CLR activities you will use.

Step 2: Quality: List any questions or uncertainties you have about doing the CLR activities, so they can be addressed beforehand.

Step 3: Strategy: What is your intent and purpose with the use of the CLR activities listed above? Take the activities in your CLR Toolbox above and categorize them according to Validating and Affirming (VA) and Building and Bridging (BB).

Do the best you can. Don't worry if you are unsure. We will discuss this at your debriefing.

Reflection: How are you feeling about this lesson?

The lesson plan preview guides you through the process of infusing CLR into lessons. Key to your initial success is filling the proverbial instructional toolbox, which means that you are going to have to be willing to experiment and fail, then try again and again. The CLR-infusing process is recursive with a series of reiterations. Give yourself time. You can do it!

Tips for Infusing CLR With Students

As you begin the CLR infusion process, there should be some thought about how to introduce the concept of CLR to your students. One of the most frequent questions I get from teachers is, *How do I discuss CLR with my students?* Needless to say, you will

Remember the formula:
Quantity + Quality + Strategy = CLR

want to clue your students in on your CLR journey. There is not a hard and fast way of rolling out CLR to your students. Here, I am providing you with tips that I have gleaned from teachers who have successfully implemented CLR.

Tip 1: Introduce and Use CLR Terminology

A frequent question I get from practitioners is, *Do I use the same terminology found in the book and professional development with my students?* My answer is yes, absolutely. Introducing CLR is simply telling your students that you plan to validate, affirm, build, and bridge them when you talk to them, in how you relate to them, and in how you teach them. Explain what cultural responsiveness is in general, but be more specific when you discuss the concept of VABB. Talk about how we all have different cultural behaviors based on who we are and that some of those behaviors can be misunderstood or misinterpreted in some settings, which then leads to defining situational appropriateness. For "getting to know you" activities, the Rings of Culture (Appendix C) is a great tool as it allows students to discuss their cultural differences broadly. At the beginning of the school year, be explicit about defining school culture as a culture linked to academic settings and the dominant (mainstream) culture. Most importantly, distinguish culture from race and racism. As you roll out the CLR activities with structure and procedures, tell your students what cultural behaviors you are validating and affirming as well as the ones you are building and bridging to school culture and expectations.

Tip 2: Explicitly Validate and Affirm Your Students—*Be You*

The explicit validation and affirmation of your students around their cultural behaviors is the key to CLR. VA-ing your students triggers the building and bridging and, by extension, your students' buy-in to being situationally appropriate. Your VA has to be intentional and purposeful, consistent and authentic, and proactive and reactive (i.e., using teachable moments). When do your students have the opportunity to be who they are in the instructional context? *BeYou* is the acronym that I share with teachers to actively encourage their students to view their cultural and linguistic behaviors as assets and not liabilities in school. Carrie Eicher, assistant principal in the North St. Paul-Maplewood Oakdale School District in Minnesota, created *BeYou*. It stands for:

B—Be

E—Engaged

Y—Your

O—Own

U—Unique way

BeYou as a concept is a challenge to us all to ensure that students can be who they are at school. It is a direct rebuttal to the often-used SLANT protocol (**S**it up tall, **L**isten, **A**sk questions, **N**od your head, and **T**rack the teacher) that has become ubiquitous in schools. Note that there are many variations of SLANT. We want students to BeYou (VA) and to SLANT (BB) situationally. As it stands now, the use of SLANT is imbalanced when looking through a CLR lens. Its overemphasis on the alignment with school cultural behaviors and expectations can be limiting or detrimental to efforts to embrace students' home cultures. BeYou is not meant to counter efforts to build and bridge toward situational appropriateness; it is intended to create more structured opportunities at school for students to be themselves culturally and linguistically.

Tip 3: Hold Your Students Accountable with Procedures and Structures

An annoying misconception about CLR is that it breeds classroom chaos, wild and out-of-control behaviors, and low expectations. None of these is true. It frustrates me when I see teachers not holding their students to the same standard with

CLR activities that they do with other classroom activities or when teachers couch CLR as the "fun" time compared to the traditional time, when the students should be more serious. When done correctly, CLR is about high expectations, a set of how-to procedures for every activity, and structures that support an organized and efficient classroom dynamic. This is why you have to plan ahead with CLR, not engage in random acts of teaching. This is why you have to be intentional and purposeful with your CLR, not haphazard. This is why you have to believe in the validation aspect of CLR, not just be wooed by the student engagement aspect of CLR. All of the CLR activities have rules, structures, and expectations. Teach them to your students!

Tip 4: Give Your Students Opportunities to Practice Situational Appropriateness

When do your students have the opportunity to practice situational appropriateness? Do you treat CLR and situational appropriateness like you treat practicing reading, math, choir, or art? Students need to practice navigating their cultural behaviors in the context of school culture. These opportunities should come proactively through planned instruction that includes the process of validation, affirmation, building, and bridging (or creating juxtapositions). Recall that an instructional juxtaposition is when you intentionally align a VA activity up against a BB activity, or vice versa. By creating juxtapositions, you allow students to toggle between home culture behaviors and school culture behaviors and expectations.

Another way to provide practice in situational appropriateness is to be reactive by taking advantage of teachable moments. There are countless interactions, happenings, and instances that occur in the milieu of a classroom on any given day. Within those events, "students will be students," which includes engaging in behaviors that are culturally inappropriate. You, in effect, have to become a cultural detective in your classroom. When you recognize these behaviors, use them as opportunities for students to practice cultureswitching. You can focus on specific behaviors, like tone of voice, eye contact, or conversational patterns, and discuss with your students their comfort zone with these behaviors in the context of school culture. Find out where they feel like they need skill-building or more practice. Create rubrics or scales for students to self-assess their situational appropriateness. In collaboration with Paddy Greeley, literacy coach in Madison School District, and Lydia McClanahan, I created a scale for situational appropriateness and suggested opportunities for practice (see Appendix I).

Tip 5: Give Your Students a Voice in the Work of Equity and CLR

When students buy into CLR and understand its purpose, the door is opened for giving them voice to the work. Instructionally, the penultimate goal is when your students can tell you what protocols for responding and discussing would be best to use for a particular task. In other words, your students are able to tell how they learn best and what activities work for them around certain cultural behaviors and the situation. Beyond instruction, students are also given voice by becoming active participants in equity and responsiveness. They can do so by forming organizations, clubs, and groups that meet to discuss school- and society-related issues of race, culture, and equity. They meet with teachers to discuss how the school and district can be more culturally and linguistically responsive. A great example of students having voice is Hopkins High School in Hopkins, Minnesota, where the students, led by Felicia Homberger and other responsive teachers, began "HHS Responds." The students meet on a regular basis to offer input on school events and activities, and through collaboration with the teachers, there is more inclusiveness for all students. The students at Hopkins High School have accomplished great things through their organizing, including petitioning their district to install gender-neutral restrooms (prior to the national controversy stemming from North Carolina's passage of House Bill 2 in 2016).

In sum, your students should be partners with you in their experience of responsiveness. CLR instruction is transparent. There are no teacher secrets here. You want your students to know that there is a "method to your madness" with all the activities that you are using. Nothing happens by accident. Let them know that they are a part of the "madness" in every way and you want to empower and inspire them to be better personally and academically.

Pause to Ponder

How have you engaged your students in discussions about CLR? How has that impacted the effectiveness of your CLR-infused lessons and your students' success?

Observing CLR Success

Invariably, a question will be asked about results with CLR. It is a fair question. When considering how CLR garners positive results—or dare I say, data—I provide four windows. Two are qualitative and two are quantitative. From a research perspective, however, what must be accepted is that CLR represents a mediated effect on overall achievement (Hattie 2012). This means that CLR influences variables that can directly impact achievement (e.g., test scores). For example, without dispute, the number one difference-maker on student outcomes is high-quality instruction (Hattie 2012; Marzano, Marzano, and Pickering 2003). CLR influences high-quality instruction. Another case of direct impact on student success is the positive-relationship factor. CLR influences positive relationships with students. In the final analysis, CLR is part of the building blocks that will be a part of your overall success. Here are the four ways you can see how CLR is influencing the areas that directly impact your intended results.

Qualitative 1: Teacher Satisfaction/Perception

Overwhelmingly, teachers report their high satisfaction with CLR pedagogy and practices. Most can quickly see the benefit because CLR is something that brings instant change. They don't have to wait for the test results because they immediately see the difference in how their students are engaged. I use two surveys to gauge teacher satisfaction with CLR professional development, focusing on what they feel has been beneficial (perceptions). Based on this data, nearly 90 percent of the teachers who experience CLR through some form of professional learning claim it was beneficial to their mindsets and skillsets.

Qualitative 2: Change in Conversational Climate

The climate in which conversations about race, culture, language, diversity, equity, and other sensitive issues take place is critical. Schools and teachers self-report this data, and the results show a positive change in their school climate around issues related to cultural and linguistic responsiveness. Folks feel more comfortable with their discomfort around certain topics, particularly if they're race-related. CLR has contributed to a stronger learning community where collaboration and connectivity along the lines of culture and language are more valued. I love it when the liberating power of CLR is realized—when a staff no longer feels the burden of talking about race, when they are not afraid to admit their first thoughts (hidden biases), and when they come to a point of increased validation and affirmation.

Quantitative 1: Decreased Send-outs or Referrals

Schools report that when they honestly and authentically adopt the principles of culturally responsive classroom management, which includes continuously grappling with the difference between culturally inappropriate and unacceptable behaviors, they have fewer referrals to the office. I have had schools report that they cut office referrals by more than half after implementing CLR. One district (which I will not name) questioned the veracity of the results of a school whose drop in referrals was so dramatic. In many cases, fewer referrals can be linked to fewer suspensions. But sometimes, I believe that we become too wrapped up in the numbers. Remember that the goal of CLR is to adjust teaching practices to address the needs of students who are culturally misunderstood. When that is done, more students stay in the classroom.

Quantitative 2: Student Engagement Surveys

In collaboration with graduate studies at the University of California, Los Angeles, we have developed surveys to assess student engagement. Students offer their opinions on how engaging the instruction they receive is through the lens of cultural and linguistic responsiveness. The surveys, typically done anonymously, are administered to students either before or after their teachers' CLR training (pre/post) or through comparisons. The pre-survey occurs before the CLR teacher participates in the CLR cadre, and the post-survey occurs after two instructional cycles (i.e., two rounds of coaching). The comparison surveys are also done after a teacher completes CLR training and coaching. In these surveys, we compare CLR cadre classrooms with non-CLR cadre classrooms. I have been able to do these in two places, and in both cases, the CLR classroom tended to have higher engagement levels according to the students.

Let it be known that I agree with anyone who says that with a deep investment and implementation of CLR, you should see results quantitatively and qualitatively. You should be able to assure all stakeholders and funding sources that the efforts are valuable. Keep in mind, though, that CLR is an effective contributor to those variables that directly impact student achievement. While data is important, there is nothing that replaces seeing results up close and in action. I had this opportunity from 2003 through 2013 as the cofounder of the Culture and Language Academy of Success, the flagship laboratory school for cultural and linguistic responsiveness in the Los Angeles Unified School District (LAUSD).

The Story of the Culture and Language Academy of Success (CLAS)

CLAS was born out of a need and a vision. Understanding the need was simple: LAUSD as an institution, like many other districts across the country, was struggling to close the so-called achievement gap, particularly with African American students. Despite countless attempts in the form of programs, forums, and initiatives, little progress was being made. The vision for CLAS grew out of the frustration of a group of educators working with a program originally known as the Language Development Program of African American Students (LDPAAS). Directed by Dr. Noma LeMoine, a nationally renowned expert and my mentor, LDPAAS focused on increasing student achievement for African American students by using the tenets of culturally and linguistically responsive teaching. As program coordinator for Dr. LeMoine, I was responsible for designing and conducting professional development programs, writing curricula and instructional materials, and working with teacher leaders at school sites. LDPAAS evolved into the Academic English Mastery Program (AEMP), where the focus was broadened to include a variety of student populations, namely Mexican American, Hawaiian American, and American Indian.

Despite our hard work and satellite success in the AEMP schools, we invariably hit the proverbial glass ceiling within the LAUSD bureaucracy. Collectively, we knew that if given an authentic opportunity without the constraints of the traditional (though failing) institution, we could develop a school-wide model for culturally and linguistically responsive teaching. At the time, between 2002 and 2003, the best avenue for change was through development of a charter school, which was then (as opposed to now) a politically viable means for an alternative school. Together, Janis Bucknor, Anthony Jackson, and I wrote a proposal to the California Department of Education for a charter school start-up grant. We were awarded the grant, and CLAS was opened in the fall of 2003 with 140 students and six classrooms. As of fall 2010, we had grown to over 300 students and 15 classrooms. CLAS was the living embodiment of a school-wide implementation of culturally and linguistically responsive teaching and learning. A visitor could go into any classroom and see culturally and linguistically responsive teaching at work. CLAS was a laboratory school where we experimented with instructional innovations, differentiated instruction, classroom management, and other school-related topics. CLAS remains one of the only national models of school-wide CLR implementation.

CLAS closed its doors in June 2013 for fiscal reasons, but its success still reigns. There are countless stories of students and their families who attribute their academic accomplishment to their experiences at CLAS, including my own family, since my children attended CLAS. Today, CLAS alumni are attending Ivy League schools, studying abroad, pursuing the arts, and attending Historically Black Colleges and Universities (HBCUs) such as Spelman College and Fisk University. My personal testimony is my daughter, Imani, who will begin law school in the fall of 2017. I know a big part of her success has been because of CLAS and cultural responsiveness. Families contact me regularly to express gratitude for the educators at CLAS who, through validation, affirmation, building, and bridging, taught their children situational appropriateness and established a foundation for academic success.

Final Words

Anyone who knows me knows that I am not one for drawn-out endings. So, I am going to say what I always say to end. Thank you for being a part of this journey to responsiveness with me, and for your participation and contribution to the CLR Community—or what we now call *VABB Nation*. This work is about your students first and foremost, and if we keep them and their success as the prize, then we know where our eyes belong. And to keep your eyes on the prize, all you have to do is validate, affirm, build, and bridge! Now, go be VABBulous!

References Cited

Allen, Janet. 2008. *More Tools for Teaching Content Literacy*. Portland, ME: Stenhouse Publishers.

Alvermann, Donna E., and Shelley Hong Xu. 2003. "Children's Everyday Literacies: Intersections of Popular Culture and Language Arts Instruction." *Language Arts* 81 (2): 145–155.

Anderson, J. A. 1995. "Literacy and Education in the African-American Experience." In *Literacy Among African-American Youth: Issues in Learning, Teaching, and Schooling*, edited by Vivian L. Gadsen and Daniel A. Wagner, 27. Cresskill, NJ: Hampton.

Ball, Arnetha F., and Cynthia A. Tyson, eds. 2011. *Studying Diversity in Teacher Education*. Lanham, MD: Rowman & Littlefield.

Banaji, Mahzarin R., and Anthony G. Greenwald. 2013. *Blindspot: Hidden Biases of Good People*. New York: Delacorte Press.

Baugh, John. 2004. "Standard English and Academic English (Dialect) Learners in the African Diaspora." *Journal of English Linguistics* 32 (3): 198–209.

Beck, Isabel L., Margaret G. McKeown, and Linda Kucan. 2002. *Bringing Words to Life*. New York: The Guilford Press.

Blachowicz, Camille, and Peter J. Fisher. 2006. *Teaching Vocabulary in All Classrooms*. Upper Saddle River, NJ: Pearson Education.

Boykin, A.W. (1983). "The Academic Performance of Afro-American Children." In *Achievement and Achievement Motives: Psychological and Sociological Approaches*, edited by Janet T. Spence. San Francisco: W.H. Freeman.

Bromley, Karen. 2007. "Nine Things Every Teacher Should Know About Words and Vocabulary Instruction." *Journal of Adolescent & Adult Literacy* 50 (7): 528–537.

Brooks, Gwendolyn. (1966) 1973. "We Real Cool." In *The Poetry of Black America: Anthology of the 20th Century,* edited by Arnold Adoff. New York: Harper Teen.

Cooperative Children's Book Center, School of Education, University of Wisconsin-Madison. 2014. "Children's Books By and About People of Color Published in the United States: Statistics Gathered by the Cooperative Children's Book Center, School of Education, University of Wisconsin-Madison." http://ccbc.education.wisc.edu/books/pcstats.asp.

Corson, David. 1997. "Non-Standard Varieties and Educational Policy." In *Encyclopedia of Language and Education*, edited by Ruth Wodak and David Corson, 1: 99–109. Dordrecht, Netherlands: Kluwer Academic Publishers.

Cronbach, Lee J. 1942. "An analysis of techniques for diagnostic vocabulary testing." *Journey of Educational Research* 36 (3): 206–217.

Dean, Ceri B., Elizabeth Ross Hubbell, Howard Pitler, and Bj Stone. 2013. *Classroom Instruction that Works: Research-Based Strategies for Increasing Student Achievement.* Alexandria, VA: Association for Supervision and Curriculum Development.

Delpit, Lisa, and Joanne Kilgour Dowdy. 2002. *The Skin That We Speak: Thoughts on Language and Culture in the Classroom.* New York: The New Press.

Dillard, J. L. 1972. *Black English: Its History and Usage in the United States.* New York: Random House.

Dolan, Lawrence J., Sheppard G. Kellam, C. Hendricks Brown, Lisa Werthamer-Larsson, George W. Rebok, Lawrence S. Mayer, Jolene Laudolff, Jaylan S. Turkkan, Carla Ford, and Leonard Wheeler. 1993. "The Short-Term Impact of Two Classroom-Based Preventive Interventions on Aggressive and Shy Behaviors and Poor Achievement." *Journal of Applied Developmental Psychology* 14 (3): 317–345.

Emmer, Edmund T., Carolyn M. Evertson, and Murray E. Worsham. 2003. *Classroom Management for Secondary Teachers.* 6th ed. Boston: Allyn & Bacon.

Fan, Chih-Chieh. 2014. "Perceived Classroom Management and Student Learning Motivation in Social Studies of Taiwan Junior High School Students." *European Journal of Research in Social Sciences* 2 (3): 40–51.

Fatlu, Indrel, and Irene Rodgers. 1984. "The Iceberg Concept of Culture." In *American Field Scholarship Orientation Handbook* 4.

Feldman, Kevin, and Kate Kinsella. 2003. "Narrowing the Language Gap: Strategies for Vocabulary Development," accessed August 2, 2001, http://www.ela.fcoe.org/sites/ela.fcoe .org/files/Narrowing%20Vocab%20Gap%20KK%20KF%201.pdf.

Fought, Carmen. 2003. *Chicano English in Context.* London: Palgrave Macmillan UK.

Frayer, Dorothy A., Wayne. C. Frederick, and Herbert J. Klaumeier. 1969. "A Schema for Testing the Level of Concept Mastery." *Working Paper No. 16.* Madison, WI: Wisconsin Research and Development Center for Cognitive Learning.

Garan, Elaine M., and Glenn DeVoogd. 2008. "The Benefits of Sustained Silent Reading: Scientific Research and Common Sense Converge." *The Reading Teacher* 62 (4): 336–344.

Gardner-Chloros, Penelope. 2009. *Codeswitching.* Cambridge: Cambridge University Press.

Gay, Geneva. 2000. *Culturally Responsive Teaching: Theory, Research, and Practice.* New York: Teachers College Press.

Gladwell, Malcolm. 2005. *Blink: The Power of Thinking Without Thinking.* New York: Little, Brown and Company.

Gonzales, Ambrose E. 1922. *The Black Border: Gullah Stories of the Carolina Coast.* Columbia SC: The State Company.

Good, Thomas L., and Jere E. Brophy. 1977. *Educational Pyschology: A Realistic Approach.* New York: Holt, Rinehart & Winston.

Goodwin, Bryan. 2011. *Simply Better: Doing What Matters Most to Change the Odds for Student Success.* Alexandria, VA: Association for Supervision and Curriculum Development.

Graves, Michael F., 2006. *The Vocabulary Book: Learning & Instruction.* New York: Teachers College Press.

Graves, Michael F. and Susan Watts-Taffe. 2002. "The Place of Word Consciousness in a Research-Based Vocabulary Program." In *What Research Has to Say about Reading Instruction,* 3rd ed., edited by Alan. E. Farstrup and S. Jay Samuels, 140–165. Newark, DE: International Reading Association.

Gregory, Anne, Russell J. Skiba, and Pedro A. Noguera. 2010. "The Achievement Gap and the Discipline Gap: Two Sides to the Same Coin?" *Educational Researcher.* doi: 10.3102/0013189X09357621.

Griffin, Gary A., Robert Hughes, and Jeanne Martin. 1982. "Knowledge, Training, and Classroom Management." Research and Development Center for Teacher Education, The University of Texas at Austin.

Hale-Benson, Janice E. 1986. *Black Children: Their Roots, Culture and Learning Styles.* Rev. ed. Baltimore, MD: Johns Hopkins University Press.

Hammond, Zaretta L. 2015. *Culturally Responsive Teaching and the Brain: Promoting Authentic Engagement and Rigor Among Culturally and Linguistically Diverse Students.* Thousand Oaks, CA: Corwin.

Harris, Violet. 1999. *Teaching Multicultural Literature in Grades K–8*. Norwood, MA: Christopher-Gordon Publishers, Inc.

Hattie, John. 2012. *Visible Learning for Teachers: Maximizing Impact on Learning*. New York: Routledge.

Herskovits, Melville. 1941. *The Myth of the Negro Past*. Massachusetts, Beacon Press.

Hobbs, Renee. 2010. *Digital and Media Literacy: A Plan of Action*. Washington, DC: The Aspen Institute.

Hollie, Sharroky. 2012. Culturally and Linguistically Responsive Teaching and Learning: Classroom Practices for Student Success. Huntington Beach, CA: Shell Education.

———. 2015. *Strategies for Culturally and Linguistically Responsive Teaching and Learning*. Huntington Beach, CA: Shell Education.

Hollins, Etta R. 2008. *Culture in School Learning: Revealing the Deep Meaning*. Mahwah, NJ: Erlbaum.

Hooks, Bell. 2003. *Rock My Soul: Black People and Self-Esteem*. New York: Atria.

Hughes, Langston. (1951) 1990. *Montage of a Dream Deferred: Selected Poems of Langston Hughes*. New York: Vintage.

Irvine, Jacqueline Jordan. 1991. *Black Students and School Failure: Policies, Practices, and Prescriptions*. New York: Praeger.

Jackson, Robyn R. 2009. *Never Work Harder Than Your Students and Other Principles of Great Teaching*. Alexandria, VA: Association for Supervision and Curriculum Development.

Jensen, Eric. 2005. *Teaching with the Brain in Mind*. 2nd ed. Alexandria, VA: Association for Supervision and Curriculum Development.

Johann Friedrich Blumenbach and the Emergence of Scientific Anthropology. "Introduction," https://www.blumenbach.info/introduction.

Johnson, David W., and Roger T. Johnson. 1987. *Learning Together and Alone: Cooperative, Competitive, and Individualistic Learning*. Upper Saddle River, NJ: Prentice-Hall, Inc.

Johnson, David W., Roger T. Johnson, and Edythe Johnson Holubec. 1994. *Cooperative Learning in the Classroom*. Alexandria, VA: Association for Supervision and Curriculum Development.

Jordan, Cathie. 1984. "Cultural Compatibility and the Education of Hawaiian Children: Implications for Mainland Educators." *Educational Research Quarterly* 8(4): 59–71.

Kagan, Dr. Spencer, and Miguel Kagan. 2009. *Kagan Cooperative Learning*. San Clemente, CA: Kagan Publishing.

Kane, Thomas J., Eric S. Taylor, John H. Tyler, and Amy L. Wooten. 2011. "Identifying Effective Classroom Practices Using Student Achievement Data." *Journal of Human Resources* 46 (3): 587–613.

Kindle, Karen. 2012. "Vocabulary Development During Read-Alouds: Primary Practices." In *Issues and Trends in Literacy Education, 5th ed.*, edited by Richard D. Robinson, Michael C. McKenna, and Kristin Conradi. Upper Saddle River, NJ: Pearson.

Knight Commission on the Information Needs of Communities in a Democracy. 2009. "Informing Communities: Sustaining Democracy in the Digital Age." Washington, DC: The Aspen Institute.

Kotulak, Ronald. 1996. *Inside the Brain: Revolutionary Discoveries of How the Mind Works*. Kansas City, MO: Andrew McMeel.

Krashen, Stephen D. 2004. *The Power of Reading: Insights from the Research*. Portsmouth, NH: Heinemann.

Labov, William. 1972. "Academic Ignorance and Black Intelligence." In *Atlantic Monthly* (June).

Ladson-Billings, Gloria. 1994. *The Dreamkeepers: Successful Teachers of African American Children*. San Francisco, CA: Jossey-Bass.

Leap, William L. 1993. *American Indian English*. Salt Lake City, UT: University of Utah Press.

LeMoine, Noma. 1999. *English for Your Success*. Maywood, NJ: People's Publishing Group.

Levine, Mel. 2002. *A Mind at a Time*. New York: Simon & Schuster.

Lietz, Petra. 2006. "A Meta-analysis of Gender Differences in Reading Achievement at the Secondary School Level." *Studies in Educational Evaluation* 32 (4): 317–344.

Marzano, Robert J. 2009. *Designing and Teaching Learning Goals and Objectives*. Bloomington, IN: Solution Tree Press.

———, ed. 2010. *On Excellence in Teaching*. Bloomington, IN: Solution Tree Press.

Marzano, Robert J., Jana S. Marzano, and Debra J. Pickering. 2003. *Classroom Management That Works: Research-Based Strategies for Every Teacher*. Alexandria, VA: Association for Supervision and Curriculum Development.

Marzano, Robert J., and Debra J. Pickering. 2005. *Building Academic Vocabulary: Teacher's Manual*. Alexandria, VA: Association for Supervision and Curriculum Development.

May, Laura A., Gary E. Bingham, and Meghan L. Pendergast. 2014. "Culturally and Linguistically Relevant Read Alouds." *Multicultural Perspectives* 16 (4): 210–218.

Molinsky, Andy. 2013. *Global Dexterity: How to Adapt Your Behavior Across Cultures without Losing Yourself in the Process*. Brighton, MA: Harvard Business Review Press.

Moos, Rudolf H. 1979. *Evaluating Educational Environments*. San Francisco: Jossey-Bass.

Muhammad, Anthony, and Sharroky Hollie. 2011. *The Will to Lead, the Skill to Teach: Transforming Schools at Every Level*. Bloomington, IN: Solution Tree Press.

Murphy, Michael. 2009. *Tools & Talk: Data, Conversation, and Action for Classroom and School Improvement.* Oxford, OH: National Staff Development Council.

National Center for Educational Statistics. 2008. "The Reading Literacy of U.S. Fourth-Grade Students in an International Context." U.S. Department of Education. http://nces.ed.gov/pubs2008/2008017.pdf.

National Reading Panel. 2000. *Report of the National Reading Panel: Teaching Children to Read. Report of the Subgroups.* Washington, DC: U.S. Department of Health and Human Services, National Institutes of Health.

New American Foundation. 2008. "Changing the Odds for Children at Risk." http://www.newamerica.net/events/2008/changing_odds.

Nieto, Sonia. 1999. *The Light in Their Eyes: Creating Multicultural Learning Communities.* New York: Teachers College Press.

Nobles, Wade W. 1987. "Psychometrics and African American Reality: A Question of Cultural Antimony." In *Negro Educational Review* 38 (2–3): 45–55.

Ogbu, John U. 1978. *Minority Education and Caste: The American System in Cross-Cultural Perspective.* New York: Academic Press.

Paris, Django, and H. Samy Alim. 2014. "What Are We Seeking to Sustain Through Culturally Sustaining Pedagogy? A Loving Critique Forward." In *Harvard Educational Review* 84 (1).

Peterson, Bob. 2008. "Whitewashing the Past." *Rethinking Schools Online* 23 (1).

Powell, Rebecca, and Elizabeth Rightmyer. 2011. *Literacy for All Students: An Instructional Framework for Closing the Gap.* New York: Routledge.

Ramírez, Manuel, and Alfredo Castañeda. 1974. *Cultural Democracy, Bicognitive Development, and Education.* New York: Academic Press.

Rasinski, Timothy, Nancy Padak, Rick M. Newton, and Evangeline Newton. 2007. *Greek and Latin Roots: Keys to Building Vocabulary*. Huntington Beach, CA: Shell Education.

Raziq, Abdul, and Raheela Maulabakhsh. 2015. "Impact of Working Environment on Job Satisfaction." *Procedia Economics and Finance* 23: 717–725.

Reutzel, D. Ray, Parker C. Fawson, and John A. Smith. 2008. "Reconsidering Silent Sustained Reading: An Exploratory Study of Scaffolded Silent Reading." *The Journal of Educational Research* 102 (1): 37–50.

Richardson, Joan. 2006. "Snapshots of Learning." *Tools for Schools* 10 (1): 1–3. Oxford, OH: National Staff Development Council.

Rogers, Fred. 2003. *The World According to Mister Rogers: Important Things to Remember*. New York: Hachette Books.

Roskos, Kathleen, and Susan B. Neuman. 2011. "The Classroom Environment: First, Last, and Always." *The Reading Teacher* 65 (2): 110–114.

Ross, Howard J. 2014. *Everyday Bias: Identifying and Navigating Unconscious Judgments in Our Daily Lives*. Lanham, MD: Rowman and Littlefield.

Shade, Barbara J., Cynthia Kelly, and Mary Oberg. 1997. *Creating Culturally Responsive Classrooms*. Washington, DC: American Psychological Association.

Singleton, Glenn E. 2015. *Courageous Conversations About Race: A Field Guide for Achieving Equity in Schools*. Thousand Oaks, CA: Corwin.

Slade, Malcolm, and Faith Trent. 2000. "What the Boys Are Saying: An Examination of the Views of Boys about Declining Rates of Achievement and Retention." *International Education Journal* 1 (3): 201–229.

Slavin, Robert E. 2010. "Co-operative Learning: What Makes Group-Work Work?" In *The Nature of Learning: Using Research to Inspire Practice*, 161–178. Paris, France: OECD Publishing.

Smith, E. A. 1992. "African-American Language Behavior: A World of Difference." Paper presented at the Claremont Reading Conference, Claremont, CA.

Smith, Howard L. 1998. "Literacy and Instruction in African American Communities: Shall We Overcome?" In *Sociocultural Contexts of Language and Literacy,* edited by Bertha Pérez, 189–222. Mahwah, NJ: Lawrence Erlbaum Associates.

Smitherman, Geneva. 1998. "Ebonics, King, and Oakland: Some Folk Don't Believe Fat Meat *Is* Greasy." *Journal of English Linguistics* 26 (2): 97–107. Thousand Oaks, CA: SAGE Publications.

Spring, Joel. 1994. *Deculturalization and the Struggle for Equality: A Brief History of the Education of Dominated Cultures in the United States.* New York: McGraw-Hill.

Stahl, Steven A. 1999. *Vocabulary Development.* Cambridge, MA: Brookline Books.

Sussman, Robert Wald. 2014. *The Myth of Race: The Troubling Persistence of an Unscientific Idea.* Cambridge, MA: Harvard University Press.

Syrus, Publilius. ThinkExist.com. "Publilius Syrus quotes," accessed June 22, 2011, http://en.thinkexist.com/quotation /speech_is_the_mirror_of_the_soul-as_a_man_speaks/149277 .html.

Tate, Marcia L. 2010. *Worksheets Don't Grow Dendrites: 20 Instructional Strategies that Engage the Brain.* Thousand Oaks, CA: Corwin Press.

Torgesen, Joseph, and Roxanne Hudson. 2006. "Reading Fluency: Critical Issues for Struggling Readers." In *Reading Fluency: The Forgotten Dimension of Reading Success*, edited by S. Jay Samuels and Alan A. Farstrup. Newark, DE: International Reading Association.

Trelease, Jim. 2001. *The Read-Aloud Handbook*. New York: Penguin Books.

Valenzuela, Angela. 1999. *Subtractive Schooling: U.S.-Mexican Youth and the Politics of Caring*. Albany, NY: State University of New York Press.

Villegas, Ana Maria, and Tamara Lucas. 2004. "Diversifying the Teacher Workforce: A Retrospective and Prospective Analysis." *Yearbook of the National Society for the Study of Education* 103 (1): 70–104.

———. 2007. "The Culturally Responsive Teacher." In *Educational Leadership* 64 (6): 28–33. Alexandria, VA: Association for Supervision and Curriculum Development.

Villicana, Adrian J., Luis M. Rivera, and Nilanjana Dasgupta. 2011. "The Effect of a Group-Affirmation on Prejudice." *Psychology Student Research Journal*: 31–37.

Wilhelm, Jeffrey D. 2007. "Imagining a New Kind of Self: Academic Language, Identity, and Content Area Learning." In *Voices from the Middle* 15 (1): 44–45. Urbana, IL: National Council of Teachers of English.

Williams, James D. and Grace Capizzi Snipper. 1990. *Literacy and Bilingualism*. New York: Longman Publishing Group.

Williams, Robert L., ed. 1975. *Ebonics: The True Language of Black Folks*. St. Louis, MO: Institute of Black Studies.

Wolfe, Patricia. 2001. *Brain Matters: Translating Research into Classroom Practice*. Alexandria, VA: Association for Supervision and Curriculum Development.

Yopp, Ruth Helen and Hallie Kay Yopp. 2007. "Ten Important Words Plus: A Strategy for Building Word Knowledge." In *The Reading Teacher* 61 (2): 157–160. International Reading Association. Hoboken, NJ: Wiley.

Zeichner, Kenneth. 2003. "The Adequacies and Inadequacies of Three Current Strategies to Recruit, Prepare, and Retain the Best Teachers for all Students." *The Teachers College Record* 105 (3): 490–519.

Glossary of Terms

CLR, as we have defined it, comes with a set of terms that have particular meanings in relation to the approach. Some of the terms are defined traditionally, but some are not. The glossary is provided to add a layer of clarity to your overall understanding of the language surrounding cultural responsiveness.

academic language—the language used in textbooks, in classrooms, and on tests; different in structure and vocabulary (e.g., technical terms and common words with specialized meanings) from Standard English

academization—an activity in which student slang terms are translated into academic language which maintains the concept conveyed in the slang; the process is an example of building and bridging

accuracy—describes students' ability to recognize words and read them instantly; as students become more fluent readers, they demonstrate automaticity in recognizing words.

African American Language/African American Vernacular/ Black English—the systematic, rule-governed language that represents an infusion of the grammatical substratum of West African languages and the vocabulary of English

assimilation—the cultural absorption of a minority group into the main cultural body where people of different backgrounds see themselves as part of a larger national family

227

attention signal—an agreed upon verbal or non-verbal cue used to bring the students back to focus when they are engaged as opposed to when they are working individually or when they are off-task; should be used during three specific contexts:

- To clarify directions already given or to give further direct instruction

- To transition during the lesson from step one to step two and so on

- To bring the lesson, activity, or class time to a close

Blumenbaching—unknowingly supporting the idea that the Caucasian race is the most beautiful, mainly through visuals, texts, and media; reinforcing a racial supremacy dynamic that is institutional

bootstrapper—a person who believes the path they took should be the one others take because the rationale is that if they did not experience it, their students do not need to experience it

cissexual/cisgender man (cisman)—a nontranssexual man; a man whose assigned male gender is consistent with his personal sense of self

codeswitching/cultureswitching—the act of switching from one cultural or linguistic behavior to another for the purpose of being situationally appropriate

conceptually coded—focused on the abstract, conceptual meaning of words versus the technical definition; used in responsive vocabulary to build on the students' conceptual knowledge of words

contrastive analysis—the practice of comparing and contrasting the linguistic structure of two languages; academic term for language codeswitching

cultural determinations—decisions or behaviors based on cultural identities as opposed to racial identities; provides the rationale for why people do things based on who they are culturally

culturally authentic text—text, including words and graphics, that realistically presents the norms, morés, traditions, customs, and beliefs of the culture in focus

culturally generic text—text, including words and graphics, that reflects common cultural ground; features characters that are members of racial minority groups, but details that define the characters culturally are usually limited or nonexistent

culturally neutral text—text, including words and graphics, that features characters and themes that are about people of color but fundamentally are about something else; traditional fairy tales and folktales are common examples in which characters are shown as people of color

cultural resonance—when certain cultural phenomenon, occurrences, and/or activities have a particular meaning that reverberates in our souls

culturally responsive methodology—similar to responsive methodology but includes elements of culture, such as language, rhythm, sociocentrism, and communalism

culture—a set of guidelines, both explicit and implicit, that individuals inherit as members of a particular group that tells them how to view the world, how to experience it emotionally, and how to behave in it; it is learned behavior

Culture and Language Academy of Success (CLAS)—a Kindergarten through Grade 8 charter school in Los Angeles founded by Sharroky Hollie, Janis Bucknor, and Anthony Jackson. It operated for ten years (2003–2013) and served as a laboratory school for CLR pedagogy.

deficit thinking—holding on to a set of negative beliefs, attitudes, and knowledge in a way that blames the students, the parents, or the community for the failure of the students

doubter—a skeptic or disbeliever

ethnocultural behaviors—characteristics of cognitive, affective, and physiological behaviors that serve as relatively stable indicators of how learners perceive, interact with, and respond to the learning environment

hater—a person who brings unnecessary drama and stress to a situation; a person who always finds something wrong, and negative energy is their response

hegemony—leadership or dominance, especially by one country or social group over others

hidden bias—the unconscious prejudice, misinterpretation, misperception, judgment, and ignorance that we naturally bring to contexts depending on filters and belief systems; known as our first thought, not our last thought

home language—the language utilized by family members and others in the home; the language that identifies someone with their community

involuntary immigrant—defined by John Ogbu (1978); any person who historically came into their United States citizenship via enslavement or conquest; their collective common experience in the United States is one of the systematic denial of their indigenous culture and language

juxtaposition—a situation in which a culturally responsive or responsive activity is used right after or before a traditional activity. Through continuous exposure, students are taught situational appropriateness.

language—a linguistic entity defined around the parameters of phonics, markers, grammar, vocabulary, nonverbal uses, and discourse styles

Mexican American Language/Chicano English—the systematic, rule-governed language spoken by the Chicano and/or Mexican American community united by common ancestry in the Southwestern United States and/or Mexico

mindset shift—the constant, ongoing shift in your prejudice, misunderstandings, misperceptions, misinterpretations, bias, and ignorance about the cultures and languages of others. This shift is required to be culturally responsive.

movement—an element of kinesthetic learning in which students and teachers can move their bodies and move around a space; involves movement of big muscles

nonstandard languages/unaccepted languages—languages that are not accepted or acknowledged by mainstream culture. These languages are linguistically legitimate, following grammatical structures and rules just as "standard" language does.

offen-sensitiveness—an overly emotional reaction to concepts or materials that have been presented unemotionally. Reaction may be in the form of an inappropriate question, a comment, or, in rare cases, a behavior.

offen-sitive—being overcome by a mixed feeling or emotion of being too sensitive or unnecessarily offended

pedagogy—the how, what, and why of instructional methodology

personal dictionary—a tool to help students interpret academic vocabulary (i.e., content-specific words) by creating an illustration and a personal connection; based on the Frayer model (Frayer, Frederick, and Klaumeier 1969)

personal thesaurus—a tool to help students develop knowledge of synonyms and antonyms

prosody—refers to stress, intonation, and pauses (known as reading with expression or feeling)

protocols—clearly defined expectations of behavior that are specific within a culture, community, or situation, including school and individual classrooms. They can be micro or macro.

race—socially constructed story of human geography and denotable phenotypes or variations among peoples. It has nothing to do with our behaviors culturally.

random urgency—the situation in which any student can be called on at any time, and the students do not resist being called upon because they believe the process is fair and random

rate—the speed at which a person reads. As students become fluent in reading, they learn to adjust their rate according to the purposes for reading and the nature of the selection.

read-alouds—cultural storytelling where reading aloud replicates the cultural base that comes from oral traditions and affirming verbal cultures

relexification—formation of a hybrid language. The deep grammatical structure of the indigenous languages was retained over time and meshed with the vocabulary of the dominant language or culture.

responsive methodology—student-centered learning. There is less teacher talk, more student-student interactions, and lowered affective filter while learning.

responsiveness—the validation and affirmation of indigenous (home) culture and language for the purpose of building and bridging the student to success in the culture of academia and mainstream society

Rings of Culture—the layered identities or cultures that make up who we are, e.g., gender, nationality, religion, ethnicity, class, and age; these identities, examined in isolation, say something about who we are and why we enact certain behaviors; in order to be a responsive educator, it is critical to account for the multiple, overlapping identities within students and to be mindful that race does not determine any of our behaviors because race is not a culture.

school language—the language utilized in the context of school, commonly associated with Standard English

sentence lifting—the use of literature, poetry, songs, plays, student-elicited sentences, or prepared story scripts that incorporate specific contrasts of home- and target-language rule forms

situational appropriateness—the concept of determining what cultural or linguistic behavior is most appropriate for the situation. Students make choices around cultural and linguistic behaviors based on the situation without sacrificing what they consider to be their base culture or language.

Standard English—the English language that is uniform with respect to spelling, grammar, pronunciation, and vocabulary; the well-established language used in formal and informal speech and writing; widely recognized as acceptable wherever English is spoken and understood

Standard English Learner (SEL)—a student whose home language differs in variety from Standard English and has been generally unaccepted by school as an institution. This student typically has strong Basic Interpersonal Communication Skills (BICS) and weak Cognitive Academic Language Proficiency (CALP).

subtractive bilingualism—the case in which learning a second language interferes with the first language. The second language replaces the first language.

subtractive schooling—the divestment of students of important social and cultural resources, leaving them progressively vulnerable to academic failure and the discouragement of cultural identity

traditional methodology—a strategy that delegitimizes students' cultures by historical, institutional, and structural racism, stereotypes, and generalizations primarily carried forth through mainstream media

twister—a person who takes the facts and twists them to fit their agenda; this person will only tell half of the story; an expert decontextualizer

underserved—a student who is unsuccessful and the school is not responding appropriately to bring that student success

Validate, Affirm, Build and Bridge (VABB)

Validate and Affirm (VA)—make culturally and linguistically legitimate and positive that which has been illegitimate and negative by the institution of education and mainstream media; understanding the complexity of culture and the many forms it takes (including age, gender, and social class), which will then create opportunities for making meaningful experiences in school

- *Validation*—the intentional and purposeful legitimatization of the home culture and language of students

- *Affirmation*—the intentional and purposeful effort to reverse the negative stereotypes of nonmainstream cultures and languages portrayed in historical perspectives

Build and Bridge (BB)—the cultural knowledge that needs to be developed and connected to academic use within the school context after students' cultures have been validated and affirmed

- *Building*—understanding and recognizing the cultural and linguistic behaviors of students and using those behaviors to foster rapport and relationships with them

- *Bridging*—providing the academic and social skills students will need to have success beyond the classroom; evident when students demonstrate they can navigate school and mainstream culture successfully

voluntary immigrant—defined by John Ogbu in 1978; a person who historically has been introduced to the United States and was marked by entry through Ellis Island or Angel Island, and their experience has been one of successful assimilation into the United States culture

Rings of Culture Diagram

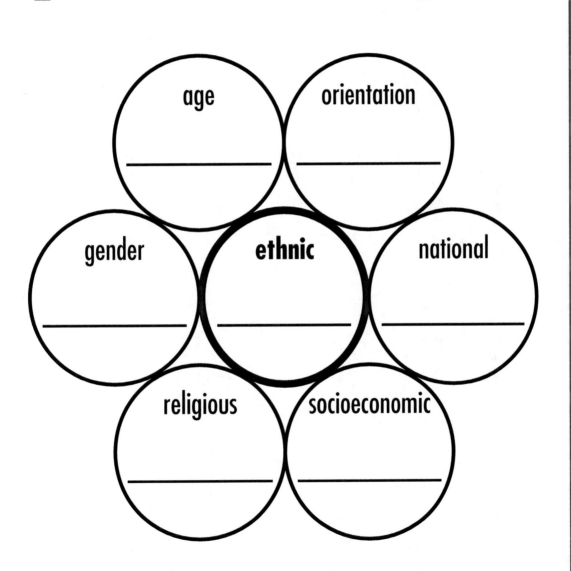

Responsive Dots: Assessing Literature for CLR

Directions: Use the chart below to help determine the cultural authenticity of texts you are considering for use in instruction. Fill in the dot next to each question to which you answer yes. The more dots filled in, the more responsive your text.

Title: _____

Author: _____

Question	Yes Marks the Dot!	Notes
1. Does the text support the literacy skills and assessment for content that you are teaching/introducing/reinforcing?	O	
2. Does the text present persons, animals, subjects, or issues in the context of race, diversity, or tokenism (perfunctory inclusion)?	O	
3. Is the content, subject, or point of the text relevant to the experiences, interests, and knowledge of the target audience (your students)?	O	
4. Is the text explicitly linked to any of the Rings of Culture?	O	
5. Does the text recognize and/or display superficial cultural behaviors with purpose (see the Iceberg Concept of Culture)?	O	
6. Is the text from an author, publisher, or source that has proven, reliable, and accurate cultural knowledge? Has the book received awards indicating cultural relevance/validation?	O	
7. Does the text recognize or display shallow and/or deep cultural behaviors with purpose (see the Iceberg Concept of Culture)?	O	
8. Is the context (setting, situation, and/or environment) authentically culturally based?	O	
9. Is home language authentically represented in the text?	O	
10. Does the text validate and affirm cultural and linguistic behaviors explicitly?	O	

How culturally responsive is the text? (Circle One)

7–10 dots = Culturally Authentic   4–6 dots = Culturally Generic   1–3 dots = Culturally Neutral

CLR Strategies

This appendix offers a sampling of CLR protocols, activities, and strategies for several different areas of CLR focus, including student engagement, attention signals, read-aloud activities, literacy strategies, and writing activities.

Protocols for Increasing Student Engagement

Protocol: **Let Me Hear You**
Description: Students respond concurrently, orally, and/or with movement to a speaker— the teacher or another student—to an improvised or pre-taught "call," such as "Got it?/Yes."

Why use it:	**It is best to use this when:**
• To actively engage all students • To validate and affirm culturally different forms of discourse, particularly as an aspect of codeswitching	• Getting students' attention • Transitioning between activities • Showing appreciation or acknowledgment

Protocol: My Turn, Your Turn

Description: This protocol is used for participation and discussion when it is appropriate for one person to speak at a time. The teacher states explicitly that one person will talk at a time to answer a question, give instruction, or present to the class. If any students "jump in" at an inappropriate time, the teacher reminds students of what is appropriate by saying in call and response "My turn," with students responding in unison, "Your turn."

Why use it:	It is best to use this when:
• To practice explicit turn taking, particularly as an aspect of codeswitching • To help students practice turn taking without jumping in when they feel engaged	• It is important for one speaker to be heard, such as during direct instruction, presentations, guest speakers, etc.

Protocol: Whip Around

Description: The teacher asks a question that requires a short answer, such as, *What adjective describes the main character?* Beginning on one side of the room, each student takes a turn answering the question, moving quickly around the room in an orderly fashion until each student has responded.

Why use it:	It is best to use this when:
• To practice explicit turn taking, particularly as an aspect of codeswitching • To validate everyone's responses • To practice precise, focused responses	• Checking whole-group understanding after a reading selection, directed instruction, or presentation • Needing brief, quick responses from all students

Protocol: Give a Shout Out

Description: Students softly shout out responses at the same time. The teacher can record shout-outs on the board, if appropriate. Posed questions can require either one correct answer or a variety of short answers.

Why use it:	It is best to use this when:
• To actively engage all students • To validate and affirm culturally different forms of discourse, particularly as an aspect of codeswitching	• Checking for understanding on short 1–2 word answers (e.g., multiplication facts, brainstorming short 1–2 word answers) • Checking responses (such as synonyms with the Personal Thesaurus)

Protocol: Train or Pass It On

Description: Students call on one another to answer and/or ask questions. Students do not raise their hands but are encouraged to call on a variety of people in the classroom. Students can also "pass" on a question by calling on another student for help or to answer. Remind students that if they "pass," the beanbag will eventually return to them, so they need to be prepared to contribute the next time around. Note: This can also be used with a small soft object that students can toss to each other.

Why use it:	It is best to use this when:
• To hold all students accountable for participation through nonvolunteerism • To validate and affirm culturally different forms of discourse, particularly as an aspect of codeswitching • To provide for improvisation and variety • To provide an opportunity for students to control participation	• Checking for understanding, individually or collectively • A student has been selected via another protocol but needs assistance

Effective Attention Signals

Effective use of responsive attention signals is not as easy as it may seem. What most teachers miss are the necessary nuances as well as the intentional and strategic use of responsive attention signals. Without considering these important subtleties in or during lesson planning, the desired outcome—increased student engagement—will remain elusive. You must be intentional and purposeful with your use of the signals, whether they are call-and-response or not. The bottom line is, when calling your students to attention, why not do it responsively?

Call and Response Attention Signals

The following example illustrates how to use an attention signal to refocus the students' attention on the teacher after a discussion or activity.

Example: When I say listen, you say up

Teacher: When I say 'listen,' you say 'up.' Listen

Students: up!

Teacher: Listen

Students: up!

No asterisk = Come to quiet, show praise or agreement, fun

* = Ending the lesson or activity

** = Transitioning

*** = Beginning the lesson

**** = Focusing

1   When I say listen, you say up****

2   Time for/Lunch*

3   Time to/End*

4   A little bit softer now/Shout; A little bit louder now/Shout**

5   Do your work/I know (To the tune of "You're a Jerk" by New Boyz)***

242

6   Teach me how to/Teach me how to multiply (To the tune of "Teach Me How to Dougie" by Cali Swag District)

7   Are you ready/Yes I'm ready, to learn***

8   Se puede/Si, se puede

9   Hocus/Pocus, Everybody focus****

10 Macaroni and cheese/Everybody freeze****

11 Hawthorne (school name)/Eagles (mascot)

12 My turn/Your turn**

13 Peace/Quiet; Clapping/Clap back****

14 R.E.S.P.E.C.T./Find out what it means to me, Shhh!

15 Aye go/Aye may

16 The title of a book/Repeat or complete the title

17 When I say _____/You say _____

18 Let's get it started/In here***

19 Learn it up kids/I'm about to; Learn it up kids/'Cause that's what I was born to do

20 Bring it back now/I'll show you how***

21 What's/Up? ****

22 Chicka-Chicka/Boom-Boom

23 When I say holla/You say back

24 You are smart/And we know it; You are smart/So let's show it***

25 When I move you move/Just like that**

26 Tell me when to go/Go, go, go, go**

27 I like to move it, move it/Move it**

28 Bottoms up, bottoms up/Get your bottoms up**

29 Get up, stand up/Stand up for your rights**

30 Lean wit it/Rock wit it

31 Aloha!/Aloha!****

32 Don't just stand there/Bust a move**

33 It's like that/And that's the way it is

Culturally Responsive Read-Aloud Activities

Name: Teacher Reads Aloud

Description: The teacher reads the text aloud, modeling the prosodic features of the language.

How-To Steps: The students listen and follow along in their books while the teacher reads to students.

Pros: All readers benefit from hearing a proficient reader: low affective filter.	**Cons:** The students may want to participate but are required to listen; lack of student participation.

What Makes It Culturally Responsive: In effect, when teachers read aloud, it has the same result as storytelling for students in their communities. Listening to an adult read an engaging story reminds students of having listened to a care provider at home tell a story.

Name: Train Reading (Proficient Readers Only Read)

Description: Just as a train has an engine, cars, and a caboose, the teacher starts as the first reader as the engine and chooses the proficient readers to be the cars and caboose.

How-To Steps: The teacher chooses readers prior to the reading, and when the teacher directs, the next student follows, and so on. Teacher chooses three to five students ahead of time and tells them that they will read when directed.

Pros: Proficient readers can model fluency; prosodic features.	**Cons:** Struggling readers will want to read (need to increase fluency); lack of equitable participation.

What Makes It Culturally Responsive: Train Reading provides an opportunity for readers to accomplish a task together for a common purpose. Students who have this experience not only feel validated for their reading ability but also have a sense of identity that they are leaders in the class. This gets buy-in from the students who are affirmed and recognized for something they do well.

Name: **Jump-In Reading**	
Description: The students have the autonomy to choose when they would like to participate and read aloud by "jumping-in."	
How-To Steps: The student reads, and another student can jump in when there is a stop period. The student can stop and go with the silence (it's perfectly acceptable). Students must read at least one sentence, or they can read for as long as they want or until someone jumps in. Having moments of silence allows students to think and reflect about what was just read. If two or more jump in at the same time, one student shall defer to the other.	
Pros: Highly engaging; low affective filter; student-centered.	**Cons:** Struggling readers will want to read; lack of equitable participation.
What Makes It Culturally Responsive: Jump-In Reading simulates more naturally how a conversation occurs in some languages. The appropriate time to "jump in" during a conversation is culturally and linguistically based. The appropriate time to jump in during a conversation is different for various cultures. In the culture of school and mainstream culture, jumping in is considered rude and interrupting. Jump-In Reading is a build-and-bridge strategy that validates and affirms the home culture for transitioning to the culture of school.	

Name: **Fade In, Fade Out**	
Description: The teacher uses nonverbal cues to choose students to read. Students must be able to read and listen for another reader's cues.	
How-To Steps: The teacher walks around the room and touches the shoulder of a student who starts to read with a whisper and gradually increases the volume to a normal reading voice. As the first student reads, the teacher touches another student's shoulder, and that student begins fade-in. The student who is reading then fades out, going from normal volume to a whisper. The reader starts to read over the first reader, who begins to fade out.	
Pros: Models fluency in a strong way.	**Cons:** High affective filter, students have little choice; struggling readers will want to read; lack of equitable participation.
What Makes It Culturally Responsive: Fade-In and Fade-Out reading gives an opportunity for students to work together toward a common goal.	

Name: **Echo Reading**	
Description: The teacher reads and students echo.	
How-To Steps: The teacher reads one sentence, paragraph, or section and then stops. Students echo the teacher by reading the same sentence in the same way.	
Pros: Great for modeling prosody; sense of cooperation; low affective filter.	**Cons:** Student participation
What Makes It Culturally Responsive: Echo-Read is a strategy that is often used with struggling readers. This strategy has a low affective filter, as students do not feel pressured to read correctly, as they just have to echo what they hear.	

Name: **Buddy Reading (Paired Reading)**	
Description: Proficient readers read to less-proficient readers. This can be done with peers or by pairing upper-grade students with lower-grade students. Students keep the same buddy for the entire grading period.	
How-To Steps: The teachers assign students as buddies who will read the text together. Proficient readers are paired with nonproficient readers to ensure that the text is being read by each group, even if it is one student reading and the other listening.	
Pros: The students are motivated to work with peers, engaging; low affective filter; student-centered.	**Cons:** The teacher must actively check up on each group to ensure that students in pairs are reading.
What Makes It Culturally Responsive: Buddy Read gives students the opportunity to engage in text with another peer to create a fun experience while reading. Reading is not an isolating experience; rather, students have a peer with whom they can share a story.	

Name: Choral Reading	
Description: Teachers lead students to read aloud together.	
How-To Steps: Just as a choir sings in unison, the teacher leads the students to read together in one voice. The teacher points out where to start in the passage and cues students to read. All students are expected to read together in unison.	
Pros: Low affective filter	**Cons:** Student engagement
What Makes It Culturally Responsive: Choral Reading provides students with the opportunity to read collaboratively.	

Name: Radio Reading	
Description: Proficient readers are chosen to read a text with different voices. They can choose an emotion to relay, such as happy, sad, or sleepy. Alternatively, they can choose a voice type, such as an old woman or a baby.	
How-To Steps: The teacher must choose proficient readers that read expressively beforehand, so the student can practice their voice of choice.	
Pros: High engagement	**Cons:** Limited to proficient readers; possible to lose track of story line and focus on the reader.
What Makes It Culturally Responsive: Radio Reading provides students with the opportunity to showcase a talent and affirm something they are good at. Also shows that reading can be fun and enjoyable and can lead to dramatic interpretation, which many students have an affinity toward.	

Culturally Responsive Literacy Activities

Literacy Strategy Activity: Phonograms—Hink-Pinks, Hinky-Pinkies, Hinkety-Pinketies

CR Element(s): Preference for rhythmic and sociocentric learning activities

Steps:

1. Before reading, the teacher uses a picture walk to introduce a book that incorporates multiple rhyming words.

2. The teacher encourages students to listen to the story and explains that they are going to be listening for words that sound alike at the end, such as *frog* and *log*. The teacher reads the story while the class listens.

3. During reading, the teacher briefly pauses several times to get the students to name a word that rhymes with a word from the story.

4. After reading, the teacher explains that he or she is going to give some clues, and the class will have to think of rhyming words to guess the riddle. At least one of the words the students will be guessing should come from the story. For example, if the book included a fish, one clue and answer could be *a dream or request made by a water animal from our story.* (fish/wish)

5. For those learners having difficulty guessing the answers to the riddles, the teacher can provide one of the words in the hink pink (the rhyming words that answer the clue) and the students can guess the second rhyming word.

6. The teacher could begin with the riddles in this way to provide scaffolding. Gradually, the teacher would give the clues as written and let the class guess both rhyming words. Eventually, students can create their own riddles with rhyming words as answers.

7. Pairs of words that are one-syllable answers to riddles are called *hink-pinks*, while answers of two syllables are called *hinky-pinkies*, and three-syllable answers are called *hinkety-pinketies*. (For example: *frog-log* (hink-pink), *gory-story* (hinky-pinky), and *robbery-snobbery* (hinkety-pinkety)

Recommended Uses: Postreading, word recognition, and vocabulary building

Literacy Strategy Activity: SQ3R

CR Element(s): Provides support for inductive learning by structuring how to identify and remember important information

Overview:

SQ3R stands for

- **Survey**: The reader previews the material to develop a general outline for organizing information.

- **Question**: The reader raises questions with the expectation of finding answers in the material to be studied.

- **Read**: The reader next attempts to answer the questions formulated in the previous step.

- **Recite**: The reader then deliberately attempts to answer out loud or in writing the questions formulated in the second step.

- **Review**: The reader finally reviews the material by rereading portions of the assignment in order to verify the answers given during the previous step.

Steps:

1. Lead students in a survey of a reading selection. Pay special attention to headings, subheadings, topic sentences, and highlighted words.

2. Build a question for each heading and subheading in the text selection. These questions will be answered during the reading of the text.

3. Ask students to read the selection carefully, keeping the questions in mind as they read.

4. Have students "recite" the answers to the questions by verbalizing them in a group discussion or writing them down. This act of restating thought in spoken or written form reinforces learning.

5. Repeat this process for all of the questions.

6. Finally, have students review all of their spoken or written answers. Once SQ3R has been modeled several times to students, the teacher can provide students with the SQ3R Guide Sheet. This worksheet contains the cues to be used at each step.

Recommended Uses: Before, during, and after reading expository text

Literacy Strategy Activity: Reciprocal Teaching

CR Element(s): Preference for cooperative and sociocentric learning environments

Overview:

Reciprocal teaching involves teachers and students analyzing and discussing a segment of text to bring meaning to it. Four strategies structure the discussion: summarizing, generating questions, clarifying, and predicting. The teacher and students alternate assuming the instructor role to lead the discussion.

The teacher and students take turns assuming the role of the teacher in leading this dialogue. The purpose of reciprocal teaching is to facilitate a group effort between teacher and students as well as among students in the task of bringing meaning to the text. Each strategy was selected for the following purposes:

Summarizing provides the opportunity to identify and integrate the most important information in the text.	**Question generating** reinforces the summarizing strategy and carries the learner one more step along in the comprehension activity.
Steps:	**Steps:**
1. Distribute selected text to students.	1. Have students identify the kind of information that is significant in the text to provide the substance for a question.
2. Encourage students to summarize across sentences, paragraphs, and the passage as a whole.	2. Have students create questions and a self-test to ascertain that they can indeed answer their own questions.
When students first begin the reciprocal-teaching procedure, their efforts are generally focused at the sentence and paragraph levels. As they become more proficient, they are able to integrate at the paragraph and passage levels.	Question generating is a flexible strategy to the extent that students can be taught and encouraged to generate questions at many levels.

Clarifying is an activity that is particularly important when working with students who have a history of comprehension difficulty.

Steps:

1. Explain to students that the purpose of reading is not to say the words correctly and that it is acceptable if the text does not make sense to them.

2. Remind students that when they are asked to clarify, their attention is called to the fact that there may be many reasons why text is difficult to understand (e.g., new vocabulary, unclear reference words, difficult concepts).

Clarifying alerts to the effects of such impediments to comprehension and to take the necessary measures to restore meaning.

Predicting occurs when students hypothesize what the author will discuss next in the text.

Steps:

1. Review the relevant background knowledge that students already possess regarding the topic of study.

2. Explain to students that they have a purpose for reading: to confirm or disprove their hypothesis. Tell students that they will be able to link their new knowledge with the knowledge they already possess.

The predicting strategy also facilitates use of text structure as students learn that headings, subheadings, and questions embedded in the text are useful means of anticipating what might occur next.

Recommended Uses: Before, during, and after reading

Literacy Strategy Activity: Anticipation/Reaction Guide

CR Element(s): Preference for sociocentric learning activities

Overview:

An Anticipation/Reaction Guide utilizes a twin strategy to increase reading comprehension. It stimulates prior knowledge and experiences before reading and then reinforces key concepts after reading.

Steps:

1. Outline the main ideas in a reading selection. Write the ideas in a short list (no more than five or six points), using clear declarative statements. Do not include generalizations or abstractions in this list.

2. Rewrite the main statements in the form of questions to prompt the students' prior knowledge and to elicit students' reactions and predictions.

3. Have students write responses to each of the questions. These written responses should include any necessary explanation or evidence.

4. Allow students to openly discuss their answers/predictions prior to reading. Note any recurring themes in the discussion. Also, note any opposing or contradictory points of view.

5. Have students read the selected passage. Instruct students to make comments on their written answer sheet, noting agreement and disagreement between their answers and the author's message or purpose.

Recommended Uses: Before and after reading

Literacy Strategy Activity: **Hot Seat**
CR Element(s): Preference for sociocentric and performance-based learning activities
Steps: 1. Students read part or all of a selected piece of literature. 2. Divide the class into groups of 3–5 students. Each student selects a character whose persona he or she will adopt and prepares for an interrogation from the rest of the class. 3. Have all students (working independently or in small groups) prepare questions for each character. Questions may focus on recalling the story or deal with a character's emotions. Hot Seat formats vary with the group of students. Teachers may ask a panel of characters to assume the "hot seat" or limit it to individuals. Variation: Use puppets, character masks, or murals as a lead-in.
Recommended Uses: After reading

Literacy Strategy Activity: **Tea Party**
CR Element(s): Preference for interpersonal sociocentric kinesthetic learning activities
Steps: A Tea Party serves as a valuable "intro" activity before students even see the book and gives the students a "taste" of the book, novel, or play. 1. Distribute quotes from the text, and revisit them in context during the actual reading, providing many opportunities for an "Ah-ha!" 2. Encourage students to share their thoughts.
Recommended Uses: Before reading

Acrostics: Poems created by writing a name or concept down the left side of a page. For each letter, write a word or phrase that describes the name or concept to you.

Alternative Endings: Students develop a new ending for a written or oral story.

Brainstorming: Students are given a topic that they discuss with peers in a small group. They use the language that is most comfortable for them. As ideas arise, students record the ideas in standard-language form. The teacher facilitates a whole-group discussion of the topic, using standard language.

Character Portraits: Concentrating on the roles of specific characters, students create pictures of the characters and describe how they fit into the story.

Character Profiles: Students develop a short description of a character, using nonstandard language and/or standard language.

Culture Bits: Short bits of cultural information are provided to students at the beginning, the middle, or the end of class. Students must take notes and discuss the cultural topic.

Dictation: The teacher selects a passage and reads it three times, first at normal speed, then a little slower, and finally at normal speed again. Students listen to the first reading, write the sentence(s) during the second reading, and confirm their recorded sentence(s) as they listen to the third reading.

Discovery Words: Word-webs concept; circles of words that are acquired outside of the school setting.

Draw It: Teachers choose a target sentence from a reading selection; students write the selected sentence and their meaning of the sentence and draw a pictorial representation.

Interviews: Students prepare a set of open-ended questions revolving around a cultural topic. They use the questions to interview people within their family and community.

Journal Writing: Students engage in free writing about a specific topic or a meaningful experience in either nonstandard or standard language.

Predicting: Students consider what will occur next in a reading selection and write their predictions in their own words and/or translate their prediction in standard-language form.

Question Circle: Students are seated in a circle. Each student has a sheet of paper and writes a question at the top of that paper. They then pass their paper to the left. Each student answers the question on the sheet they receive.

Scrambled Sentences: Students rearrange a list of scrambled words to form a sentence that makes sense.

Story-Retelling: Students retell a story in oral or written form using nonstandard language or standard language. They may share their retelling with a partner.

Summarizing: Students write a short description of a reading selection. The summary can also be provided orally.

Culturally Authentic Texts

This list of titles was curated by Lydia McClanahan, educator and consultant for the Center for Culturally Responsive Teaching and Learning.

Book	Rings of Culture	Ethnicity	Themes	Grade Level	Genre
Alexander, Kwame. 2014. *The Crossover*. New York: Houghton Mifflin Harcourt Books.	youth, gender, ethnicity, socioeconomic	Black	sports, family, loss, change	4–10	novel in verse
Alexie, Sherman. 2009. *The Absolutely True Diary of a Part-Time Indian*. New York: Little, Brown Books for Young Readers.	youth, gender, ethnicity, socioeconomic	American Indian/Indigenous	coming of age	9–12	realistic fiction
Alexie, Sherman, and Yuyi Morales. 2016. *Thunder Boy Jr.* New York: Little, Brown Books for Young Readers.	ethnicity, age, gender, nationality	American Indian	family traditions, American Indian heritage, identity, importance of names, father/son relationship	K–4	picture book
Allen, Crystal. 2016. *The Magnificent Mya Tibbs: Spirit Week Showdown*. New York: Balzer & Bray.	nationality, gender, age, ethnicity	Black	school fun, friendship, family, small town life, mean girl troubles, overcoming conflict	3–6	realistic fiction
Alvarez, Julia. 2010. *Return to Sender*. New York: Yearling Books.	ethnicity, nationality, youth	Mexican/Mexican American	undocumented workers, family, understanding, courage, loss, overcoming fear	4–7	realistic fiction

Book	Rings of Culture	Ethnicity	Themes	Grade Level	Genre
Andrews, Troy, and Bryan Collier. 2015. *Trombone Shorty.* New York: Harry N. Abrams.	ethnicity, age, nationality, gender	Black	music, creativity, New Orleans jazz, life of Trombone Shorty	1–4	biography
Asim, Jabari. 2016. *Preaching to the Chickens: The Story of Young John Lewis.* London: Nancy Paulsen Books.	nationality, religion, gender, ethnicity, socioeconomic	Black	biography of young John Lewis, growing up, living on a farm, following your dreams, hard work, family, responsibility	2–5	biographical picture book
Baker, Darryl, and Qin Ling. 2016. *Kamik Joins the Pack.* Iqaluit, NU, CAN: Inhabit Media.	ethnicity, age, gender, nationality	Inuit	Inuit traditions, dog sledding, family and traditions	K–3	realistic fiction
Bolden, Tonya. 2002. *Tell All the Children Our Story: Memories and Mementos of Being Young and Black in America.* New York: Harry N. Abrams.	nationality, ethnicity, gender, socioeconomic	Black	American children from colonial times to present	4–8	nonfiction
Bolden, Tonya. 2005. *Maritcha: A Nineteenth-Century American Girl.* New York: Harry N. Abrams.	nationality, ethnicity, gender	Black	biographical, Marticha Redmond Lyons, born free during slavery	4–8	historical nonfiction
Bolden, Tonya. 2005. *Portraits of African American Heroes.* London: Puffin Books.	nationality, ethnicity, gender	Black	biographical	4–8	nonfiction

Book	Rings of Culture	Ethnicity	Themes	Grade Level	Genre
Bolden, Tonya. 2007. *The Champ: The Story of Muhammad Ali.* New York: Dragonfly Books.	nationality, religion, gender, ethnicity	Black	Muhammad Ali's life, civil rights	1–5	biography
Bolden, Tonya. 2013. *Emancipation Proclamation: Lincoln and the Dawn of Liberty.* New York: Harry N. Abrams.	nationality, ethnicity	Black/ White	Emancipation Proclamation	5–9	nonfiction
Bolden, Tonya. 2014. *Searching for Sarah Rector: The Richest Black Girl in America.* New York: Harry N. Abrams.	nationality, ethnicity, gender, socioeconomic	Black	biographical, Sarah Rector, African American history	6–8	historical, nonfiction
Bolden, Tonya. 2016. *How to Build a Museum: Smithsonian's National Museum of African American History and Culture.* New York: Viking Books for Young Readers.	nationality, ethnicity	Black	the building of Smithsonian's National Museum of African American History and Culture	5–12	nonfiction
Bolden, Tonya. 2017. *Pathfinders: The Journey of 16 Extraordinary Black Souls.* New York: Harry N. Abrams.	ethnicity, nationality	Black	biographical	5–8	historical/ nonfiction

Book	Rings of Culture	Ethnicity	Themes	Grade Level	Genre
Booth, Coe. 2007. *Tyrell*. New York: Push.	age, gender, socioeconomic, ethnicity, nationality	Black	homelessness, addiction, incarcerated black men, urban life, choices and consequences, trying to escape the cycle of poverty	9–12	realistic fiction
Booth, Coe. 2015. *Kinda Like Brothers*. New York: Scholastic Inc.	socioeconomic, age, gender, ethnicity, nationality	Black	foster families, dealing with resentment, peer rivalries, sharing attention and space, special needs children, choices and consequences, urban life	4–6	realistic fiction
Bruchac, Joseph, and Bill Farnsworth. 2015. *The Hunter's Promise: An Abenaki Tale*. Bloomington, IN: World Wisdom, Inc.	ethnicity, age, gender, nationality, religious	Abenaki	love, nature, family, keeping promises, tradition	2–5	folktale
Bryan, Ashley. 2016. *Freedom Over Me: Eleven Slaves, Their Lives and Dreams Brought to Life*. New York: Atheneum/ Caitlyn Dlouhy Books.	nationality, socioeconomic, ethnicity	Black	slave life, history of slavery in America, biographies of 11 slaves, hope for freedom, self-identity, self-concept, developing skills/talents	3–7	historical/ biographical picture book
Canales, Viola. 2007. *The Tequila Worm*. New York: Wendy Lamb Books.	ethnicity, nationality, age, gender, socioeconomic	Mexican/ Mexican American	life in the barrio, family, friendship, self-acceptance, cultural identity, education, fitting in, hopes/dreams	5–8	realistic fiction

Book	Rings of Culture	Ethnicity	Themes	Grade Level	Genre
Charleyboy, Lisa, and Mary Beth Leatherdale, eds. 2016. *Dreaming in Indian: Contemporary American Indian Voices*. Toronto, ON, CAN: Annick Press.	youth, gender, ethnicity, socioeconomic	American Indian/First Nations	various	9–12	Anthology
Choi, Yangsook. 2003. *The Name Jar*. New York: Dragonfly Books.	ethnicity, nationality, age, gender	Korean	cultural identity and acceptance, being the new kids, fitting in, prejudice and bullying, struggling through change, self-love, heritage, family, friendship	K–2	picture book
Cisneros, Sandra. 1991. *The House on Mango Street*. London: Vintage Press.	ethnicity, socioeconomic, youth	Mexican/Mexican American	identity, coming of age, family, friendship, community hopes/dreams, love	5–12	fiction/vignettes
Clark, Kristin Elizabeth. 2016. *Freakboy*. New York: Square Fish Books.	gender, sexual orientation, youth	White	LGBTQ, gender identity, self-love, acceptance, coming of age, family, friendship, overcoming fear/challenges, honesty	9–12	realistic fiction

Book	Rings of Culture	Ethnicity	Themes	Grade Level	Genre
Cline-Ransome, Lesa, and James E. Ransome. 2015. *My Story, My Dance: Robert Battle's Journey to Alvin Ailey.* New York: Simon & Schuster Books for Young Readers.	age, ethnicity, socioeconomic, religion, nationality	Black	biography of Robert Battle, overcoming physical challenges, creativity, dance, family love, cultural identity, following your dreams	2–5	biographical picture book
Coates, Ta'Nehisi, and Brian Stelfreeze. *Black Panther: A Nation Under Our Feet, Book 1.* New York: Marvel.	youth, nationality	African	superheroes, facing challenges, courage, facing enemies, survival	3–12	comic book
Copeland, Misty, and Christopher Myers. 2014. *Firebird.* G. P. Putnam's Sons Books for Young Readers.	gender, ethnicity, nationality	Black	following your dreams, overcoming stereotypes and prejudice, dance, creativity, self-concept, hard work and confidence, not giving up on your dreams	2–6	biographical picture book
de la Peña, Matt. 2010. *Mexican Whiteboy.* New York: Ember.	youth, ethnicity, socioeconomic, gender, nationality	Mexican/ Mexican American	sports, identity, acceptance, coming of age, fitting in, friendship, relationships, absent fathers	7–12	fiction
de la Peña, Matt. 2015. *Last Stop on Market Street.* New York: G. P. Putnam's Sons Books for Young Readers.	age, ethnicity, religious, gender, socioeconomic	Black	family, Sundays, urban life, grandparents, giving back, being grateful	K–2	picture book

Book	Rings of Culture	Ethnicity	Themes	Grade Level	Genre
de la Peña, Matt. 2015. *The Living*. New York: Ember.	age, gender, socioeconomic, ethnic	Mexican/ Mexican American	survival, coming of age, adventure, social class differences	9–12	adventure
Draper, Sharon. 1998. *Forged by Fire*. New York: Simon Pulse.	youth, ethnicity, socioeconomic, gender	Black	loss, abuse, coming of age, family, loss, identity	7–12	realistic fiction
Dunn, Anne M. 2016. *Fire in the Village: New and Selected Stories*. Duluth, MN: Holy Cow! Press.	nationality, ethnicity, age, gender, socioeconomic, religious	American Indian	various	9–12	short stories
Dupuis, Jenny Kay, Kathy Kacer, and Gillian Newland. 2016. *I Am Not a Number*. Toronto, ON, CAN: Second Story Press.	nationality, age, ethnicity, gender, socioeconomic	American Indian	American Indian history, injustice, identity, residential schools, resilience, overcoming prejudice	3–6	historical fiction
Erdrich, Louise. 2002. *The Birchbark House*. New York: Hyperion Books.	youth, nationality, gender, ethnicity	First Nations/ Ojibwe	relationship between humans and nature, family, tradition, Ojibwe culture/language	4–7	historical fiction

Book	Rings of Culture	Ethnicity	Themes	Grade Level	Genre
Faruqi, Reem, and Lea Lyon. 2015. *Lailah's Lunchbox: A Ramadan Story.* Thomaston, ME: Tilbury House Publishers.	religion, age, gender, ethnicity, nationality	Middle Eastern	Ramadan, fasting, being the new kid, being different, meeting new friends, family, identity and self-acceptance, feelings about fitting in	K–3	picture book
Fehlbaum, Beth. 2015. *Big Fat Disaster.* New York: Simon Pulse.	gender, socioeconomic, youth	White	body image, eating disorder, abuse, acceptance, love, acceptance, depression, bullying	9–12	realistic fiction
Flake, Sharon. 2007. *Money Hungry.* New York: Hyperion Books.	ethnicity, age, gender, socioeconomic	Black	inner city life, overcoming poverty/homelessness, evaluating priorities/values, coming of age, fear of being poor, friendship/family conflict, generosity vs. stinginess	6–9	realistic fiction
Flake, Sharon. 2007. *The Skin I'm In.* New York: Hyperion Books.	ethnicity, age, gender, socioeconomic	Black	self-love, identity/self-acceptance, struggles of adolescence, popularity, bullying, fitting in, believing in yourself, cultural identity, friendship, family conflict, colorism	5–9	realistic fiction
Flake, Sharon. 2011. *You Don't Even Know Me: Stories and Poems About Boys.* New York: Jump at the Sun.	age, gender, ethnicity	Black	black male lives, coming of age, choices, stereotypes, overcoming obstacles, urban life, identity	7–12	short stories/ poems

Book	Rings of Culture	Ethnicity	Themes	Grade Level	Genre
Flett, Julie. 2014. *We All Count: A Book of Cree Numbers*. Vancouver, BC, CAN: Native Northwest.	ethnicity, age	Cree	counting, Cree life	PreK–2	board book
Frame, Jeron Ashford, and R. Gregory Christie. 2008. *Yesterday I Had the Blues*. Berkeley, CA: Tricycle Press.	age, ethnicity, nationality, gender, socioeconomic	Black	colors, urban life, family, feelings, identity	1–4	picture book
Frazier, Sundee T. 2008. *Brendan Buckley's Universe and Everything in It*. New York: Yearling Books.	ethnicity, gender, age, nationality	Black/White	biracial identity, family conflict, intergenerational relationships, overcoming estrangement/prejudice, love of science, being true to who you are, interracial marriage	3–7	realistic fiction
Frazier, Sundee T. 2013. *Brendan Buckley's Sixth-Grade Experiment*. New York: Yearling Books.	ethnicity, gender, age, nationality	Black/White	biracial identity, family and conflict, friendship, awkwardness of adolescence, adopting a child, meeting parental expectations, self-identity, love of science	3–7	realistic fiction
Gansworth, Eric. 2015. *If I Ever Get Out of Here*. New York: Arthur A. Levine Books.	ethnicity, socioeconomic, youth	American Indian/First Nations	coming of age, identity, music, friendship, life on the reservation, education	7–12	realistic fiction

Book	Rings of Culture	Ethnicity	Themes	Grade Level	Genre
Garza, Xavier. 2011. *Maximilian and the Mystery of the Guardian Angel: A Bilingual Lucha Libre Thriller*. El Paso, TX: Cinco Puntas Press.	ethnicity, nationality, age, gender, socioeconomic	Mexican/ Mexican American	Mexican wrestling/lucha libre, mystery, adventure	4–7	adventure fiction
Golio, Gary. 2010. *Jimi: Sounds like a Rainbow: A Story of the Young Jimi Hendrix*. New York: Clarion Books.	nationality, gender, age	Black	music, creativity, Jimi Hendrix life	4–8	biographical
Gonzales, Mark, and Mehrdokht Amini. 2017. *Yo Soy Muslim: A Father's Letter to His Daughter*. New York: Salaam Reads.	religion, age, ethnicity, gender, nationality	Mexican/ Mexican American	cultural identity, being a Mexican American Muslim, family, self-love/acceptance, overcoming prejudice, father/ daughter relationship	PreK– 2	picture book
Gray, Monique, and Julie Flett. 2016. *My Heart Fills with Happiness*. Victoria, BC, CAN: Orca Book Publishers.	ethnicity, nationality, age, gender, socioeconomic	American Indian	family, cultural traditions, daily experiences of indigenous children	K–3	board book
Grimes, Nikki. 2002. *My Man Blue*. London: Picture Puffin Books.	ethnicity, gender, age, socioeconomic, nationality	Black	urban life, absent father, father figures, positive male role model, friendship	2–5	poetry

Book	Rings of Culture	Ethnicity	Themes	Grade Level	Genre
Grimes, Nikki. 2011. *Planet Middle School*. New York: Bloomsbury USA Children's Literature.	gender, age, ethnicity, socioeconomic, nationality	Black	adolescence, growing up, basketball, being a tween, first crush, middle school, friendship, family, identity	5–9	novel in prose
Grimes, Nikki. 2016. *Garvey's Choice*. Honesdale, PA: Wordsong.	gender, age, ethnicity, socioeconomic, nationality	Black	overcoming stereotypes, not living up to parents' expectations, being compared to a sibling, being a nerd, self-love, bullying, being overweight, being true to who you are	4–8	novel in verse
Grimes, Nikki. 2017. *One Last Word: Wisdom from the Harlem Renaissance*. New York: Bloomsbury USA Children's Literature.	nationality, ethnicity	Black	Harlem Renaissance	5–8	poetry
Herrington, John. 2016. *Mission to Space*. Ada, OK: White Dog Press.	nationality, gender, age	Chickasaw	first American Indian to fly to space shares information	2–5	nonfiction picture book
Highway, Tomson, and Brian Dienes. 2010. *Fox on the Ice (Maageesees Maskwameek Kaapit)* (Songs of the North Wind trilogy #1). Markam, ON, CAN: Fifth House Publishing.	ethnicity, nationality, age, gender, socioeconomic	Cree	ice fishing, family, Cree traditions, adventure	K–2	picture book

Book	Rings of Culture	Ethnicity	Themes	Grade Level	Genre
Jackson, Richard, and Jerry Pinkney. 2016. *In Plain Sight: A Game*. New York: Roaring Brook Press.	age, ethnicity, nationality	Black	family, intergenerational connections, aging	PreK–2	realistic fiction picture book
John, Antony. 2010. *Five Flavors of Dumb*. New York: Speak.	ability (deaf), gender, youth, socioeconomic	White	accepting challenges, coming of age, music, deaf life/culture	9–12	realistic fiction
Johnson, Angela. 2010. *The First Part Last*. New York: Simon & Schuster.	youth, gender, ethnicity, socioeconomic	Black	coming of age, teen pregnancy, responsibility, loss, choices, dealing with change	8–12	realistic fiction
Jones, Traci L. 2010. *Standing Against the Wind*. New York: Square Fish Books.	youth, socioeconomic, gender, ethnicity	Black	coming of age, facing challenges, overcoming obstacles, education, family, bullying, fitting in, achieving dreams	6–8	realistic fiction
Kahn, Hena, and Mehrdokht Amini. 2015. *Golden Domes and Silver Lanterns: A Muslim Book of Colors*. San Francisco: Chronicle Books.	religion, age, ethnicity, gender	Middle Eastern	Islamic practices/life, family, colors, identity, self-concept, acceptance, religous practices, love	PreK–2	picture book

Book	Rings of Culture	Ethnicity	Themes	Grade Level	Genre
Kahn, Hena, and Mehrdokht Amini. *Amina's Voice*. 2017. New York: Salaam Reads.	religion, age, ethnicity, gender, nationality	Pakistani-American	self-acceptance, islamic practices/life, family, identity, acceptance of others, community, overcoming tragedy/bias, self-love, love of others, surviving middle school, cultural differences	3–7	realistic fiction
Kaluk, Celina, and Alexandria Neonakus. 2016. *Sweetest Kulu*. Iqaluit, NU, CAN: Inhabit Media.	ethnicity, age, gender, nationality	Inuit	lullaby, babies	PreK–2	board book
Kilodavis, Cheryl, and Suzanne DeSimone. 2010. *My Princess Boy*. New York: Aladdin Books.	gender, age, nationality	Black/White	gender identity, transgender, acceptance, family love, biracial identity	PreK–3	picture book
Kuntz, Doug, and Amy Shrodes. 2017. *Lost and Found Cat: The True Story of Kunkush's Incredible Journey*. New York: Crown Books for Young Readers.	youth, nationality, ethnicity, gender	Iraqi	change, loss, facing hardship, family, having hope	K–3	biographical
Lainez, René, and Joe Cepeda. 2013. *From North to South (Del Norte al Sur)*. New York: Children's Book Press.	ethnicity, nationality, socioeconomic, age	Latino/ Mexican/ Salvadoran	realities of deportation, family separation, undocumented immigrant life, having hope, family love	K–3	picture book

Book	Rings of Culture	Ethnicity	Themes	Grade Level	Genre
Langston-George, Rebecca, and Janna Bock. 2016. *For the Right to Learn: Malala Yousafzai's Story*. North Mankato, MN: Capstone Publishers.	religion, gender, age, ethnicity, nationality	Pakistani	education, gender equality, overcoming prejudice, courage, standing up for your beliefs, defying the Taliban	3–5	biographical picture book
Laskin, Pamela L. 2017. *Ronit & Jamil*. New York: Katherine Tegen Books.	ethnicity, religious, nationality, age, gender	Israeli/ Palestinian	modern day Romeo & Juliet, forbidden love, Israeli/ Palestinian conflict, family conflict, following your heart	8–12	novel in verse
Levinson, Cynthia. 2012. *We've Got a Job: The 1963 Birmingham Children's March*. Atlanta: Peachtree Publishers.	nationality, ethnicity, youth	Black	civil rights movement, coming of age, U.S. history, prejudice, discrimination	5–12	nonfiction
Levinson, Cynthia. 2017. *The Youngest Marcher: The Story of Audrey Faye Hendricks, a Young Civil Rights Activist*. New York: Atheneum Books for Young Readers.	youth, nationality, ethnicity, gender	Black	courage, civil rights, freedom, having hope	K–4	biography
Lewis, John, Andrew Aydin, and Nate Powell. 2013–2016. *March (Trilogy)*. Marietta, GA: Top Shelf Productions.	nationality, ethnicity	Black	civil rights	8–12	graphic novel

Book	Rings of Culture	Ethnicity	Themes	Grade Level	Genre
Magoon, Kekla. 2010. *The Rock and the River*. New York: Aladdin Books.	ethnicity, age, nationality, socioeconomic, gender	Black	Civil Rights Movement vs. Black Power Movement, cultural identity, protest, family conflict, police brutality, coming of age, urban life, cultural conflict, father/son relationships, forms of protest	7–12	historical fiction
Magoon, Kekla. 2015. *How It Went Down*. New York: Square Fish Books.	socioeconomic, ethnicity, youth	Black/ Puerto Rican/ White	killing of black males, urban life, community, protest, equality, identity	7–12	realistic fiction
Medina, Meg. 2013. *The Girl Who Could Silence the Wind*. Somerset, MA: Candlewick Press.	age, ethnicity, nationality, socioeconomic, religious	Cuban/ Cuban American	folklore, family, spiritual beliefs, loss, coming of age, young love	8–11	magical realism
Medina, Meg. 2014. *Milagros: Girl from Away*. North Charleston, SC: CreateSpace.	age, ethnicity, gender, socioeconomic	Latin Caribbean/ Mexican	adventure, cultural identity, immigrant life, new beginnings, survival, family, friendship	4–8	fantasy adventure
Medina, Meg. 2014. *Yaqui Delgado Wants to Kick Your Ass*. Somerset, MA: Candlewick Press.	age, socioeconomic, gender, nationality	Cuban/ Cuban American	bullying, coming of age, absent fathers, courage, identity, overcoming fear and obstacles, choices, family	7–12	realistic fiction

Book	Rings of Culture	Ethnicity	Themes	Grade Level	Genre
Medina, Meg. 2015. *Mango, Abuela, and Me*. Somerset, MA: Candlewick Press.	age, ethnicity, nationality	Cuban/ Cuban American	family, communication, cultural connection/ understanding, love, intergenerational relationships	PreK– 2	picture book
Medina, Meg. 2016. *Burn, Baby, Burn*. Somerset, MA: Candlewick Press.	age, ethnicity, nationality, gender, socioeconomic	Cuban/ Cuban American	NYC Summer of 1977, Son of Sam, coming of age, family, friendship, love, fear, hopes/ dreams	9–12	historical fiction
Medina, Meg. 2016. *Tía Isa Wants a Car*. Somerset, MA: Candlewick Press.	age, ethnicity, nationality, socioeconomic	Cuban/ Cuban American	family, love, work ethic, immigrant life, sacrifice and priorities, cooperation, hopes and dreams	PreK– 2	picture book
Menon, Sandhya. 2017. *When Dimple Met Rishi*. New York: Simon Pulse.	ethnicity, age, nationality, gender	Indian	romance, arranged marriage, self-concept, family, breaking with tradition, being true to who you are, cultural identity	9–12	realistic fiction
Minnema, Cheryl Kay, and Wesley Ballinger. 2014. *Hungry Johnny*. St. Paul, MN: Minnesota Historical Society Press.	ethnicity, age, gender, nationality	Ojibwe	family, community, contemporary daily Ojibwe life, patience, intergenerational relationships	PreK– 2	realistic fiction picture book

Book	Rings of Culture	Ethnicity	Themes	Grade Level	Genre
Mock, Janet. 2014. *Redefining Realness: My Path to Womanhood, Identity, Love & So Much More.* New York: Atria Books.	gender, socioeconomic, ethnicity	Black/ Hawaiian	LGBTQ, gender identity, self-love, acceptance, coming of age, family, friendship, overcoming fear/challenges, honesty	9–12	memoir
Moon, Sarah, and James Lecesne, eds. 2012. *The Letter Q: Queer Writers' Notes to Their Younger Selves.* New York: Arthur A. Levine Books.	gender identity, sexual orientation, youth	various	identity, acceptance, coming out, self-love, bullying, LGBTQ perspective/issues, coming of age	9–12	anthology
Morales, Yuyi. 2008. *Just in Case: A Trickster Tale and Spanish Alphabet Book.* New York: Roaring Brook Press.	age, ethnicity	Mexican	folktale, alphabet	PreK–2	picture book
Morales, Yuyi. 2014. *Viva Frida.* New York: Roaring Brook Press.	ethnicity, nationality	Mexican	creativity, Frida Kahlo	K–3	biographical
Morales, Yuyi. 2015. *Niño Wrestles the World.* New York: Square Fish Books.	ethnicity, age, nationality	Mexican/ Mexican American	Lucha Libre wrestling, playtime, imagination	PreK–3	picture book
Morales, Yuyi. 2016. *Just a Minute: A Trickster Tale and Counting Book.* San Francisco: Chronicle Books.	age, ethnicity	Mexican/ Mexican American	folktale, counting	PreK–2	folktale

Book	Rings of Culture	Ethnicity	Themes	Grade Level	Genre
Morales, Yuyi. 2016. *Little Night/Nochecita*. New York: Square Fish Books.	age, ethnicity	Mexican/ Mexican American	bedtime, folktale, bilingual	PreK–2	picture book
Morales, Yuyi. 2016. *Rudas: Niño's Horrendous Hermanitas*. New York: Roaring Brook Press.	ethnicity, age, nationality	Mexican/ Mexican American	siblings, Lucha Libre, playtime, imagination	PreK–3	picture book
Myers, Walter Dean. 2004. *Monster*. New York: Amistad Press.	ethnicity, age, nationality, gender, socioeconomic	Black	inner-city life, juvenile detention, surviving choices/ consequences, overcoming the cycle of poverty, mass incarceration, coming of age	7–12	realistic fiction
Nelson, Kadir. 2013. *Nelson Mandela*. New York: Katherine Tegen Books.	ethnicity, nationality, age, socioeconomic, gender	South African	life of Nelson Mandela, determination, overcoming prejudice, self-concept, family, South African heritage	1–5	biographical picture book
Nicholson, Hope, ed. 2016. *Love Beyond Body, Space, and Time: An Indigenous LGBT Sci-Fi Anthology*. Winnipeg, MB, CAN: Bedside Press.	orientation, gender, age, nationality	American Indian/ Indigenous	LGBT, sci-fi, various	9–12	sci-fi anthology
Oh, Ellen, ed. 2017. *Flying Lessons and Other Stories*. New York: Crown Books for Young Readers.	nationality, ethnicity, gender, age, religion	Various	various themes	4–6	fiction

Book	Rings of Culture	Ethnicity	Themes	Grade Level	Genre
Older, Daniel Jose. 2016. *Shadowshaper*. New York: Scholastic Inc.	gender, ethnicity, youth	Black-Puerto Rican	coming of age, ancestors, art, family, identity, self-acceptance, responsibility, community, facing fear, preserving one's heritage	7–12	fantasy
Peete, Holly Robinson, and Ryan Elizabeth Peete. 2010. *My Brother Charlie*. New York: Scholastic Inc.	ability, age, ethnicity, gender	Black	autism, being different, family love, acceptance, sibling love	PreK–2	picture book
Perdomo, Willie. 2005. *Visiting Langston*. New York: Square Fish Books.	nationality, ethnicity, gender	Black	poetry, Harlem renaissance, Langston Hughes	2–4	biographical fiction
Perkins, Mitali. 2004. *Monsoon Summer*. New York: Laurel-Leaf Books.	age, ethnicity, nationality, gender, socioeconomic	Indian/ Indian American	change, cultural identity, friendship, family, understanding cultural differences	7–11	realistic fiction
Perkins, Mitali. 2005. *The Not-So-Star-Spangled Life of Sunita Sen*. New York: Little, Brown Books for Young Readers.	age, nationality, ethnicity, gender	Indian/ Indian American	cultural identity, coming of age, family, biculturalism, change, friendship, cultural appreciation	6–9	realistic fiction
Perkins, Mitali. 2008. *Rickshaw Girl*. Watertown, MA: Charlesbridge Publishing.	age, ethnicity, nationality, gender, socioeconomic	Indian	identity, family, responsibility, gender equality, work ethic, life in India	2–5	realistic fiction

Book	Rings of Culture	Ethnicity	Themes	Grade Level	Genre
Perkins, Mitali. 2010. *Secret Keeper*. New York: Ember.	age, gender, nationality, socioeconomic	Indian	family, change, socioeconomic hardship, gender equality, challenging traditions, coming of age, self-determination, friendship, life in India	7–10	realistic fiction
Perkins, Mitali. 2012. *Bamboo People*. Watertown, MA: Charlesbridge Publishing.	nationality ethnicity, age	Indian	coming of age, ethnic conflict, effects of war, child soldiers, family, friendship, loyalty	7–10	realistic fiction
Perkins, Mitali. 2015. *Tiger Boy*. Watertown, MA: Charlesbridge Publishing.	age, socioeconomic, ethnicity, nationality	Indian	nature, life in India, poor economic conditions, climate change, education, animal reserve, responsibility, family, choices	3–6	realistic fiction
Perkins, Mitali, ed. 2016. *Open Mic: Riffs on Life Between Cultures in Ten Voices*. Somerville, MA: Candlewick Press.	age, ethnicity, gender, nationality	various	various stories of bridging cultures	6–12	anthology
Pinkney, Angela Davis. 2015. *The Red Pencil*. New York: Little, Brown Books for Young Readers.	religious, youth, gender, nationality	Sudanese	refugee life, living through war/violence, change, facing challenges, loss, having hope	3–7	realistic fiction

Book	Rings of Culture	Ethnicity	Themes	Grade Level	Genre
Quintero, Isabel. 2014. *Gabi, A Girl in Pieces*. El Paso, TX: Cinco Puntos Press.	youth, ethnicity, socioeconomic, gender	Mexican American	identity, coming of age, family, friendship, overcoming challenges, education, hopes/dreams, love	7–12	realistic fiction
Quintero, Sofia. 2015. *Show and Prove*. New York: Knopf Books for Young Readers.	age, ethnicity, nationality, socioeconomic	Puerto Rican/Black/Jamaican/White	Bronx life in the '80s, hip-hop/break dancing, overcoming stereotypes/prejudice, friendship, family, grief/loss, cultural identity, meeting family expectations, hopes and dreams	7–12	historical fiction
Reynolds, Jason. 2015. *When I Was the Greatest*. New York: Atheneum Books for Young Readers.	ethnicity, age, gender, socioeconomic	Black	urban life, Brooklyn, coming of age, responsibility, family, choices and consequences, friendship, loyalty	7–12	realistic fiction
Reynolds, Jason. 2016. *As Brave As You*. New York: Atheneum/Caitlyn Dlouhy Books.	age, ability, ethnicity, gender	Black	family, courage, loss, coming of age	5–8	realistic fiction
Reynolds, Jason. 2016. *Ghost (Track series)*. New York: Atheneum/Caitlyn Dlouhy Books.	youth, socioeconomic, ethnicity, nationality	Black	overcoming challenges, identity, community, track, coming of age, finding your talent, running track	5–8	realistic fiction

Book	Rings of Culture	Ethnicity	Themes	Grade Level	Genre
Reynolds, Jason. 2016. *The Boy in the Black Suit.* New York: Atheneum/Caitlyn Dlouhy Books.	age, ethnicity, gender, socioeconomic	Black	overcoming grief/loss, coming of age, family, responsibility, love, friendship, substance abuse	7–12	realistic fiction
Reynolds, Jason, and Brendan Kiely. 2015. *All American Boys.* New York: Atheneum/Caitlyn Dlouhy Books.	youth, gender, ethnicity, socioeconomic	Black/White	police brutality, race relations, protest, stereotypes	8–12	realistic fiction
Rivera, Gabby. 2016. *Juliet Takes a Breath.* New York: Riverdale Avenue Books.	gender, sexual orientation, youth	Puerto Rican	sexual orientation, coming of age, acceptance, identity, self-love	10–12	realistic fiction
Robertson, David Alexander, and Julie Flett. 2016. *When We Were Alone.* Winnipeg, MB, CAN: HighWater Press.	ethnicity, nationality, age, gender, socioeconomic, religious	American Indian	family, intergenerational relationships, history of residential schools, native heritage/tradition	K–3	board book
Rodgers, Greg, and Leslie Stall Widener. 2014. *Chukfi Rabbit's Big, Bad Bellyache: A Trickster Tale.* El Paso, TX: Cinco Puntos Press.	ethnicity, age, gender	Choctaw	community, hard-work vs. laziness, learning lessons about greediness	K–5	picture book
Rodman, Mary Ann, and E.B. Lewis. 2007. *My Best Friend.* London: Puffin Books.	age, ethnicity, gender, socioeconomic	Black	summertime, friendship, being an outsider, being disappointed, self-confidence, acceptance	1–4	realistic fiction

Book	Rings of Culture	Ethnicity	Themes	Grade Level	Genre
Rodriguez, Cindy L. 2015. *When Reason Breaks*. New York: Bloomsbury Children's Books.	age, gender, ethnicity, nationality, socioeconomic, orientation	Latino/White	depression/anxiety, attempted suicide, self-concept, identity, friendship, family, coming of age, Emily Dickinson's poetry, bicultural identity, teenage angst	9–12	realistic fiction
Saenz, Benjamin Alire. 2012. *Aristotle and Dante Discover the Secrets of the Universe*. New York: Simon & Schuster Books for Young Readers.	ethnicity, gender, orientation	Mexican American	coming of age, identity, LGBTQ, acceptance, love, family, friendship	9–12	realistic fiction
Saenz, Benjamin Alire. 2017. *The Inexplicable Logic of My Life*. New York: Clarion Books.	age, ethnicity, orientation	Mexican American	coming of age, adoption, family, identity, friendship, loss	9–12	realistic fiction
Santiago, Esmeralda. 2006. *When I Was Puerto Rican: A Memoir*. Cambridge, MA: Da Capo Press.	ethnicity, gender, nationality, youth, socioeconomic	Puerto Rican	coming of age, family, change, education, overcoming obstacles	7–12	memoir
Shabazz, Ilyasah, and Kekla Magoon. 2016. *X: A Novel*. Somerville, MA: Candlewick Press.	nationality, ethnicity, religious, socioeconomic, age, gender	Black	identity, coming of age, notions of success, family, responsibility, change, black life, civil rights, being black in America	8–10	historical fiction

Book	Rings of Culture	Ethnicity	Themes	Grade Level	Genre
Shakur, Tupac. 2009. *The Rose That Grew from Concrete*. New York: MTV Books.	youth, ethnicity, socioeconomic, nationality	Black	injustice, overcoming obstacles, poverty, love, relationships, identity, coming of age, equality	7–12	poetry
Shange, Ntozake, and Kadir Nelson. 2004. *Ellington Was Not a Street*. New York: Simon & Schuster Books for Young Readers.	ethnicity, nationality, age, gender, socioeconomic	Black	community, segregation, rich African American history, black innovators, family, cultural identity, self-concept, Harlem	3–8	picture book
Sharon Flake. 2007. *Who Am I Without Him? Short Stories About Girls and the Boys in Their Lives*. New York: Jump at the Sun.	age, gender, ethnicity	Black	love, coming of age, relationships, self-worth, choices, friendship, identity	7–12	short stories
Shraya, Vivek. 2016. *The Boy and the Bindi*. Vancouver, BC, CAN: Arsenal Pulp Press.	age, gender, ethnicity, religion	Indian	Hindu culture, gender identity/questioning, family love and acceptance, self-concept	PreK–3	picture book
Silvera, Adam. 2015. *More Happy than Not*. New York: Soho Teen.	age, orientation, ethnicity, socioeconomic	Puerto Rican	grief and loss, suicide, relationships, family, gender identity, sexual orientation, happiness, coming of age	10–12	realistic fiction
Silvera, Adam. 2017. *History Is All You Left Me*. New York: Soho Teen.	age, orientation, ability	White	loss & grief, LGBTQ, change, love, friendship, mental illness	10–12	realistic fiction

Book	Rings of Culture	Ethnicity	Themes	Grade Level	Genre
Smith, Cynthia Leitich. 2000. *Jingle Dancer*. New York: HarperCollins.	age, ethnicity, nationality, gender	Creek	Creek heritage/traditions, family, community, intergenerational relationships, jingle dancing	K–3	picture book
Smith, Cynthia Leitich. 2002. *Indian Shoes*. New York: HarperCollins.	age, ethnicity, nationality, gender, socioeconomic	Seminole/ Cherokee	grandparent/grandchild relationship, heritage, urban life, family heritage, identity, priorities, contemporary American Indian life, family tradition	3–5	realistic fiction
Smith, Cynthia Leitich. 2014. *Feral Nights* (Feral Trilogy Book 1). Somerville, MA: Candlewick Press.	ethnicity, age, religion nationality	Black/ American Indian/ White	mystery, murder, shape-shifting, friendship, romance, loyalty, adventure, identity, self-acceptance, prejudice/bias, adoption	8–12	realistic/ fantasy fiction
Starr, Arigon, ed. 2014. *Tales of the Mighty Code Talkers*, vol. 1. Albuquerque, NM: Native Realities.	ethnicity, nationality, gender	Choctaw	history of Choctaw code talkers, WWI, Korea, American Indian heroes	5–12	historical graphic novel
Tafolla, Carmen. 2009. *What Can You Do with a Paleta?* Berkeley, CA: Tricycle Press.	ethnicity, age, nationality, socioeconomic	Mexican/ Mexican American	barrio life, summer fun, bilingual	PreK–2	picture book
Thomas, Angie. 2017. *The Hate U Give*. New York: Balzer & Bray.	youth, nationality, ethnicity,	Black	racism, police violence, Black Lives Matter, education, poverty/marginalization	10–12	realistic fiction

Book	Rings of Culture	Ethnicity	Themes	Grade Level	Genre
Tingle, Tim. 2008. *Crossing Bok Chitto: A Choctaw Tale of Friendship and Freedom*. El Paso, TX: Cinco Puntos Press.	nationality, age, ethnicity, gender	American Indian/ Choctaw/ Black	Choctaw culture, slavery, friendship, intersection of Southern American Indians and slaves, humanity, resilience, compassion/connections between cultures	2–6	historical fiction
Tingle, Tim. 2013. *Danny Blackgoat: Navajo Prisoner (PathFinders)*. Summertown, TN: 7th Generation.	nationality, ethnicity, gender, religion, age	Navajo	Overcoming oppression/ prejudice, family, Navajo life/ culture, Long Walk of 1864, Civil War, prejudice, genocide, identity, coming of age	6–10	historical fiction/ adventure
Tingle, Tim. 2014. *House of Purple Cedar*. El Paso, TX: Cinco Puntos Press.	nationality, ethnicity, age, religion	Choctaw	Choctaw cultural identity, prejudice/violence against American Indians, racial tension, survival	9–12	historical fiction
Tingle, Tim. 2014. *No Name (PathFinders)*. Summertown, TN: 7th Generation.	age, ethnicity, socioeconomic, nationality, gender, religion	Choctaw	Choctaw life/culture, water rights, alcoholism, marginalization of American Indians, basketball, friendship, family, resilience, survival	6–10	realistic fiction
Tingle, Tim. 2015. *How I Became a Ghost: A Choctaw Trail of Tears*. Van Nuys, CA: Roadrunner Press.	nationality, age, ethnicity, gender	American Indian/ Choctaw	historical tragedy, Trail of Tears, innocence, resilience, Choctaw storytelling, Choctaw history/culture	4–7	historical fiction/ fantasy

Book	Rings of Culture	Ethnicity	Themes	Grade Level	Genre
Ursu, Anne. 2015. *The Real Boy.* Boston: Walden Pond Press.	age, gender, socioeconomic, ability	various	autism, being different, self-acceptance, fantasy, defeating evil	3–7	fantasy
Van Camp, Richard, and Julie Flett. 2013. *Little You.* Victoria, BC, CAN: Orca Book Publishers.	ethnicity, nationality, age, gender	American Indian	rhymes, baby/toddlers, parent child relationship	K–2	board book
Van Camp, Richard, and Julie Flett. 2016. *We Sang You Home.* Victoria, BC, CAN: Orca Book Publishers.	ethnicity, nationality, age, gender, socioeconomic	American Indian	family, new baby, parent/child relationships, love	K–2	board book
Venkatraman, Padma. 2015. *A Time to Dance.* New York: Speak.	ethnicity, ability, gender, religion, age, nationality	Indian	overcoming tragedy, dancing, following your passion, being true to who you are, family pressure, identity, living as an amputee	6–12	novel in verse
Watson, Renée. 2017. *Piecing Me Together.* New York: Bloomsbury USA Children's Literature.	socioeconomic, age, ethnicity, nationality, gender	Black/White	cultural identity, defying stereotypes, family, friendships, being different/not fitting in, bias, acceptance, overcoming socio-economic challenges, education	8–12	realistic fiction

Book	Rings of Culture	Ethnicity	Themes	Grade Level	Genre
Weatherford, Carol Boston. 2016. *Freedom in Congo Square*. New York: Little Bee Books.	nationality, ethnicity, youth, religion	Black	slavery, New Orleans Congo Square	1–3	narrative nonfiction picture book
Weatherford, Carol Boston. 2017. *The Legendary Miss Lena Horne*. New York: Atheneum Books for Young Readers.	nationality, gender, ethnicity	Black	Lena Horne's life, civil rights	3–5	biography
Weatherford, Carol Boston, and Kadir Nelson. 2006. *Moses: When Harriet Tubman Led Her People to Freedom*. New York: Hyperion Books.	ethnicity, nationality, gender, socioeconomic	Black	life of Harriet Tubman, slavery, courage, freeing the slaves, determination, cultural heritage	2–5	historical fiction
Williams-Garcia, Rita. 2011. *One Crazy Summer* (first of a trilogy). New York: Amistad Press.	nationality, ethnicity, socioeconomic, gender	Black	coming of age, family, identity, Black Panthers, facing change/ challenges	5–9	historical fiction
Williams-Garcia, Rita. 2017. *Clayton Byrd Goes Underground*. New York: Amistad Press.	age, ethnicity, socioeconomic, nationality	Black	family, intergenerational relationships, music, grief and loss, self-identity, healing, running away	3–7	realistic fiction

Book	Rings of Culture	Ethnicity	Themes	Grade Level	Genre
Williams, Karen, Khadra Mohammed, and Catherine Stock. 2009. *My Name Is Sangoel.* Grand Rapids, MN: Eerdmans Books for Young Readers.	ethnicity, nationality, socioeconomic, age, gender	Sudanese	refugee life, living through war/violence, being different, immigrant experience, beginning a new life, struggling with change, cultural identity/differences	1–3	picture book
Woods, Brenda. 2003. *The Red Rose Box.* London: Puffin Books.	age, ethnicity, nationality, gender	Black	freedom from segregation, Jim Crow South, finding new family, struggling through loss/grief, love	4–6	historical fiction
Woods, Brenda. 2012. *Saint Louis Armstrong Beach.* London: Puffin Books.	age, ethnicity, socioeconomic, nationality	Black	Hurricane Katrina, family, identity, survival, music, relationships	3–6	historical fiction
Woods, Brenda. 2015. *The Blossoming Universe of Violet Diamond.* London: Puffin Books.	age, ethnicity, nationality, gender	White/Black	being biracial, finding your heritage, self-identity, loss of a parent, intergenerational relationships, journey to self, family love and acceptance, prejudice, standing out/fitting in	4–6	realistic fiction
Woods, Brenda. 2016. *Zoe in Wonderland.* London: Nancy Paulsen Books.	age, gender, ethnicity	Black	curiosity, adolescence, friendship and loss, self-identity, family bonds, realities of cancer/Alzheimer's	3–6	realistic fiction

Book	Rings of Culture	Ethnicity	Themes	Grade Level	Genre
Woodson, Jacqueline. 2015. *Visiting Day*. London: Puffin Books.	ethnicity, nationality, age, socioeconomic	Black	family, incarceration, intergenerational relationships, father/daughter relationship, unconditional love, hope, overcoming challenges	K–3	realistic fiction
Woodson, Jacqueline. 2016. *Brown Girl Dreaming*. London: Puffin Books.	gender, youth, ethnicity, nationality	Black	coming of age, change, family, identity, loss	7–12	novel in verse
Yang, Gene Luen. 2008. *American Born Chinese*. New York: Square Fish Books.	ethnicity, gender, nationality	Chinese/ Chinese American	acceptance, identity, stereotypes	9–12	graphic novel
Yoon, Nicola. 2016. *The Sun Is Also a Star*. New York: Delacorte Press.	ethnicity, age, nationality, socioeconomic, gender	Jamaican/ Korean/ White	undocumented/deportation, interracial romance, family expectation, self-identity, cultural identity, life in Brooklyn, following your dreams, challenging family tradition, friendship	8–12	realistic fiction
Zoboi, Ibi. 2017. *American Street*. New York: Balzer & Bray.	ethnicity, age, nationality, religion	Haitian	coming of age, change, urban life, making good choices, family	9–12	realistic fiction

CLR Lesson Planning Template

Lesson: _____

Step 1—Quantity: What's in your CLR Toolbox?

❏ Attention Signals
❏ Protocols for Responding
❏ Protocols for Discussion
❏ Movement
❏ Extended Collaboration
❏ Leveling Words
❏ Context Clues
❏ Personal Thesaurus/Personal Dictionary
❏ Use of Culturally Authentic Texts
❏ Read-Alouds
❏ Literacy Activities
❏ Situational Appropriateness Writing

Step 2—Quality: What is my accuracy and fidelity in using CLR activities?

Notes:

Questions:

Reflection:

Step 3—Strategy: What is my intent and purpose with the use of CLR activities?

Validating and Affirming What activities validate/ affirm cultural behaviors?	**Building and Bridging** What activities build/bridge to academic culture?

Reflection

CLR Learning Environment Survey

CLR Learning Environment Survey

Teacher _____ Grade/Class _____

Observer_____ Date of Observation _____

Observe the learning environment in your colleague's classroom by rating its cultural responsiveness on two levels:

- **Quantitative:** Is the environmental feature in place? Yes or No
- **Qualitative:** aspects of responsiveness, including creativity, presentation, and student friendliness

Rate the quality of responsiveness on a five-point scale from very responsive (5) to least responsive (1).

Add comments or suggestions to discuss with the teacher whose classroom you have observed.

Print-Rich Environment

Quantitative: Is the 70:30 ratio of authentic to commercially produced print resources evident in the classroom?

Yes or No (circle one)

Qualitative: Rate the level of responsiveness (creativity, presentation, and student friendliness).

Very Responsive				Least Responsive
5	4	3	2	1

Comments/Suggestions:

_____

_____

_____

Learning Centers

Quantitative: Are a variety of learning centers present? Is space set up for them to be organized?

Yes or No (circle one)

Qualitative: Rate the level of responsiveness (creativity, presentation, and student friendliness).

Very Responsive   **Least Responsive**
    5   4   3   2   1

Comments/Suggestions:

_____

_____

_____

Culturally Colorful

Quantitative: Does the room feature a variety of colors that are relevant to various cultures or to the culture/activities of the school?

Yes or No (circle one)

Qualitative: Rate the level of responsiveness (creativity, presentation, and student friendliness).

Very Responsive   **Least Responsive**
    5   4   3   2   1

Comments/Suggestions:

_____

_____

_____

Optimally Arranged

Quantitative: Does the room arrangement facilitate ease of movement, management, and presentations?

Yes or No (circle one)

Qualitative: Rate the level of responsiveness (creativity, presentation, and student friendliness).

Very Responsive   **Least Responsive**

     5   4   3   2   1

Comments/Suggestions:

_____

_____

_____

Multiple Libraries

Quantitative: Do the library resources support a focus on multiple literacies and cultures?

Yes or No (circle one)

Qualitative: Rate the level of responsiveness (creativity, presentation, and student friendliness).

Very Responsive   **Least Responsive**

     5   4   3   2   1

Comments/Suggestions:

_____

_____

_____

Technology

Quantitative: Are technology resources present and ready for use?

Yes or No (circle one)

Qualitative: Rate the level of responsiveness (creativity, presentation, and student friendliness).

Very Responsive   **Least Responsive**
5   4   3   2   1

Comments/Suggestions:

_____

_____

_____

Relevant Bulletin Boards

Quantitative: Are the bulletin boards relevant to the content areas and the cultural diversity of the students?

Yes or No (circle one)

Qualitative: Rate the level of responsiveness (creativity, presentation, and student friendliness).

Very Responsive   **Least Responsive**
5   4   3   2   1

Comments/Suggestions:

_____

_____

_____

Plan for Using Survey Findings

What are the strengths in the learning environment?

_____

_____

_____

_____

_____

_____

_____

What are the limitations in the learning environment?

_____

_____

_____

_____

_____

_____

_____

_____

What are your plans for using the survey findings?

_____

_____

_____

_____

_____

_____

_____

_____

Situational Appropriateness Practice

Managing levels of situational appropriateness through daily instructional opportunities supports students by equipping them with choices. These choices will support students in negotiating school culture and eventually the multitudes of cultures outside of school. Students will encounter cultural misunderstandings throughout their lives. Opportunities to practice and discuss situational appropriateness offer students skills to navigate cultural misunderstandings. Always, always begin with validation and affirmation; teaching situational appropriateness serves as a tool for classroom management that is responsive to students' needs.

The following content was developed by Paddy Greely, consultant for the Center for Culturally Responsive Teaching and Learning.

Instructional Opportunities	Engage in Situational Appropriateness
Active Listening A way of communicating that goes beyond hearing to understanding the message being delivered. This form of listening often comes with its own set of protocols that vary from teacher to teacher but may include making eye contact, paraphrasing, and questioning.	Hold a discussion in which students determine the appropriate behaviors for active listening. For example, the teacher might ask, "How will we show one another that we are listening today?" relative to: • the topic • the classroom • one-on-one discussion After students have determined the appropriate behaviors, engage them in a discussion around *why* these are appropriate behaviors for the particular situation.

Instructional Opportunities	Engage in Situational Appropriateness
Collaboration An extended form of small group work that may take place over several hours, class periods, or days. Collaboration is predicated on the idea of group member interdependence and group members working together on tasks using higher-level thinking, such as synthesizing or evaluating.	At its heart, collaboration is culturally responsive because it calls into play cultural and linguistic behaviors, such as sociocentrism, communalism, and differing discourse styles. Validate and affirm the cultural behaviors as assets by identifying them as learning targets and debriefing after collaboration time on the process. For example, "Today we focused on communalism. How did it work when you focused on group goals instead of individual goals?"
Discussing and Responding Opportunities to discuss and respond are typically brief collaborations to scaffold learning.	Maximize the quality and quantity of CLR Discussion and Response protocols used in the classroom. Juxtapose validating and affirming protocols with building and bridging protocols. This honors who the students are culturally and linguistically and provides scaffolding for them to practice languages and behaviors that may be used outside of their home cultures.
Independent Work Time Students work independently, applying and practicing new learning and skills.	Infuse independent work time with validating and affirming protocols that align with learning targets. For example, use Shout Out and Silent Appointment interspersed throughout a long period of independent work. The protocols provide choice and allow for movement. The brief collaboration supports sociocentric learners who learn best when talking.
Interactive Modeling* A Responsive Classroom practice that involves a seven-step modeling process to teach a new skill or behavior.	Use interactive modeling to teach the behaviors appropriate for given situations, e.g., the library and the playground.

Instructional Opportunities	Engage in Situational Appropriateness
Morning Meeting* A Responsive Classroom routine used to build community in the classroom, and it includes the following components: • Greeting • Sharing • Group Activity • Morning Message	Home languages and cultural greetings of students are learned, authentically included, and celebrated. Activities validate and affirm cultural and linguistic behaviors from students' home cultures. Students have the opportunity to share meaningful stories from their home life and cultures.
Movement Students take breaks or get up and move around at designated times throughout the day or a class period.	Intentionally planned to enhance and support learning, strategic use of movement taps into students' cultural identities by validating and affirming them through a kinesthetic, sociocentric, or communalistic lens. Validate and affirm the cultural behaviors as assets by identifying them as learning targets and debriefing after movement on the process. For example, use Corners with Musical Shares. After the lesson, debrief with students by asking, "How did the protocols support your learning? How did they validate you culturally or linguistically?"
Take A Break* A Responsive Classroom behavior time-out in which a student leaves the group and sits in an identified space to reflect on misbehavior for the purpose of identifying the appropriate behavior and returning to the group.	Through one-on-one dialogue, the student helps the teacher determine if this is an appropriate strategy for the individual. Students from homes that subscribe to communalism may feel that this strategy is unfair because the student is being isolated from the community, whereas students from homes that subscribe to individualism may find that this strategy works as intended. By asking questions, the teacher prompts the students to be metacognitive about what behaviors are appropriate for a given situation and which strategies will support the student in returning to learning.

Instructional Opportunities	Engage in Situational Appropriateness
Voice Levels A tool used to teach students appropriate voice levels for different situations. Each level is explicitly taught and modeled. A chart defining situationally appropriate voice levels is then posted and referenced as a classroom management tool.	Invite students to be part of the process of determining what each voice level means. After the tool is established, engage students in a decision-making process around the appropriate voice level for a given situation. For example, "What voice level is appropriate for walking to recess? Why is this the appropriate voice level for walking in the hallway to recess?" After students provide the rationale, trust that the students can and will achieve the behavior, allowing the students to act upon their decision.
Y Chart* A Responsive Classroom *Looks Like, Sounds Like, Feels Like* Chart for revisiting rules and expectations	Like interactive modeling, this is another tool to use when teaching behaviors appropriate for certain situations.

*A component of the Positive Behavioral Interventions & Supports (PBIS) framework.

Situational Appropriateness Scale

The following scale is provided to assist teachers and students with evaluating students' success in achieving situational appropriateness. The scale should never be used for punishing students or identifying wrong behaviors. It is a reflective tool for teachers to use to consider next steps for teaching.

Scale	Descriptor	Example
Achieving Situationally Appropriate Behavior and Language	The student is situationally appropriate in nearly all contexts within the school culture. Most of the time, the student recognizes the appropriate cultural or linguistic behavior for a situation, such as voice level, protocols for discussions, conversations, and responses, movement within the classroom (when and how), conduct in communal spaces (e.g., hallways and playgrounds) and outside the classroom (e.g., during lunch, recess, dismissal).	The student flexibly moves through situations, identifying the appropriate language and behavior for each environment. The student demonstrates this by shifting from a whisper voice in the library to a moderate voice while walking through the hall talking with a teacher. On the playground, the student interacts with peers using home language and a louder voice.

Scale	Descriptor	Example
Practicing Situationally Appropriate Behaviors and Language	The student practices situational appropriateness for some of the contexts within the school culture. Some of the time, the student recognizes the appropriate cultural or linguistic behavior for a situation, such as voice level, protocols for discussions, conversations, and responses, movement within the classroom (when and how), conduct in communal spaces (e.g., hallways and playgrounds) and outside the classroom (e.g., during lunch, recess, dismissal).	The student understands some of the appropriate behaviors for large group instruction. The student demonstrates this by sitting and listening while the teacher talks. The student uses hand raising to participate in discussions. Sometimes the student also taps rhythmically on the floor and moves to the beat.
Developing Situationally Appropriate Behaviors and Language	The student is working on situational appropriateness for many of the contexts within the school culture. In a few contexts, the student recognizes the appropriate cultural or linguistic behavior for a situation, such as voice level, protocols for discussions, conversations, and responses, movement within the classroom (when and how), conduct in communal spaces (e.g., hallways and playgrounds) and outside the classroom (e.g., during lunch, recess, dismissal).	The student understands a few of the appropriate behaviors for independent work time. The student demonstrates this by frequently getting up and walking around the room and spontaneously shouting out questions and comments. The student is focused on the task and completes the assigned work.

Scale	Descriptor	Example
Struggling with Situationally Appropriate Behaviors and Language	The student struggles with situational appropriateness for most of the contexts within the school culture. The student does not recognize the appropriate cultural or linguistic behavior for a situation, such as voice level, protocols for discussions, conversations, and responses, movement within the classroom (when and how), conduct in communal spaces (e.g., hallways and playgrounds) and outside the classroom (e.g., during lunch, recess, dismissal).	The student demonstrates the cultural behavior of communalism in all situations. The student demonstrates this by yelling across the lunchroom to help a friend at a different table. In the classroom, the student jumps in with an answer when her cousin is put on the spot. The student does not understand why these behaviors are viewed as inappropriate.

Using the Scale

When using the Situational Appropriateness Scale in classrooms, teachers should consider not only the level of the student but also the implicit and explicit messages that the student is receiving about behaviors, whether from school, the community, or the media. The teacher must start with validation and affirmation to ensure students know that they are not being asked to compromise their home culture in any way.

As the teacher begins the lessons on situational appropriateness, all dialogue about behaviors and languages must occur without judgment. Students should not be made to feel as if their home culture is beneath, less than, or lower than school culture.

The following questions are offered for reflection to support the teacher and the student through the process:

For the teacher:

- How can I support the student responsively?
- Have I taught the student the skills needed to be situationally appropriate?

For the student:

- Do I have the knowledge and skills to be situationally appropriate?
- If so, am I intentionally choosing *not* to be situationally appropriate? Why?

Additional Resources

Strategies for Culturally and Linguistically Responsive Teaching and Learning (Hollie 2015) is a resource of instructional activities in the areas of responsive management, responsive academic vocabulary, responsive literacy, and responsive language and learning environment. The chart below shows where CLR activities that are mentioned in this book are elaborated on in this additional resource.

CLR Activities	*Strategies for Culturally and Linguistically Responsive Teaching and Learning* References
Attention Signals	Chapter 1, page 25
Responding Protocols	Chapter 2, page 45
Discussion Protocols	Chapter 2, page 45
Movement Activities	Chapter 3, page 81
Extended Collaboration	Chapter 4, page 109
Leveling of Vocabulary	Chapter 5, page 129
Use of Context Clues	Chapter 6, page 141
CLR Vocab Tools (Personal Dictionary and Personal Thesaurus)	Chapter 7, page 163
Use of CLR Texts	Chapter 8, page 175
Use of Engaging Read Alouds	Chapter 9, page 189
Effective Literacy Activities	Chapter 10, page 209
Effective Writing Activities	Chapter 10, page 209
Use of Code Switching and Situational Appropriateness	Chapter 11, page 247

For additional resources from the Center for Culturally Responsive Teaching and Learning, visit www.culturallyresponsive.org